THE TWO HARMONIES

Poetry and Prose
in the Seventeenth Century

THE TWO HARMONIES

POETRY AND PROSE IN THE
SEVENTEENTH CENTURY

BY

K. G. HAMILTON

CLARENDON PRESS · OXFORD
1963

Oxford University Press, Amen House, London E.C. 4

GLASGOW   NEW YORK   TORONTO   MELBOURNE   WELLINGTON
BOMBAY   CALCUTTA   MADRAS   KARACHI   LAHORE   DACCA
CAPE TOWN   SALISBURY   NAIROBI   IBADAN   ACCRA
KUALA LUMPUR   HONG KONG

Printed in Great Britain by
W. & J. Mackay and Co. Ltd., Chatham

Preface

THIS study had its origins in a long-standing interest in the nature of poetry as a unique form of discourse, and, more immediately, in the problems associated with lecturing on the poetry of the seventeenth century to students to whom 'poetry' is likely to mean either Romantic or modern poetry, and who in consequence find their ideas as to what poetry should be inadequate for an appreciation of Dryden in particular.

I have tried to do two main things: firstly, to bring together in a convenient and coherent form a large amount of scattered material, primary and secondary, with a bearing on seventeenth-century ideas of the nature and function of poetry—this in itself would, I hoped, be valuable to students of the period, and because of this interest in the subject from a teaching point of view the background and bibliographical material is sometimes more detailed than the strict requirements of the argument might have demanded; and secondly, from this material to draw some conclusions about the history of literary theory which have not, I think, been so far explicitly stated, and, incidentally, to re-examine some of the conclusions arrived at in other studies of the period. The work would thus serve, I hope, both as a reference book for the study of certain aspects of literary history and theory, and at the same time present its own views on the significance of the material.

I have been very much indebted in this study to other scholars who have worked in this and related fields. I trust that this indebtedness is adequately recorded in the footnotes, but I would particularly mention here W. J. Ong, S.J., George Williamson, Norman Maclean, Bernard Weinberg, D. L. Clark, W. S. Howell, D. F. Bond, and R. F. Jones. Indeed, part of my aim has been to make more widely known, in relation to my own particular interest, the work of these scholars, and I should like to help lead students to those studies to which I have myself been indebted. However, as far as this study itself is concerned, my interest in the work of other scholars has been most often from a point of view or with a significance which they have not been directly or primarily concerned to develop. Many of my most stimulating ideas have come, in fact, not from any single work, but from the light thrown on the subject when several studies have been considered together.

For the purpose of quotation I have endeavoured always to use the original text, or a scholarly modern edition thereof, and the actual source is indicated on the first occasion on which the work is mentioned in the footnotes; it also appears in the Bibliography. All quotations, with a few very minor exceptions, are repeated in the form in which they appear in the source indicated in the appropriate note—I have not myself modernized or translated any passages, but where this has already been done in the text which I have used it has been retained.

K.G.H.

University of Queensland
1962.

Contents

CHAPTER ONE

The Proper Style in Poetry and Prose

A T the end of the seventeenth century, when the old master John Dryden came to write his *Fables*, he declared that he found the thoughts 'come crowding in so fast upon me, that my only difficulty is to choose or to reject, to run them into verse, or to give them the other harmony of prose . . .'[1] In the twentieth century, except perhaps in a limited field of the drama, the choice between verse and prose has little reality. The two forms have moved apart to a point where their field of effective contact is small. For Dryden, however, this seems not to have been the case; the literary tradition in which he wrote apparently allowed a greater degree of homogeneity between the various arts of discourse.

The later seventeenth century was, of course, essentially an age of prose—this has long been an accepted convention of literary history. Dryden and Pope, according to Matthew Arnold, are 'classics not of our poetry but our prose';[2] and, though twentieth-century criticism may profess not to accept this view, the essentially prosaic quality of Augustan poetry is still often tacitly accepted, or is explained away only with difficulty. For the seventeenth century itself the fashion was for prose—so much so that the fad was parodied by a playwright of the period:

JORDAN: I . . . but ask you what this is you speak to me and I to you?
LUCIA: What is it? 'tis English.
JORDAN: True, but what else?
LUCIA: Nothing else, 'tis every word English.

[1] Dryden, Preface to *Fables, Ancient and Modern* (London, 1700); ed. W. P. Ker, *Essays of John Dryden* (2 vols., Oxford, 1900), ii, 249.
[2] Matthew Arnold, 'The Study of Poetry', in *Essays in Criticism, Second Series*, ed. S. R. Littlewood (London, 1938), p. 25.

JORDAN: What are these words? LUCIA: These? JORDAN: Yes; What?

LUCIA: Letters make Syllables, Syllables Words, Words Sentences, and Sentences a Discourse.

JORDAN: And this is all you know? LUCIA: Yes.

JORDAN: God help your head, what a fine fellow should I be, were I as ignorant as yourself?

LUCIA: Where lies my ignorance? What is it I said, say you?

JORDAN: 'Twas Prose you Fool. LUCIA: Prose!

JORDAN: Yes Prose: all that is Prose is not Verse, and all that is Verse is not Prose. . . .[1]

The problem posed by the distinction of verse from prose—or rather of 'poetry' from prose—is not so simple as 'Mr. Jordan' might like to suggest. It is a distinction whose analysis involves the whole attitude of the period towards discourse in general and towards the nature and function of poetry and prose as forms of discourse. This analysis—and what can be learned about poetry from the making of it—will be the concern of this study.

The emphasis on prose, particularly on prose as a plain, straight-forward, accurate means of communication, will be a primary concern of what follows, but not for its own sake. The real interest is in seventeenth-century poetry. Yet it must be stressed that this is not intended as a study of the general history of poetic theory in the seventeenth century, or of poetry as part of the whole seventeenth-century pattern of ideas.[2] Its aim is limited to delineating the course

[1] From *Mamamouchi: or, The Citizen turn'd Gentleman: A comedy*, by Edward Ravenscroft (London, 1675); adapted from Molière's *Bourgeois Gentilhomme*.

[2] Poetry as part of the history of ideas in the seventeenth century has been the immediate or partial concern of a number of important and influential studies: e.g.

H. Baker, *The Wars of Truth* (London, 1952).

P. Cruttwell, *The Shakespearean Moment* (London, 1954).

S. L. Bethell, *The Cultural Revolution of the Seventeenth Century* (London, 1951).

H. J. C. Grierson, *Cross Currents of Literature of the Seventeenth Century* (London, 1929).

M. M. Mahood, *Poetry and Humanism* (London, 1950).

Basil Willey, *The Seventeenth Century Background* (London, 1934); and *The Eighteenth Century Background* (London, 1940).

These studies have all been valuable for the present work, whose subject,

of, and to some extent accounting for, certain developments in poetic theory associated particularly with the emergence of modern science and its emphasis on 'utilitarian' prose. Much that may be important for the formation of seventeenth-century concepts of poetry will thus of necessity be passed over, for it is certainly not intended to suggest that all the happenings in literary theory or practice during this period can be accounted for in terms of the developments with which this study is concerned. It is indeed not intended to *prove* anything. What is suggested is that these new attitudes to prose seem on the face of them to be important for the history of poetry, and that accordingly their study may yield some further insight into the nature of seventeenth-century practice as well as theory.

'One of the most interesting things in the history of English poetry', it has been claimed, 'is the change in style which took place in the seventeenth century. Briefly it may be described as a process of simplification. It parallels a similar change in prose . . .'[1] This is one side of the picture. But provision must also be made, at least in the opinion of such an eminent seventeenth-century scholar as R. F. Jones, for the growing consciousness in the seventeenth century of prose as a separate literary form, distinct from poetry. Prose, Jones believes, 'as a distinct type of literature was emerging in much more definite outline; its own peculiar properties were beginning to

---

however, they do not approach directly. It has been touched on in passing by studies (which will be referred to from time to time) by R. F. Jones, M. W. Croll, G. E. Williamson, and others, D. L. Clark's *Rhetoric and Poetry in the Renaissance* (New York, 1922) stops before reaching the period of this study and is more limited in its aims. W. S. Howell's *Logic and Rhetoric in England 1500–1700* (Princeton, 1956) and K. R. Wallace's *Francis Bacon on Communication and Rhetoric* (Chapel Hill, 1943) both intentionally exclude any direct consideration of poetry. Studies which most directly parallel the present one are those of W. J. Ong on the influence of Ramism (see below, pp. 109–19). One specialized study which seeks to relate poetry to a particular form of discourse—religious meditation—may be mentioned—that of L. Martz, *The Poetry of Meditation* (New Haven, 1954). For a further bibliography of works concerned particularly with the connexion of poetry and rhetoric see below, p. 47.

[1] R. L. Sharp, *From Donne to Dryden* (Chapel Hill, 1940), p. ix.

receive attention'.[1] Why, it might be asked, should prose and poetry undergo a noticeably parallel change in style at a time when, more distinctly than hitherto, they were beginning to be thought of as separate forms of discourse? Apparently there were influences at work which kept poetry and prose together, as well as those that were tending to separate them.

The parallel development of prose and poetry is, in fact, something much more extensive than this simplifying of style, and it goes back well beyond the seventeenth century. In one respect at least it goes back to the fourteenth century or earlier, from which time there was a conscious tendency to consider the vernacular, whether in verse or prose, as too harsh, too crude and base, for writing with any literary pretensions. Partly a matter of affected self-depreciation, from which even Chaucer was not altogether free, and partly one of popular attitude, this idea could still be accepted by Ascham in the middle of the sixteenth century; his *Toxophilus*, he declared, would have been more honourably written in Latin or Greek and he adds that 'in the Englishe tonge . . . [everything is done] in a maner so meanly, both for the matter and handelynge, that no man can do worse'.[2] It was an attitude, however, that came

---

[1] R. F. Jones, 'The Attack on Pulpit Eloquence in the Restoration', *JEGP*, xxx (1931), 205–6.

Attention has been given to the development of 'plain' style in prose in a number of important studies. See particularly:

M. W. Croll, 'Attic Prose in the Seventeenth Century', *SP*, xviii (1921), 79–128.

M. W. Croll, 'The Baroque Style in Prose', in *Studies in English Philology*, ed. Kemp Malone and M. B. Ruud (Minneapolis, 1929), pp. 427–56.

R. F. Jones, 'Science and English Prose Style in the Third Quarter of the Seventeenth Century', *PMLA*, xlv (1930), 977–1009.

R. F. Jones, 'Science and Language in England of the mid-Seventeenth Century', *JEGP*, xxxi (1932), 315–31.

K. R. Wallace, *Francis Bacon on Communication and Rhetoric*, op. cit.

G. E. Williamson, 'Senecan Style in the Seventeenth Century', *PQ*, xv (1936), 321–51.

G. E. Williamson, *The Senecan Amble: A Study in Prose Form from Bacon to Collier* (London, 1951).

[2] Roger Ascham, *Toxophilus: or, The Schole of shootinge conteyned in two bookes* (London, 1545); ed. A. M. Wright, *The English Writings of Roger Ascham* (Cambridge, 1904), p. xiv.

more and more under fire during the sixteenth century, and during the last quarter of the century poets and prose writers alike were praised for overcoming the lack of literary distinction in the native language. Works such as the prose writings of John Lyly and Spenser's *Shepheardes Calendar* were each seen as demonstrating the power of the vernacular for artistic eloquence.[1]

The seventeenth-century trend towards a simpler style in poetry and prose belongs essentially to the later part of the century. For the earlier seventeenth century the 'curt' or 'Senecan' style in prose, the forerunner of the later plain style, has been seen as part of a movement which also affected poetry, and indeed all the arts. A foremost authority on the development of prose style in this period, Professor Morris Croll, has declared that '. . . the change that takes place in the prose style of the same period—the change, that is, from Ciceronian to anti-Ciceronian forms and ideas—is exactly parallel with those that were occurring in the other arts . . .'[2] Thus it is not surprising to find Croll writing of Senecan prose style in terms that suggest a strong relationship with metaphysical poetry. The following passage could, for instance, very well be thought of as coming from a critique of the poetry of John Donne, written perhaps in the spirit of Eliot's theory of the 'undissociated sensibility':

Their purpose was to portray, not a thought, but a mind thinking, or, in Pascal's words, *la peinture de la pensée*. They knew that an idea separated from the act of experiencing is not the idea that was experienced. The ardour of its conception in the mind is a necessary part of its truth; and unless it can be conveyed to another mind in something of the form of its occurence, either it has changed into some other idea or it has ceased to be an idea, to have any existence whatever except a verbal one. It was the latter fate that happened to it, they believed, in the Ciceronian periods of sixteenth-century Latin rhetoricians. The successive processes of revision to which these periods had been submitted had removed them from reality by just so many steps. For themselves, they preferred to present the truth of experience in a less concocted form, and deliberately chose as the

[1] See R. F. Jones, *The Triumph of the English Language* (London, 1953).
[2] M. W. Croll, 'The Baroque Style in Prose', op. cit., p. 429.

moment of expression that in which the idea first clearly objectified itself in the mind, in which, therefore, each of its parts still preserves its own peculiar emphasis and an independent vigour of its own—in brief, the moment in which the truth is still *imagined*.[1]

This may be to read Senecan prose with the same twentieth-century expectations as have been attributed to Eliot in his reading of the poetry of Donne.[2] Nevertheless, the appearance of a similar reading, even if it turns out to be a misreading, of both the prose and the poetry of the same period may yet be significant. And in a similar strain Ruth Wallerstein has seen a connexion between both metaphysical poetry and Senecan prose style on the one hand and Augustinian neo-Platonism on the other;[3] while George Williamson has shown the connexion between Senecan 'pointed' style and the antithetic style of wit described in earlier poetic theory by Puttenham and beginning to appear in the early seventeenth-century couplets of Drayton and Ben Jonson. 'These shaping figures', he writes, referring to Puttenham's summary of many of the figures of classical rhetoric, 'produce the antithetic pattern of the curt Senecan period and the neo-classical couplet; they are most brilliantly displayed in the character writing and occasional verse of the seventeenth century.'[4] Here once again reference is being made to both prose and poetry in order to illustrate a common development.

At the risk of some oversimplification it is possible to see three periods in this parallel process of development of prose and poetry during the period *c.* 1575 to the end of the seventeenth century:

i. In prose, Ciceronian imitation and Euphuism, differing in structure but alike in the emphasis on verbal qualities.

In poetry, the elaborate, florid harmonies and ornamentation associated with Spenser, and like its contemporary prose, prompted by a desire to make English a fit vehicle for literary expression.

ii. In prose, the various forms of Senecan style (curt, obscure,

[1] Ibid., pp. 430–1. [2] By, for example, Frank Kermode, in 'Dissociation of Sensibility', *KR*, xix (1957), 169–94.

[3] Ruth Wallerstein, *Studies in Seventeenth Century Poetic* (Wisconsin, 1950), p. 55.

[4] G. E. Williamson, 'The Rhetorical Pattern of Neo-Classical Wit', *MP*, xxxiii (1935), 66.

loose, etc.) which cultivate wit but primarily for the sake of thought or 'point'.

In poetry, first metaphysical and later antithetic wit, where again the poetry resembles the prose in seeming to have been partly dictated by a desire to make words a more direct expression of thought.

iii. In both poetry and prose, an emphasis on simplicity, clarity, intelligibility, propriety, naturalness, refinement, ease, &c.

These changes may be seen as successive stages in a cyclical process of action and reaction, in which the Romantic Movement was to be the next stage: the metaphysicals and Senecans revolting against Elizabethan verbalism, the neo-classicists against metaphysical extravagance, the Romantics against neo-classic aridity, the reaction in each case being against the tag end of the former stage which has lost its initial inspiration. This at least is the conventional explanation accepted by literary historians.

The latest stage in this cyclical process, however, presents a different pattern from that of the earlier changes. The Romantic Movement affected only poetry and certain special kinds of literary prose with relatively close affinities to poetry. In this respect it was far less all-embracing in its effects on the arts of discourse than were the movements of the sixteenth and seventeenth centuries. These latter movements not only revealed parallel manifestations in prose and in poetry, but within prose their effects were largely indiscriminate. Thus Euphuism and Ciceronian imitation in the sixteenth century are accepted as having affected to a greater or lesser extent not only rhetorical exercises like Lyly's *Euphues* and the oratory of Hooker, but also prose in almost all its forms and uses, except perhaps the most unselfconscious and non-literary. And much the same thing may be claimed for the two following stages in the process of change—that is, those changes in style which took place in the earlier and later seventeenth centuries respectively.

The changes of the later seventeenth century were impermanent, like their predecessors, but only as they applied to poetry; for prose they remained relatively permanent. By the middle of the nineteenth century Dryden's poetry, for the time being at least, could be regarded as being not really poetry at all; his prose, on the other hand, has remained widely accepted as having helped largely to establish the modern norm. It would seem that the reforms of the later seventeenth century were found to be satisfactory for prose, but not for poetry. Hence prose discourse has remained relatively stable, while in poetry neo-classicism has been supplanted by Romanticism and the variety of modern aesthetic theories (Imagism, Expressionism, Symbolism, Realism, &c.) that have sprung from it —or have reacted against it.

The picture is thus one of poetry and prose developing along more or less parallel paths until some time after the end of the seventeenth century, when poetry tends to diverge while prose continues straight ahead. This eventual divergence of poetry from prose may serve to explain why R. L. Sharp, in a passage from his study of seventeenth-century poetry, following the lines quoted earlier in this chapter in which he comments on changes in the style of poetry and prose, should have found the tendency towards a simpler poetry 'more surprising and puzzling' than the parallel change in prose. 'Prose, as distinguished from poetry', he says, 'is primarily the language of statement. Poetry, however, we normally expect to be something else.'[1] But 'our' expectations regarding the nature of poetry are not necessarily those of the seventeenth century; as stated by Sharp at least, they may imply distinctions between poetry and prose which the seventeenth century apparently did not hold.

Indeed, if the outline of development suggested above is accepted, it would seem desirable to re-examine the proposition that the later seventeenth century developed a growing consciousness of the distinction between poetry and prose. Did this consciousness, as something new, in fact develop significant proportions before the beginnings of Romanticism in the eighteenth century? Would it be possible, without being inconsistent, to accept the proposition that prose developed as a more distinct form of discourse in the later seventeenth century, without at the same time accepting as a consequence the simultaneous development of a conscious

[1] R. L. Sharp, *From Donne to Dryden*, op. cit., p. ix.

distinction between poetry and prose? Might not the latter, rather than accompanying the former, have followed from it, not immediately but ultimately, the developments in prose having been of such a kind that the traditionally close relationship of poetry and prose could not be sustained indefinitely?

Style, superficially at least, is the most obvious basis for a distinction between poetry and prose. And, even though the question of the styles most appropriate to poetry and prose respectively may not ultimately prove to have the most important bearing on the problem of seventeenth-century distinctions between the two forms, it has the advantage of being relatively tangible, and is also something that was of primary interest to the seventeenth century itself.

The problem, however, is not whether the seventeenth century made a distinction between the styles of poetry and prose. It concerns rather the nature and extent of the distinction. Some such distinction had always been made, changing and often vague as it may have been. To be of any significance, seventeenth-century distinctions must in some way have been more fundamental, or at least different from those that had been made hitherto.

The attempt to formulate principles of English poetic technique, as distinct from such poetic applications of rhetoric as Stephen Hawes's *Pastime of Pleasure* (1509),[1] begins apparently with George Gascoigne's *Certayne Notes of Instruction concerning the making of Verse or Ryme in English* (1575). From this short treatise mainly concerned with prosody three excerpts might be noted as having some bearing on the author's idea of the relationship between the proper styles of poetry and prose:

And in your verses remember to place euery worde in his natural *Emphasis* or sound, that is to say, in such wise, and with such length or shortnesse, eleuation or depression of sillables, as it is commonly pronounced or vsed.[2]

[1] For a discussion of this matter see below, pp. 80–81.

[2] George Gascoigne, *Certayne Notes of Instruction concerning the making of Verse or Ryme in English, written at the request of Master Edouardo Donati* (London, 1575); ed. G. G. Smith, *Elizabethan Critical Essays* (2 vols., Oxford, 1904), i, 49.

T.H.—B

You may vse the same Figures or Tropes in verse which are vsed in prose, and in my iudgement they serue more aptly and haue greater grace in verse than they haue in prose . . .[1]

. . . Therefore euen as I haue aduised you to place all wordes in their naturall or most common and vsuall pronunciation, so would I wishe you to frame all sentences in their mother phrase and proper *Idioma;* and yet sometimes (as I haue sayd before) the contrarie may be borne, but that is rather where rime enforceth, or *per licentiam Poëticam,* than it is otherwise lawful or commendable.

This poeticall licence is a shrewde fellow, and couereth many faults in a verse; it maketh wordes longer, shorter, of mo sillables, of fewer, newer, older, truer, falser; and, to conclude, it turkeneth all things at pleasure . . .[2]

Here is the outline of a pattern that will become increasingly familiar as this study proceeds: poetry must aim generally at a natural word order and usage, but with some slight allowance by way of 'poetic licence'; and, with perhaps less restriction and greater effectiveness, it uses the same figures as prose.

Much more extensive and ambitious than Gascoigne's *Notes* is the *Arte of English Poesie,* usually ascribed to George Puttenham. First published in 1589, the *Arte* was probably composed rather earlier, possibly even earlier than Gascoigne's work.[3] It is very much in the rhetorical tradition, about one-third of its two hundred and sixty odd pages being devoted to an analysis and illustration of more than one hundred 'figures' of speech. Of these figures Puttenham (if it may be assumed for sake of convenience that he is the author) says that:

. . . the learned clerks who haue writte methodically of this Arte in the two master languages, Greeke and Latine, haue sorted all their figures into three rankes, and the first they bestowed vpon the Poet

---

[1] George Gascoigne, *Certayne Notes of Instruction concerning the making of Verse or Ryme in English, written at the request of Master Edouardo Donati* (London, 1575); ed. G. G. Smith, *Elizabethan Critical Essays* (2 vols., Oxford, 1904), i, 52.

[2] Ibid., i, 53–54.

[3] For a discussion of the authorship and date of the *Arte* see the Introduction to G. D. Willcock and A. Walker (eds.) *The Arte of English Poesie by George Puttenham* (Cambridge, 1936).

onely: the second vpon the Poet and Oratour indifferently: the third vpon the Oratour alone. And that first sort of figures doth serve th'eare onely and may be therefore called *Auricular:* your second serues the conceit onely and not th'eare, and may be called *sensable,* not sensible nor yet sententious: your third sort serues as well th'eare as the conceit, and may be called *sententious figures,* because not onely they properly apperteine to full sentences, for bewtifying them with currant & pleasant numerositie, but also giuing them eflicacie, and enlarging the whole matter besides with copious amplifications.[1]

Puttenham's division of the figures on the basis of their application by classical writers to poetry, to oratory, or to either indiscriminately, is not altogether correct. At least in their origins, that is for Gorgias the Sophist, the figures both of sense and of sound (*figurae sententiae* and *figurae dictionis*) were appropriated from poetry to the services of oratory. R. C. Jebb, in his *Attic Orators,* describes the Gorgian figures as they appear in the writings of Isocrates, the pupil of Gorgias: 'The specially Isocratean figures of language are those which depend on a parallelism. These are chiefly three. (1) A parallelism in sense—Antithesis . . . (2) A parallelism in form and size merely between two or more clauses or sentences—Parisosis. (3) A parallelism of sound—Paromoiosis: when the latter of two clauses gives to the ear an echo of the former, either in its opening or at its close or throughout.'[2] Also Professor Van Hook has traced 107 of Puttenham's 121 figures to their origins in the classical art of oratory, particularly in Quintilian;[3] and Puttenham himself, in fact, uses the distinction only to emphasize the close relationship he sees between poetry and oratory. He begins his discussion with the *auricular* figures that he believed were the special property of the poet, but then goes on to include the *sensable* and *sententious* figures in his treatment, because, as he says:

. . . if our presupposall be true, that the Poet is of all other the most auncient Orator, as he that by good & pleasant perswasions first

---

[1] Puttenham, *Arte of English Poesie* (London, 1589); ed. G. D. Willcock and A. Walker (Cambridge, 1936), pp. 159–60.

[2] R. C. Jebb, *The Attic Orators* (2 vols., London, 1893), ii, 61.

[3] La Rue Van Hook, 'Greek Rhetorical Terminology in Puttenham's *The Arte of English Poesie*', *Trans. Am. Phil. Ass*, xlv (1914).

reduced the wilde and beastly people into publicke societies and ciuilitie of life, insinuating vnto them, vnder fictions with sweete and coloured speeches, many wholesome lessons and doctrines, then no doubt there is nothing so fitte for him, as to be furnished with all the figures that be *Rhetoricall*, and such as do most beautifie language with eloquence & sententiousness.[1]

All the stylistic devices of the orator are thus to be at the disposal of the poet. And from the discussion of the figures it appears that they are in fact to be used more sparingly in prose than in poetry. Of rhyme and assonance, for example, Puttenham says: '. . . your clauses in prose should neither finish with the same nor with the like terminants, but with the contrary . . .'[2] Similarly the hyperbole ('or the over-reacher, otherwise called the loud lyer') is particularly dangerous in prose: '. . . this maner of speech is vsed, when either we would greatly aduaunce or greatly abase the reputation of any thing or person, and must be vsed very discreetly, or els it will seeme odious . . . especially in the proseman . . .'[3] The use of *parison* ('or the figure of even') is also to be limited in prose: 'In a prose there should not be vsed at once of such euen clauses past three or foure at the most.'[4] And the same is true of *antitheton* ('or the rirenconter'): '*Isocrates* the Greek Oratour was a little too full of this figure . . . & many of our moderne writers in vulgar, vse it in excesse & incurre the vice of fond affectation . . .'[5]

Puttenham assumes that metre is essential to poetry, thus taking sides in what had been since the time of Aristotle, and indeed still is, a fundamental aspect of the problem of distinguishing poetry from other forms of discourse. His argument is a rather circular one, based on what he regarded as a law of nature: '. . . God made the world by number, measure and weight: some for weight say tune, and peraduenture better.' And thus 'all things stand by proportion, and . . . without it nothing could stand to be good or beautiful'.[6] Poetry, being the highest form of discourse, must necessarily be the most 'harmonical' and show the highest degree of proportion.

[1] Puttenham, op. cit., p. 196.
[2] Ibid., p. 174.   [3] Ibid., p. 192.   [4] Ibid., p. 214.
[5] Ibid., p. 211.   [6] Ibid., p. 64.

Style, in the sense of metrical or rhythmical form, is therefore what especially separates poetry from prose and makes possible the special advantages and virtues of the former. All speech has the same objective, but poetry is more effective than prose because its metrical form makes it easier to remember and more pleasant to listen to:

Vtterance also and language is giuen by nature to man for perswasion of others, and aide of them selues, I meane the first abilite to speake. For speech it selfe is artificiall and made by man, and the more pleasing it is, the more it preuaileth to such purpose as it is intended for: but speech by meeter is a kind of vtterance, more cleanly couched and more delicate to the eare then prose is, because it is more currant and slipper vpon the tongue, and withal tunable and melodious, as a kinde of Musicke, and therefore may be tearmed a musicall speech or vtterance, which cannot but please the hearer very well. Another cause is, for that it is briefer & more compendious, and easier to beare away and be retained in memorie, then that which is contained in multitude of words and full of tedious ambage and long periods. It is beside a maner of vtterance more eloquent and rhetoricall then the ordinarie prose, which we vse in our daily talke . . . The vtterance in prose is not of so great efficacie, because not only is it daily vsed, and by that occasion the eare is ouerglutted with it, but is also not so voluble and slipper vpon the tong, being wide and lose, and nothing numerous, nor contriued into measures, and sounded with so gallant and harmonical accents, nor in fine alowed that figuratiue conueyance, nor so great licence in choise of words and phrases as meeter is.[1]

The metrical form of poetry also leads Puttenham to make an interesting contrast between the syntax of poetry and that of prose:

Much more might be sayd for the vse of your three pauses, *comma*, *colon*, & *periode*, for perchance it be not all a matter to vse many *commas*, and few, nor *colons* likewise, or long or shorte periodes, for it is diuersly vsed, by diuers good writers. But because it apperteineth more to the oratour or writer in prose then in verse, I will say no more in it, then thus, that they be vsed for a commodious and sensible distinction of clauses in prose, since euery verse is as it were a clause of it selfe, and limited with a *Cesure* howsoeuer the sense beare, perfect

[1] Ibid., p. 8.

or imperfect, which difference is obseruable betwixt the prose and the meeter.[1]

Puttenham does not develop this point any further. However, the idea that in poetry the metre to some extent replaced normal syntax was apparently commonplace, as is indicated by a passage from John Brinsley's school manual, *Ludus Literarius; or, The Grammar School* (1612), in which he suggests the teaching of versifying by having the pupils write first in prose and then turn this into poetry: 'For the making of a verse is nothing but the turning of words forth of the Grammaticall order into the Rhetoricall, in, some kind of metre; which we call verses . . .'[2]

In the first section of the Arte, that dealing with 'Poets and Poesie', Puttenham has some comments on the nature of poetry other than those concerned with technique and style; they are, however, by way of introduction only, and his concern is primarily with formal, stylistic matters. From this point of view, to summarize his statements, Puttenham sees poetry as more regularly 'proportioned' than prose, yet freer than prose in its use of the ornaments of language and in its choice of words and phrases, and perhaps less tied to the strict requirements of grammar and syntax. The similarity to the pattern established by Gascoigne is obvious.

The remainder of the sixteenth century provides only incidental material with any new bearing on the immediate problem. Thomas Nashe, for example, usually seems to identify poetry and prose so closely as to make it difficult to know which he is referring to, or whether indeed any distinction is intended in his attacks on fine writing. In this passage written in 1589 he seems to refer primarily to prose eloquence:

Indeede, I must needes say the descending yeares from the Philoso-phers *Athens* haue not been supplied with such present Orators as were able in anie English vaine to be eloquent of their owne, but

[1] Puttenham, op. cit. , p. 76.

[2] John Brinsley, *Ludus Literarius; or, The Grammar School* (London, 1612); ed. E. T. Campagnac, *Brinsley's Ludus Literarius, reproduced from the 1627 edition* (Liverpool, 1917), p. 192. The question of prose syntax in poetry has been taken up by some recent critics, notably Donald Davie, in his *Articulate Energy* (London, 1955).

either they must borrow inuention of *Ariosto* and his Countreyman, make vp choyce of words by exchange in *Tullies Tusculane* and the Latine Historiographers store-houses, similitudes, nay whole sheetes and tractacts *verbatim*, from the plentie of *Plutarch* and *Plinie*, and to conclude, their whole methode of writing from the libertie of Comical fictions that haue succeeded to our Rethoritians by a second imitation: so that well may the Adage, *Nil dictum quod non dictum prius*, bee the most iudiciall estimate of our latter Writers.[1]

However, in keeping with the mixture of sources in this passage, the discussion that follows it seems to deal indiscriminately with poetry and prose. The position is similarly indeterminate when he talks of the need for a study of the art of writing, or when he warns against irrelevance:

There is no such discredit of Arte as an ignoraunt Artificer . . . Nothing is more odious to the Auditor then the artlesse tongue of a tedious dolt, which dulleth the delight of hearing, and slacketh the desire of remembring.[2]

. . . To the eschewing therefore of the lothing hatred of them that heare them, I would wish them to learne to speake many things in few, neither to speake all things which to theyr purpose they may speake, least those things be lesse profitably spoken which they ought to speake . . .[3]

It may be accepted that Nashe was primarily an orator, and that for him the style of poetry was likely to be determined by the needs of eloquence. It is significant that he praises Gascoigne in terms that link poetry and oratory: he it was who 'first beate the path to that perfection which our best Poets haue aspired too since his departure; whereto he did ascend by comparing the Italian with the English, as *Tullie* did *Graeca cum Latinis*'.[4]

Sir John Harington, in his 'Briefe Apologie of Poetrie' (1591), is

[1] Thomas Nashe, 'To the Gentlemen Students of both Universities', prefixed to Robert Greene's *Menaphon* (London, 1589); ed. G. G. Smith, op. cit., i, 309.

[2] Thomas Nashe, *The Anatomie of Absurditie* (London, 1589); ed. G. G. Smith, op. cit., i, 334-5.

[3] Ibid., i, 335.

[4] Thomas Nashe, 'To the Gentlemen Students . . .', op. cit., i, 315.

primarily concerned with the defence of poetry, and is not prepared 'to bestow any long time to argue whether *Plato, Zenephon,* and *Erasmus* writing fictions and Dialogues in prose may justly be called Poets, or whether *Lucan* writing a story in verse be an historiographer . . .'[1] He does, however, apparently accept 'the phrase of the common sort that terme all that is written in verse Poetrie',[2] in order to claim some value for even the lowliest forms of verse; and a large part of his defence is based on the virtues of metrical composition, in terms very similar to Puttenham's:

The other part of Poetrie, which is Verse, as it were the clothing or ornament of it, hath many good vses. Of the helpe of memorie I spake somewhat before; for the words being couched together in due order, measure, and number, one doth as it were bring on another, as my selfe haue often proued, & so I thinke do many beside (though for my own part I can rather bost of the marring of a good memorie then of hauing one), yet I haue euer found that Verse is easier to learne and farre better to preserue in memorie then is prose. An other speciall grace in Verse is the forcible manner of phrase, in which, if it be well made, it farre excelleth loose speech or prose. A third is the pleasure and sweetness to the eare which makes the discourse pleasaunt vnto vs often time when the matter it selfe is harsh and vnacceptable . . .[3]

A Defence of Ryme (1603), by Samuel Daniel, is, of course, written from a special point of view, that of poetry considered specifically as verse, and accordingly begins with the definition of all verse as 'but a frame of wordes confined within certaine measure, differing from the ordinarie speach, and introduced, the better to expresse mens conceipts, both for delight and memorie.'[4] The familiar qualities of verse which enable it to delight the ear and aid the memory are especially found in rhyme:

And for our Ryme . . . dooth adde more grace, and hath more of delight than euer bare numbers, howsoeuer they can be forced to

[1] Sir John Harington, 'A Preface, or rather a Briefe Apologie of Poetrie, and of the Author and Translator', prefixed to his translation of *Orlando Furioso* (London, 1591); ed. G. G. Smith, op. cit., ii, 196.

[2] Ibid., ii, 197.   [3] Ibid., ii, 206.

[4] Samuel Daniel, *A Defence of Ryme, against a Pamphlet entituled: 'Obseruations in the Art of English Poesie'* (London, 1603?); ed. G. G. Smith, op. cit., ii, 359.

runne in our slow language, can possibly yeeld. Which, whether it be deriu'd of *Rhythmus* or of *Romance*, which were songs the *Bards* and *Druydes* about Rymes vsed, and thereof were called *Remensi*, as some Italians holde, or howsoeuer, it is likewise number and harmonie of words, consisting of an agreeing sound in the last sillables of seuerall verses, giuing both to the Eare an Echo of a delightful report, and to the Memorie a deeper impression of what is deliuered therein.[1]

The *Defence* end, however, with a plea for the use of natural words and expression in verse:

Next to this deformitie stands our affectation, wherein we always bewray our selues to be both vnkinde and vnnaturall to our owne natiue language, in disguising or forging strange or vnusuall wordes, as if it were to make our verse seeme another kind of speach out of the course of our vsuall practise, displacing our wordes, or inuenting new, onely vpon a singularitie, when our owne accustomed phrase, set in the due place, would expresse vs more familiarly and to better delight than all this idle affectation of antiquitie or noueltie can euer do.[2]

An unusual note for his time is struck by George Chapman in the Preface to his *Ovid's Banquet of Sense* (1595): 'But that Poesie should be as *peruiall* as Oratorie and plainness her special ornament, were the plaine way to barbarisme: and to make the Asse runne proude of his eares; to take away strength from Lyons, and give Cammels horns . . .'[3] Poetry and prose, particularly rhetorical prose, were very different things for Chapman:

> . . . So men, beastly giuen,
> The manly soules voice, sacred Poesie,
>   Whose Hymnes the Angels euer sing in heauen,
> Contemne, and heare not: but when the brutish noises
>   For Gaine, Lust, Honour, in litigious Prose
> Are bellow'd-out, and cracke the barbarous voices
>   Of Turkish *Stentors*, O! ye leane to those,
> Like itching Horse to blockes or high May-poles . . .[4]

---

[1] Ibid., ii, 360.   [2] Ibid., ii, 384.

[3] George Chapman, Preface to *Ovid's Banquet of Sence: A Coronet for his Mistresse Philosophie and his amorous Zodiacke* (London, 1595).

[4] George Chapman, 'The preface to the reader II' prefixed to his translation of Homer (London, 1610–16?); ed. J. E. Spingarn, *Critical Essays of the Seventeenth Century* (3 vols., Oxford, 1908), i, 81.

Yet despite such occasional discordant voices the sixteenth century, or at least the latter part of it, shows a considerable degree of uniformity in its ideas regarding the proper style of poetry and the peculiar virtues and functions of that style. Order, harmony, proportion, a certain licence, but with it an avoidance of unnaturalness: these are the characteristics sought for in poetic style, for the reason that these things are found to induce delight in the hearer and to aid him in remembering what he hears. A distinction between poetry and prose is consistently recognized, but it is not generally emphasized: poetry is simply a more rhythmically regular, though grammatically and syntactically freer and more delightful form of discourse than prose.

It now remains to be seen how far this state of affairs carries over into the seventeenth century, and how far it has been modified by the later part of that century, particularly as a result of any growing consciousness of prose as a separate form of discourse.

The prosodic tradition represented in the later sixteenth century by Puttenham's *Arte of English Poesie* appears in the latter part of the seventeenth century in such works as Poole's *English Parnassus* (1657), and Bysshe's *Art of English Poetry* (1702). Of these Bysshe's work differs from Puttenham's in that it provides a much more rigid and extensive treatment of metrics, but does not deal at all with the rhetorical figures of thought and sound, consideration of which had occupied the greater part of the earlier work.[1] Joshua Poole's *English Parnassus* lies midway between the two, in content as well as time, with considerable attention given to prosody, but with still some consideration of the figures. During the second half of the seventeenth century, indeed, the treatment of the rhetorical figures appears to have been separated from poetics and dealt with in such works as Thomas Blount's *Academie of Eloquence* (1654), and John Smith's *Mysterie of rhetorique unveil'd* (1657), the latter of which was

[1] One reason for this concentration of attention on prosody may have been that Bysshe's work was largely a direct adaptation from a French work on prosody; see A. D. Culler, 'Edward Bysshe and the Poet's Handbook', *PMLA*, lxiii (1948), 858–85.

probably the most popular rhetoric of the period, ten editions of it having appeared prior to 1721. In turn, these rhetorics concerned themselves wholly with prose oratory.

At the same time as there was this tendency to neglect the rhetorical figures in the theoretical treatment of poetry it also became fashionable, in keeping with the general derogation of rhetoric, and also perhaps as part of the reaction against the extravagance of later metaphysical wit, to disparage the type of poetic wit which relied on these rhetorical figures. Samuel Butler, for example, around 1670, allows that the figures of sound (*figurae dictionis*) are already avoided, but also objects to the continued fashion for the use of the figures of thought (*figurae sententiae*):

There are two sorts of Quibbling, the one with Words, and the other with Sense, like the Rhetoricians *Figurae Dictionis* & *Figurae Sententiae*—The first is already cried down, and the other as yet prevails; and is the only Elegance of our modern Poets, which easy Judges call *Easiness*; but having nothing in it but Easiness, and being never used by any lasting Wit, will in wiser Times fall to nothing of itself.[1]

And Dryden professes to a similar attitude towards rhetorical wit:

Tis' not the jerk or sting of an epigram, nor the seeming contradiction of a poor antithesis (the delight of an ill-judging audience in a play of rhyme), nor the jingle of a more poor paronomasia; neither is it so much the morality of a grave sentence, affected by Lucan, but more sparingly used by Virgil; but it is some lively and apt description, dressed in such colours of speech, that it sets before your eyes the absent object, as perfectly, and more delightfully than nature.[2]

This was written in 1667, and more than thirty years later, when writing of Ovid's poetry in the preface to his *Fables*, Dryden again expressed similar views about poetic wit. But this apparent divorce

[1] Samuel Butler, *Characters and Passages from Note-books;* ed. A. R. Waller (Cambridge, 1908), p. 90.
[2] Dryden, Preface to *Annus Mirabilis: The Year of Wonders MDCLXVI* (London, 1667); ed. W. P. Ker, *Essays of John Dryden*, op. cit., i, 14–15. N.B. All references to Dryden's critical writings, unless otherwise specified, will be to the Ker edition.

of poetry from rhetoric is made less significant than it might otherwise be by the fact that wit based on a marriage of the neo-classic
couplet and the figures of classical rhetoric continued in practice to
be the common characteristic of the work of poets at least until the
time of Pope, who was perhaps its most skilled exponent.[1]

In the Preface to Poole's *English Parnassus*, one J.D., who it has
been suggested may possibly have been John Dryden, declares that
'harmony, in *prose*, consists in an exact placing of the accent, and an
accurate *disposition* of the words . . . In *Poesie* it consists besides the
aforesaid conditions of Prose in measure, proportion, and Rhime.'[2]
The attitude implied here towards poetic style as differing from
prose only, or at least primarily, on formal, prosodic grounds, is the
one most likely to be stated during this period, whenever the subject is approached directly. Dryden, for example, writing some six
years after the publication of this Preface, refers to blank verse as
'measured prose';[3] that is, as being too close to prose because it
lacks the additional formality of rhyme. This treatment of form as
the distinguishing mark of poetry is not new—all the elements of it
are in Puttenham's work, though given less prominence than his
treatment of the figures, and Puttenham, together with other
sixteenth-century writers such as Chapman and Gabriel Harvey,
thought of verse as the essential ingredient of poetry. None the less
it is undoubtedly one aspect of the formalism associated with the
neo-classic movement that it should receive greater emphasis during
this period.

The general answer, then, to questions regarding the difference
between the styles of poetry and prose that could be expected in the
later seventeenth century would be that the former is more regularly proportioned, more under formal control than the latter.
However, more revealing for the present purpose are the scattered
incidental comments of poets and critics such as Cowley, Dryden,
or Dennis, when other considerations bring them back, as they tend

[1] This use of rhetorical wit in the heroic couplet is fully discussed by G. E.
Williamson, 'The Rhetorical Pattern of Neo-Classical Wit', op. cit.

[2] J.D., Preface to Poole's *English Parnassus* (London, 1657).

[3] Dryden, 'Epistle Dedicatory to the *Rival Ladies*' (London, 1664); op.
cit., i, 6.

often to do, to matters of poetic style. These comments will be found frequently to reveal a remarkable similarity to those of a century earlier.

Abraham Cowley was one who recognized a distinction between the proprieties of prose and poetry—Dr. Johnson thought that 'no author ever kept his verse and prose at a greater distance from each other'. In the manner of the sixteenth century he tended to allow a greater freedom to poetry than to prose. In a note to his imitation of Claudian in the Ode *To Mr. Hobs* (1656) he comments that: '*Tacitus* has the like expression . . . which is too *poetical* for the prose even of a Romance, much more of an *Historian*.'[1] In another note, this time to his *Davideis* (1656), he declares that an expression may be poetically though not literally true; but, he says, 'I confess indeed in a *Declamation* I like not those kind of Flowers so well.'[2] Here he is contrasting poetry and oratorical prose, and the enthusiasm of the Pindaric style is thought to be similarly unsuitable for prose: 'You may wonder, Sir, (for this seems a little too extravagant and Pindarical for Prose) what I mean by all this Preface . . .'[3] Elsewhere Cowley comments on the Pindaric style in a manner interesting for its implication of a special 'poetic logic', and also perhaps as having some relationship to Puttenham's suggestion of a difference between the syntactical arrangement of prose and that of verse:

The manner of the *Prophets* writing, especially of Isaiah, seems to me very like that of Pindar; they pass from one thing to another with almost *Invisible connexions*, and are full of words and expressions of the highest and boldest flights of *Poetry*, as may be seen in this Chapter, where there are as extraordinary Figures as can be found in any Poet whatsoever; and the connexion is so difficult, that I am forced to adde a little, and leave out a great deal to make it seem *Sense* to us, who are not used to that elevated way of expression . . . for the old fashion of writing, was like *Disputing* in *Enthymemes*, where half is left out to be

---

[1] Abraham Cowley, 'To Mr. Hobs', n. 1 to st. 6; in *Pindarique Odes, written in imitation of the stile & manner of the Odes of Pindar; The Works of Abraham Cowley* (London, 1668), p. 29.

[2] Cowley, *Davideis*, Bk. II, n. 89; op. cit., p. 89.

[3] Cowley, 'The Garden, to J. Evelyn Esquire'; in *Several Discourses by way of essays in verse and prose;* op. cit., p. 115.

supplyed by the Hearer: ours is like Syllogisms, where all that is meant is exprest.[1]

Clearly the Pindaric is for Cowley the most licensed form of poetry, and its style quite out of place in prose. In this his attitude looks forward to that of the eighteenth century towards the lyric, but at the same time he reveals his ties with his own age by his desire to modify the structure of the Pindaric style in order that it may 'seem sense to us'.

For Dryden, as it had been for Puttenham, what is proper for the ornamentation of verse may not be proper for prose. Of new words, for example, Dryden writes in 1666: '. . . you have taken notice of some words, which I have innovated (if it be too bold for me to say refined) upon his Latin; which, as I offer not to introduce into English prose, so I hope they are neither improper, nor altogether unelegant in verse'.[2] Applied to words this is perhaps a strengthening of the recurrent sixteenth-century opposition to the introduction of new words, and as such is no doubt evidence of the settling down of the vocabulary after its period of expansion through the adoption of foreign words. However, the accompanying attitude that what is suitable for poetry may not be so for prose is a familiar one.

With an even more noticeable echo of Gascoigne and Puttenham, Dryden writes in 1667 on the matter of 'poetic licence', and on the manner in which figures, while they are not to be excluded from prose altogether, have their range and force restricted by comparison with their use in poetry:

Poetic Licence I take to be the liberty which poets have assumed to themselves, in all ages, of speaking things in verse, which are beyond the severity of prose. 'Tis that particular character which distinguishes and sets the bounds betwixt *oratio soluta* and poetry. This, as to what regards the thought or imagination of the poet, consists in fiction: but then those thoughts must be expressed; and here arises two other branches of it; for if this licence be included in a single

[1] Cowley, 'The 34. Chapter of the Prophet Isaiah', n. 1 to st. 1; in Pindarique Odes . . . op. cit., p. 50.
[2] Dryden, Preface to *Annus Mirabilis*, op. cit., i, 17.

word, it admits of tropes; if in a sentence or proposition, of figures; both which are of much larger extent, and more forcibly to be used in verse than prose.[1]

Again, writing in 1668 of the prose of Sir Robert Howard, Dryden implies a similar distinction between the styles of poetry and oratory: '. . . I cannot but give this testimony of his style, that it is extreme poetical, even in oratory; his thoughts elevated sometimes above common apprehension . . .; that they are abundantly interlaced with variety of fancies, tropes, and figures, which the critics have enviously branded with the name of obscurity and false grammar.'[2]

Elsewhere in other incidental remarks Dryden reflects the same kind of opposition to the over-use of 'poetic' devices in prose. Similes may be used in prose by way of illustration, but they are not the same as argument: 'I am almost fearful of illustrating anything by similitude, lest he should confute it for an argument . . .'[3] And metaphorical expression is improper in definition, as Dryden suggests by turning to direct expression, in recognition of possible criticism, with an apologetic 'or without metaphor'.[4] These latter sorts of remarks, even allowing for their probable irony, might be seen as signs of a growing demand for exactness in prose expression, were it not for their obvious echo of the rules of logic, as Dryden would no doubt have learned them at Westminster School, along with his predecessors at that and similar institutions of learning since their foundation; in fact, they reflect only the traditional distinction between logical and rhetorical (or poetic) expression.

Thus far, in matters appertaining to style, the remarks of these seventeenth-century theorists have not shown any material clarification, beyond that achieved by Puttenham, of the distinction between poetry and prose. Indeed, rather than the tendency being

---

[1] Dryden, 'The Author's Apology for Heroic Poetry and Poetic Licence', prefixed to *The State of Innocence and Fall of Man, an Opera* (London, 1677); op. cit., i, 188–9.

[2] Dryden, 'A Defence of an Essay of Dramatic Poesy' prefixed to the Second Edition of the *Indian Emperour* (London, 1668); op. cit., i, 119.

[3] Ibid., i, 129.

[4] Dryden, Preface to *Annus Mirabilis*, op. cit., i, 14.

towards a sharper distinction of the two forms, it is towards a greater clarity in the acceptance of prose as a norm of style, from which poetry may be allowed to depart, but always at its peril. This attitude is not altogether new: Gascoigne had required the poet to 'remember to place euery worde in his natural *Emphasis* or sound, that is to say, in such wise, and with such length or shortnesse, eleuation or depression of sillables, as it is commonly pronounced or vsed', and the familiar concept of 'poetic licence' had implied a norm, departure from which this licence allowed. All that is new, perhaps, is the greater emphasis on prose usage as a guide.

Blank verse is criticized by Dryden when 'the clauses are placed unnaturally, that is, contrary to the common way of speaking'.[1] Similarly, the poet should make it his general rule that 'the words be placed as they are in the negligence of prose',[2] and they are not to be inverted for the sake of rhyme:

This is that which makes them say, rhyme is not natural, it being only so, when the poet either makes a vicious choice of words, or places them, for rhyme sake, so unnaturally as no man would in ordinary speaking; but when 'tis so judiciously ordered, that the first word in the verse seems to beget the second, and that the next, till that becomes the last word in the line, which, in the negligence of prose would be so; it must then be granted, rhyme has all the advantages of prose, besides it own.[3]

The ideal poetic style aimed at here by Dryden is very similar to that of the loose, or fluent Senecan style which tended to replace 'curt' prose as the characteristic style of the later seventeenth century, and of which Dryden himself was a leading exponent. Florid style in prose is consistently condemned by Dryden, but it is also condemned in poetry. He criticizes Shakespeare because, he says, his 'whole style is so pestered with figurative expressions, that it is as affected as it is obscure'. Wit, for Dryden, whether in prose or verse, is not to be achieved in this manner, but '. . . is best con-

---

[1] Dryden, *An Essay of Dramatic Poesy* (London, 1668); op. cit., i, 94–95.
[2] Ibid., i, 98.
[3] Dryden, Epistle Dedicatory to the *Rival Ladies*, op. cit., i, 7.

veyed to us in most easy language; and is most to be admired when a great thought comes dressed in words so commonly received . . . So that there is this difference betwixt his [Cleveland's] *Satires* and Doctor Donne's; that the one gives us deep thoughts in common language, though rough cadence; the other gives us common thoughts in abstruse words.'[1]

Similar evidence of the value placed on prose clarity in poetry is provided by Edward Phillips in the preface to his *Theatrum Poetarum* (1675). He concludes a discussion of verse forms by saying:

. . . let the fashion of the Verse be what it will, according to the different humour of the Writer, if the Style be elegant and suitable, the Verse, whatever it is, may be the better dispenc'd with; and the truth is the use of Measure alone without any Rime at all would give far more ample Scope and liberty both to Style and fancy then can possibly be observed in Rime, as evidently appears from an *English* Heroic poem which came forth not many years ago, and from the Style of *Virgil*, *Horace*, *Ovid*, and others of the *Latins*, which is so pure and proper that it could not possibly have been better in Prose . . .[2]

John Dennis's *The Impartial Critic* (1693), too, at almost the end of the period, repeats the same pattern of a recognition of some relatively minor distinctions between the styles of poetry and prose, but with an even more explicit demand for the application of prose rules to poetry. In discussing the relative merits of the styles of Waller and Dryden he writes:

Yet if any one is of Opinion that either his [Waller's] Language or Numbers are always perfect, he errs; For as there are sometimes improprieties in his Expressions, so there is a great deal of Prose in his Verse. *Mr. Dryden*, who had the good luck to come after him, has the honour to have finish'd what the other so happily begun. For as we have nothing to show, e'en in Prose, which has greater purity than some of his blank Verse, and particularly that of the *Spanish Fryar* (tho at the same time that it has the purity and easiness of Prose, it has the

---

[1] Dryden, *An Essay of Dramatic Poesy*, op. cit., i, 52.
[2] Edward Phillips, Preface to *Theatrum Poetarum; or, A Compleat Collection of the Poets* (London, 1675); ed. Spingarn, op. cit., ii, 266.

dignity and strength of Poetry), so I cannot imagine anything more perfect than his Equal numbers in Heroic Verse . . .[1]

Though this passage makes some distinction between poetry and prose, the dialogue that follows shortly after it, in which Waller's lines are subjected to close analysis, shows quite clearly what Dennis considers to be their common elements. His aim is to show the imperfections of some of Waller's lines, which he does by pointing to their shortcomings as prose:

BEAUMONT reads:

> Where e're thy Navy spreads her Canvas Wings
> Homage to thee, and Peace to all she brings.

Have you anything to say to that Couplet?

FREEMAN: Yes; if Mr. Waller had been to say that in Prose, he would have expressed himself otherwise: he would have said thus: Where e're thy Fleet goes, she carries Peace to all, and causes all to pay or to do Homage to thee: For where e're she goes she brings Homage; would not be good English in Prose.

BEAUM: Why, will you allow nothing to be said in Verse that may not be said in Prose too?

FREEM: Yes, an expression may be too florid, or too bold for Prose, and yet very becoming of Verse. But every Expression that is false English in Prose is barbarous and absurd in Verse too . . .[2]

In this last statement Mr. Freeman sums up, not only for Dennis but apparently for Dryden and Cowley and, it would probably be safe to say, for the majority of their contemporaries as well. His attitude might be compared, for example, with Dryden's comments on the 'false grammar'—including the putting of a preposition at the end of a sentence—of which he found Ben Jonson guilty in his poetry. And at the same time he is not so very far removed from Gascoigne or Puttenham. It is true that in his later (1717) remarks on Pope's

---

[1] John Dennis, 'The Impartial Critic': or, some Observations upon a late book, entituled, a short view of tragedy, written by Mr. Rymer (London, 1693); ed. E. N. Hooker, The Critical Works of John Dennis (2 vols., Baltimore, 1939), i, 14. N.B. All references to Dennis are to this edition.

[2] Ibid., i, 24.

Homer Dennis seems to imply that the difference between poetry and prose, at least in diction, lies in the use of figures:

> . . . a Translator of Homer has but one way of rendering his Diction Poetical; and that is, the frequent Use of Figures, and above all of Metaphors. And therefore, where-ever in the late translation of Homer, there is no Use of Figures, there we may justly conclude, that the Diction is Prosaick . . . Now, in the late Translation of Homer, there are, modestly speaking, Twenty Lines where there is no Figure, for One that is Figurative; and consequently, there are Twenty Prosaick Lines, for One that is Poetical.[1]

This identification of 'figurative' with 'poetic' writing, however, seems, for reasons that are as hard to understand as the argument is weak in logic, to apply only to the translation of Homer; the distinction is not elsewhere reduced to this simple formula, and antagonism to Pope may have been the reason here.

These views put forward by Dennis come, it might be remembered, from a critic who will be cited later in this study as one of those whose ideas pointed the way from neo-classicism to the new horizons of eighteenth-century poetic theory, and who therefore cannot be regarded as untypically prosaic in his attitudes.

There seems to be little evidence, at least from the writings of three such representatives and influential critics as Cowley, Dryden, and Dennis, of any material development of a distinction between poetry and prose, in matters related to style, that would serve to mark off the later seventeenth century from the last quarter of the sixteenth. The furthest extent of the distinction as it was commonly accepted might be summed up in these lines written in 1700 by one Samuel Wesley:

> 'A different Style's for *Prose* and *Verse* requir'd;
> *Strong Figures* here, Neat Plainness there desir'd:
> A different *Set of Words* to both belong,
> What *shines* in *Prose*, is *flat* and *mean* in *Song*'.[2]

---

[1] Dennis, *Remarks upon Mr. Pope's Translation of Homer* . . . (London, 1717); op. cit., ii, 123. [2] Samuel Wesley, *An Epistle to a Friend concerning Poetry* (London, 1700), ll. 154–7.

On the other hand, even among poets and critics of poetry there does appear to have been a sharper awareness of prose which can be seen as having had some influence on their attitude to poetic style. Yet once again this influence apparently did not work in the direction of a materially greater distinction between the styles of the two forms; on the contrary, it tended to strengthen the influence of prose characteristics on poetry. With this sharper awareness of prose in mind, attention will now be turned temporarily from poets and critics of poetry to those men whose primary interest was in prose, or in those things for which prose was becoming recognized as the natural medium.

In the writings of Sir Francis Bacon the early part of the seventeenth century saw one of its most influential figures in matters of discourse virtually deny that style has any essential relationship to poetry at all:

Poesy is a part of Learning in measure of words for the most part restrained, but in all other points extremely licensed, and doth truly refer to the Imagination . . . It is taken in two senses, in respect of words or matter. In the first sense it is but a character of style, and belongeth to artes of speech, and is not pertinent for the present. In the later, it is (as hath been said) one of the principal portions of learning, and is nothing else but Feigned History, which may be styled as well in prose as in verse.[1]

This again raises the old problem of the position of verse in relation to poetry, but, as will be discussed later, without Bacon's having anything new to add to it. On the immediate question of style Bacon allows at least for the traditional distinction between poetry and prose when he speaks of poetry as being 'in measure of words for the most part restrained': restrained, that is, by the demands of metrical or rhythmical form. His reference to 'licence' in the same sentence, however, seems to be to imaginative rather than to stylistic licence, to content rather than to style.

[1] Francis Bacon, *The Twoo Books of Francis Bacon, of the Proficiencie and Advancement of Learning, Divine and Humane* (London, 1605); ed. J. Spedding and R. H. Ellis, *The Philosophical Works of Francis Bacon* (5 vols., London, 1861), iii, 343.

Elsewhere Bacon has something to say of poetry as the 'measured' use of words, and of the special relationship, in poetry, between subject-matter and form, or genre. In this context poetry is one of the 'accidents of words'— sound, measure, and accent—and as such its treatment is part of grammar:

The Measure of words has produced a vast body of art; namely Poesy, considered with reference not to the matter of it (of which I have spoken above) but to the style and form of words: that is to say, metre or verse; wherein the art we have is a very small thing, but the examples are large and innumerable. Neither should that art (which the grammarians call Prosody) be confined to the teaching of the kinds and measures of verse. Precepts should be added as to the kinds of verse which best suit each matter or subject. The ancients used hexameter for histories and eulogies; elegiac for complaints; iambic for invectives; lyric for odes and hymns . . . In these things the judgement of the sense is to be preferred to the precepts of art,—as the poet says,   Coenae fercula nostrae
Mallem convivis quam placiusse cocis.[1]

Bacon, however, is essentially a rhetorician, interested in prose discourse rather than in poetry. His ideas on poetry are almost completely derived from earlier authorities, and they seem to have been inserted only for the sake of the completeness of his scheme.[2] His influence in the later seventeenth century was on men whose interest also was in prose rather than in poetry; rightly or wrongly he was hailed as the apostle of the new scientific method, and his attacks on rhetorical display for its own sake became one of the main instruments towards the development of 'plain' style in prose. The new scientists' preference for 'things' rather than words found what it wanted in Bacon's attacks on sixteenth-century 'Ciceronianism'. 'The whole inclination and bent of those times was rather towards copie than weight', declared Bacon, and this:

. . . grew speedily to excess; for men began to hunt more after words than matter; and more after the choiceness of the phrase, and the round

<hr>

[1] Bacon, *De dignitate et augmentis scientiarum* (London, 1623); op. cit., iv. 443.
[2] On this matter see M. W. Bundy, 'Bacon's True Opinion of Poetry', *SP*, xxvii (1930), 244–64; see also below, pp. 143–51.

and clean composition of the sentence, and the sweet falling of the clauses, and the varying and illustration of their works with tropes and figures, than after weight of matter, worth of subject, soundness of argument, life of invention, or depth of judgement.[1]

It is for the part he played in influencing the decline of eloquence more than for anything he had to say directly about poetry that Bacon is important for a study of seventeenth-century poetic style.

From the time of Bacon onwards the almost constant theme of those who discuss prose is the need for a plain, straightforward style. This theme is expressed in two main fields which are no doubt related, but whose degree of interdependence is immaterial for the present purpose. On the one hand plain style is associated with the development of experimental science and the scientific attitude, and its exponents are the members of the newly formed Royal Society of London, and those who come under their influence; on the other hand, the same theme appears in the attacks of church-men on 'pulpit eloquence'; in the demand for a plainer style of preaching which would bring the spirit of science to religion through scientific exactness in using words for the expression of moral and religious truths.

These movements were so widespread that they must be assumed to have had their effect on poetry. At least it can be taken as vir-tually certain that poetry was affected by the same spirit of scientific rationalism as was informing the discourse of both scientists and preachers—an amusing instance of the influence of Descartes on Dryden is provided by the opening lines of Act II, Scene I of Dryden's *State of Innocence and Fall of Man* (1667), which opens with Adam 'as newly created, laid on a bed of moss and flowers, by a rock . . . ADAM: What am I? or from whence? For that I am I know, because I think . . .' In the case of poetry this spirit was reinforced by the strengthening of the classical spirit associated with the neo-classic movement. Yet it must be remembered also that these influences were such as tended to bring poetry and prose together, rather than to distinguish the one from the other. They

[1] Bacon, *The Advancement of Learning*, op. cit., iii, 283.

are influences, indeed, which have been seen as largely responsible for giving the poetry of the later seventeenth century its essentially prosaic reputation.

For Bacon eloquence was a hindrance only to the progress of learning, not to its use:

But yet notwithstanding it is a thing not hastily to be condemned, to clothe and adorn the obscurity even of philosophy itself with sensible and plausible elocution . . . to the severe inquisitions of truth, and the deep progress into philosophy, it is some hindrance; because it is too early satisfactory to the mind of man, and quencheth the desire of further search, before we come to a just period; but then if a man be to have any use of such knowledge in civil occasions, of conference, counsel, persuasion, discourse, or the like, then shall he find it prepared to his hands in those authors which write in that manner.[1]

Bacon would, in fact, seek to extend rhetoric into the field of learned as well as of popular communication, in order to fill the gap caused by his tendency to withdraw logic into the field of inquiry rather than that of communication—but only in so far as rhetoric was used for the dissemination or recall of knowledge, and not for the progress of knowledge. To the scientists and preachers of the later part of the century, however, all eloquence, no matter what its purpose, was likely to be distrusted.

Alexander Ross, although he was no scientist—an 'Aristotelian fundamentalist' he has been called—was an early member of the group who followed Bacon in demanding an emphasis on things rather than words. 'Expect not here from me Rhetorical flourishes', he declared in 1645; 'I study matter not words.'[2] Ross here follows Bacon in his description of 'fantastical learning' when 'men began to hunt more after words than matter'; and both neatly reverse the judgement of the sixteenth-century humanist Ascham—'Ye know not what hurt ye do to learning, that care not for words but for matter.'[3] And Bishop Sprat himself, the spokesman for the Royal

[1] Ibid., iii, 284.
[2] Alexander Ross, Epistle Dedicatory to *Medicus Medicatus* (London, 1645).
[3] Roger Ascham, *The Scholemaster* (London, 1570); *English Writings*, op. cit., p. 265.

Society, pointed out in his *History of the Royal Society of London* (1667): '. . . there is one thing more, about which the Society has been most solicitous; and that is, the manner of their *Discourse*; which, unless they had been very watchful to keep in due temper, the whole spirit and vigour of their *Design*, had been soon eaten out, by the luxury and redundance of speech.'[1] Sprat states the aim of the Society in matters of discourse as that of 'bringing all things as near the Mathematical plainness, as they can; and preferring the language of Artizans, Countrymen, and Merchants, before that of Wits or Scholars'.[2] This ideal may be compared with Puttenham's warning against following 'the speach of a craftes man or carter, or other of the inferiour sort, though he be inhabitant or bred in the best towne and Citie in this Realme.'[3] Here is clear evidence of the difference between the rhetorical theory that helped shape the poetry of the sixteenth century and the attitude towards rhetoric that shaped the prose of the seventeenth.

The stylistic ideas expressed by Sprat were repeated a year later by an even more influential and energetic campaigner for plain style, John Wilkins, in his *Essay toward a Real Character and a Philosophical Language* (1668). The doctrine put forward by Wilkins again sought to avoid 'ambiguity of words by reason of Metaphor and Phraseology' by demanding an exact, orthographical correspondence between words and things—'a Real Universal Character, that should not signify words, but things and notions'.[4] Hobbes's *Leviathan* (1651) had paid tribute to the power of words, but only if they are fully under the control of the reason and purged of any figurative element:

The Light of humane minds is Perspicuous Words, but by exact definitions first snuffed, and purged free from ambiguity; Reason is the pace; Encrease of Science, the way; and the Benefit of man-kind, the end. And on the contrary, Metaphors, and senseless and am-

---

[1] Thomas Sprat, *The History of the Royal Society of London* (London, 1667), p. III.

[2] Ibid., p. 113.

[3] Puttenham, *Arte of English Poesie*, op. cit., p. 144.

[4] John Wilkins, *Essay towards a Real Character and a Philosophical Language* (London, 1668), p. 13.

biguous words, are like *ignes fatui;* and reasoning upon them, is wandering amongst innumerable absurdities; and their end, contention, and sedition, or contempt.[1]

John Locke, too, forty years later, in his *Essay concerning Human Understanding* (1690) is strongly aware of the power of words to deceive when they are elaborated beyond the demands of clarity: 'If we would speak of things as they are, we must allow that all the art of rhetoric, besides order and clearness; all the artificial and figurative application of words eloquence hath invented, are for nothing else but to insinuate wrong ideas, move the passions, and thereby mislead the judgement; and so indeed are prefect cheats . . .'[2]

The advocates of plain style in preaching are likely to be even more outspoken. Samuel Parker, who was Bishop of Oxford and also a member of the Royal Society, argued in his *Discourse of Ecclesiastical Politie* (1671) for a new law forbidding 'all fulsome and lushious Metaphors',[3] which if passed he believed would cure 'all our present Distempers'; and Robert South, perhaps the finest exponent in the seventeenth century of a sermon style that was plain without being dull and monotonous, preaching in 1686 on 'The Fatal Imposture and Force of Words', declared:

As for the meaning of the word itself, that may shift for itself, and as for the sense and reason of it, that has little or nothing to do here; only let it sound full and round, and chime right to the humour, which is at present agog, (just as a big, long, rattling name is said to command adoration even in a Spaniard), and no doubt, with this powerful, senseless engine, the rabble-driver shall be able to carry all before him, or draw all after him, as he pleases. For a plausible and magnificent word, in the mouth of an expert demagogue is a dangerous and dreadful weapon . . .

The truth is, he who shall duly consider these matters will find that

[1] Hobbes, *Leviathan* (London, 1651), ch. v (Everyman ed., London, 1914), p. 22.

[2] John Locke, *An Essay concerning Human Understanding* (London, 1690), III, x, 34; ed. A. C. Fraser (2 vols., Oxford, 1894), ii, 146.

[3] Samuel Parker, *A Discourse of Ecclesiastical Politie* (London, 1671), p. 76.

there is a certain bewitchery, or fascination in words, which makes them operate with a force beyond what we naturally give an account of.[1]

Again, some eighteen years earlier South had declared that 'if we look into the reason of the thing itself, it will be found, that all obscurity of speech is resolvable into the confusion and disorder of the speaker's thoughts . . .'[2]

Another of the advocates of plain preaching, John Eachard, finds 'Hard Words, High Notions, and Unprofitable Quotations out of learned languages' among the many grounds on which the clergy is held in contempt.[3] His view of rhetoric, however, is a relatively moderate one; he does not condemn it out of hand, for as he says: 'I have no reason, Sir, to go about to determine what style or method is best for the improvement and advantage of all people.' Nevertheless there are some kinds of rhetoric which appear foolish to everyone, amongst which 'may chiefly be reckoned these following, *harsh Metaphors, childish Similitudes and ill-applied Tales*'. Such things are judged 'absolutely ridiculous . . . by every man in the Corporation that understands plain English and common sense . . .'[4] Despite his acceptance of 'true and allowable Rhetoric', it is obvious from the tone of Eachard's pamphlet that he found little enough of it coming from England's pulpits.

Locke in *Some Thoughts Concerning Education* (1693) urged that parents whose children had a liking for poetry should see that this was 'stifled and suppressed as much as may be'.[5] But this sort of direct attack on poetry seems to have been the exception rather

---

[1] Robert South, 'The Fatal Imposture and Force of Words': sermon preached on 9th May 1686; R. South, *Sermons preached on several occasions* (7 vols., Oxford, 1823), ii, 123–4.

[2] South, 'Christ's Promise the Support of his Despised Ministers': Sermon preached at Christ's Church, Oxford, on 30th April 1668, being Ascension Day; *Dr. South's Sermons* (2 vols., Oxford, 1855), i, 519.

[3] John Eachard, 'The Grounds & Occasions of the Contempt of the Clergy and Religion enquired into in a letter written to R. L.' (London, 1670); ed. E. Arber, *An English Garner* (8 vols., London, 1895), vii, 270.

[4] Ibid., vii, 271.

[5] Locke, *Some Thoughts Concerning Education*, sect. 174; *The Works* (10 vols., London, 1812), ix, 167.

than the rule. It was eloquence, or rhetoric, rather than poetry, that the scientists and preachers attacked, and the importance of their attitude for poetry was indirect only, the result of poetry's close association with rhetoric. The result for poetry of the loss by rhetoric of its traditional status will be discussed elsewhere, particularly in relation to the concept of 'verbal utility'.[1] In the meanwhile, some measure of the likely effect may be suggested by such a remark as the following, in which Joseph Glanvill seeks to excuse part of his Preface to *The Vanity of Dogmatizing* (1661): 'That some grains may be allowed to a rhetoricall display which will not bear the rigour of a critical severity . . .'[2] Here Glanvill makes a plea for rhetoric, which though it is based on the traditional distinction between rhetorical and logical discourse, nevertheless uses terms that are very similar to many of those seen earlier in this chapter as having served to distinguish prose from poetry.

If there is this tendency to make the same kind of distinction between rhetorical and philosophic (i.e. scientific) prose as was being made between prose and poetry generally, then the result is likely to be some measure of identification of poetry with rhetorical prose: that is, with the elements of discourse that the advocates of plain style objected to. That something of the kind did, in fact, tend to occur is indicated by these regrets at the death of Cowley, contained in a postscript to a translation of Rapin made in 1672, and reflecting the current hostility to ornate pulpit style:

The death of the most excellent Mr. Cowley is very much to be lamented, which with that of his Life, gave an unhappy period to the design he had conceived to give us the pattern of several Stiles fitted for several Subjects; His example might have put some bounds to *that Poetick rage, from whose invasion our holy places have not escaped* [my italics]: Certainly none knew better than he, how modestly to confine that Wanton: And in this it may be truly affirmed, he hath left very few successors. The Stiles of our most witty men, seem the dictates of the same spirit which inspires them in their raptures.[3]

[1] See below, Chap. 3.

[2] Joseph Glanvill, *The Vanity of Dogmatizing* (London, 1661).

[3] René Rapin, *Reflections upon the Eloquence of these Times* (London, 1672), pp. 157-8.

And a little later (1684) Gilbert Burnet associated the rhymed heroic play with the extravagance of current pulpit oratory:

The English Language has wrought itself out, both of the fulsome Pedantry under which it laboured long ago, and the trifling way of dark and unintelligible Wit that came after that, and out of the course extravagance of Canting that succeeded this: but as one Extream commonly produces another, so we were beginning to fly into a sublime pitch, of a strong but false Rhetorick, which had much corrupted, not only the stage, but even the Pulpit; two places, that tho they ought not to be named together, much less to resemble one another . . .[1]

In a similar strain, Dr. South, in his plea for 'an unaffected plainness and simplicity' in the style of sermons, and for an avoidance of rhetorical ornament, declares that '. . . he who thinks to furnish himself out of plays and romances with language for the pulpit, shews himself much fitter to act a part in the revels, than for a cure of souls.'[2] Another adviser of would-be preachers, James Arderne, in 1671 warns them '. . . nor suffer your fancy to be tempted towards following of Poetick, or Romantic writings, the latter being good for nothing, and the other best in its own measures.[3]' And finally Joseph Glanvill attacks the congregations who 'come to Sermons with the same appetites and inclinations, as they go to see, and hear Plays'.[4]

In a more positive way, the same attitude seems to be behind the defence of the Biblical use of rhetorical figures, on the ground that the relevant parts of the Scriptures are, in fact, poetry. David's Psalms are 'pieces of Divine Poetry, in which Passions are wont to be expressed much otherwise than they ought to do in plain and familiar speech';[5] and '. . . there is a vast difference between

[1] Gilbert Burnet, Preface to his translation of More's *Utopia* (London, 1684).
[2] South, 'Christ's Promise the Support of his Despised Ministers', op. cit., i, 519.
[3] James Arderne, *Directions Concerning the Matter and Stile of Sermons* (London, 1671); ed. J. Mackay (Oxford, 1952), pp. 23–24.
[4] Glanvill, *An Essay concerning Preaching* (London, 1678), p. 87.
[5] S. Patrick, *A Friendly Debate between a Conformist* . . . (London, 1666), pp. 85–86.

Poetical Descriptions, such as the Book of Canticles is, and Practical Discourses for the Government of our Lives; the first requires more Garnish and Ornament, and justifies the most mysterious flights of Fancy; the second requires a plain and simple dress, which may convey the Notions with ease and perspicuity to the mind.'[1] Dr. South, too, despite his insistence on plain sermons, is prepared to defend the rhetoric of the Bible as supreme poetry:

. . . by knowledge a man informs himself, so by expression he conveys that knowledge to others; and as bare words convey, so the propriety and elegance of them gives force and facility to the conveyance. But because this is likely to have more opposers, especially such as call a speaking coherently upon any sacred subject, a blending of man's wisdom with the word, an offering of strange fire; and account the being pertinent even the next door to being profane, I say for their sake, I shall prove a thing clear in itself by Scripture, and that not by arguments, or consequences drawn from thence, but by downright instances occurring in it, and those so very plain, that even such as themselves cannot be ignorant of them. For in God's words we have not only a body of religion, but also a system of the best rhetoric: and as the highest things require the highest expressions, we shall find nothing in the Scripture so sublime in itself, but it is reached and sometimes overtopped by the sublimity of expression. And first where did majesty ever ride in more splendour than in those descriptions of the divine power in Job . . . and then for the passions of the soul; which being things of the highest transport and most wonderful and various operation in human nature, are therefore the proper object and business of rhetoric; let us take a view how the Scriptures express the most noted and powerful of them. And here, what poetry ever paralleled Solomon in his description of love.[2]

And, against his advocacy of plain style and his opposition to poetic ornament in sermons, South is prepared to defend the use of the

[1] William Sherlock, *A defence and continuation of the discourse concerning the knowledge* . . . (London, 1675), p. 168.

[2] South, 'The Scribe instructed . . .'; sermon preached on 29th July 1660; *Sermons Preached on Several Occasions*, op. cit., iii, 21–22.

imagination when preaching concerning the qualifications of a 'scribe':

Third faculty, which is invention: a faculty acting chiefly in the strength of what is offered by the imagination . . . I see not why divinity . . . should be deprived of the services of a most useful and excellent endowment of the mind, and which gives a gloss and shine to all the rest . . . if . . . we take fancy for that power or ability of the mind, which suggests apposite and pertinent expressions, and handsome ways of clothing and setting off those truths which the judgement has rationally pitched upon, it will be found full as useful as any of all the three mentioned by us in the work of preaching [judgement, memory, and invention].[1]

Indeed, it is in the attitude of such men as South to the essentially poetic qualities of the Bible that the distinctions ultimately to be reached between poetry and prose are more clearly forecast than in anything said by the seventeenth-century poets or critics themselves. This, however, goes beyond considerations of style and will therefore be left for later treatment. In the meantime it might be pointed out that the identification of poetry and Biblical rhetoric was by no means universal. Lord Shaftesbury, for example, in his *Advice to an Author*, could still write in 1711: 'For this reason 'twould be in vain for any poet or ingenious author to form his characters after the models of our sacred penmen . . . 'Tis apparent . . . that the manners, actions and characters of sacred writ are in no wise the proper subject of other authors than divines themselves . . . and are too sacred to be submitted to the poet's fancy.'[2]

To sum up then, it would seem that, to the advocates of the plain style, poetry is often on the side of the devil, though only a minor villain with whom they are not directly concerned, and whose usefulness they are even occasionally inclined to acknowledge: related to the Scriptures, indeed, poetry's role may be seen as transcending the merely useful. The resultant effect of this attitude, for poetry, is

[1] South, 'The Scribe instructed . . .'; sermon preached on 29th July 1660; *Sermons Preached on Several Occasions*, op. cit., iii, 14–15.
[2] Anthony Ashley Cooper, 3rd Earl of Shaftesbury, *Characteristicks of Men, Manners, Opinions, Times* (3 vols., London, 1711), i, 356 ff.

likely to be twofold: the general strength of the scientific, rationalist attitude, with its hostility to rhetorical ornament, will tend at first to bring the style of poetry closer to the new type of prose; but at the same time the identification of poetry with what have come to be regarded as the anti-rational elements in discourse will open the way eventually to a more complete separation of the two forms. Something of the former of these two effects has already been seen in the attitude to poetic style of such men as Dryden and Dennis; for a brief discussion of the latter, also for the moment only so far as it concerns style, the centre of attention must be shifted from the seventeenth to the eighteenth century.

The marked similarity that has been found to exist between the sixteenth and seventeenth centuries in their concepts of poetic style may be emphasized by contrast with eighteenth-century pronouncements on the same subject. For example, early in the eighteenth century (1711) Joseph Trapp was declaring language to be the differentiating mark of poetry. Lyric poetry he believed to be 'of all Kinds of Poetry, the most poetical; and . . . as distinct, both in Style and Thought, from the rest, as Poetry in general is from Prose'.[1] Like the critics of the seventeenth century, he treats poetry as 'a branch of eloquence in general', but unlike them he insists primarily on the difference between poetry and oratory:

The difference between them is very great; and Poetry has several other Characteristics besides that of Metre; a Style, for instance, peculiar to itself, Fiction, copious Descriptions, poetic Fire, and (to add no more) a certain Licence, denied to Orators, in the due Exercise of which the Poet's Art is chiefly conspicuous.[2]

Here again are the traditional elements: fiction, rhetorical amplification, poetic licence. But the emphasis on poetry's 'peculiarity' is different—or at least it is an emphasis that is unmistakably stronger.

In a similar strain is the comparison of the poet and the orator in Fénelon's *Dialogues on Eloquence* published for the first time in

[1] Joseph Trapp, *Lectures on Poetry* (London, 1742), p. 203. This work is a translation of his *Praelectiones poeticae* (1711).
[2] Ibid., pp. 34–35.

England in 1722: 'Poetry differs from simple eloquence only in this; that she paints with ecstasy and with bolder strokes.'[1] Bacon had thought poetry 'for wit and eloquence not much less than to orators' harangues',[2] and Fénelon, in this dialogue between 'A' (who appears to represent Fénelon's own views) and 'C', reverses this position:

A: The entire difference [between oratory and poetry] consists in that which I have set forth to you. Over and above orators, poets have ecstasy, and this makes them still more elevated, more lively, and more daring in their utterances. You well remember what I told you yesterday from Cicero?
C: What! Is it . . .
A: That the orator ought almost to have the diction of the poet. That 'almost' tells the whole story.[3]

The reference to Cicero is to De oratore I, xxviii, 128, where oratory is defined as demanding the acuteness of the dialectician, the knowledge of a philosopher, a tragedian's voice, the gestures of an actor, and a diction almost that of a poet. Fénelon is literally justified, but Cicero might have been surprised at the use he makes of this catalogue of the accomplishments of the ideal orator.

The poet Thomas Gray, writing in 1742, answered objections to the alleged extravagance of his own poetic style by asserting a similar gulf between poetry and prose:

The language of the age is never the language of poetry; except among the French whose verse . . . differs in nothing from prose. Our poetry, on the contrary, has a language peculiar to itself; to which almost everyone that has written has added something by enriching it with foreign idioms and derivatives; nay sometimes words of their own composition or invention.[4]

A little later in the century (1753) Bishop Robert Lowth, in his

---

[1] Fénelon, *Dialogues on Eloquence* (possibly written *c.* 1679, first published 1717, translated London, 1722); ed. W. S. Howell (Princeton, 1951), p. 48.

[2] Bacon, *The Advancement of Learning*, op. cit., iii, 346.

[3] Fénelon, op. cit., pp. 94–95.

[4] Thomas Gray, Letter of April 1742 to Mr. West; ed. P. Toynbee and L. Whibley, *Correspondence of Thomas Gray* (3 vols., Oxford, 1935), i, 192.

study of the poetry of the Hebrews, finds that poetry to deviate strongly from a normal mode of expression which he describes as 'plain, correct, chaste, and temperate', in which 'the words are uncommon neither in their meaning nor application', and 'there is no appearance of study, nor even of the least attention to the harmony of the periods': such a mode of expression as 'is disposed in such an order, and so connected by the continued succession of the different parts, as to demonstrate the clearly regular state of the author . . .'[1] From this type of discourse, which would clearly have been acceptable to the Royal Society, Hebrew poetry is found to differ, and this leads Lowth to a general statement regarding the style of poetry.

The poetry of every language has a style and form of expression peculiar to itself; forcible, magnificent, and sonorous; the words pompous and energetic; the composition singular and artificial; the whole form and complexion different from what we meet with in common life, and frequently (as with a noble indignation) breaking down the boundaries by which the popular dialect is confined. The language of reason is cool, temperate, rather humble than elevated, well arranged and perspicuous, with an evident care and anxiety lest any thing escape which might appear perplexed or obscure. *The language of the passions is totally different:* the conceptions burst out in a turbid stream, expressive in a manner of the internal conflict; the more vehement break out in hasty confusion; they catch (without search or study) whatever is impetuous, vivid or energetic. In a word, *reason speaks literally, the passions poetically* [my italics].[1]

The whole emphasis here is on the distinction between poetry and prose—'the language of the passions is totally different'. There can be no doubt of the consciousness of a distinction, and though it is seen as reflected in style it is a distinction that goes far deeper than a simple difference in style.[2]

[1] Robert Lowth, *Lectures on the Sacred Poetry of the Hebrews* (first published London, 1735, under the title *De sacra poesi Hebraeorum praelectiones academicae*); trans. G. Gregory (London, 1835), Lect. xiv, 'Of the Sublime in General and Sublimity of Expression in Particular', p. 150.
[2] For a further discussion of the significance of Lowth in the development of eighteenth-century literary theory see below, pp. 188–90.

T.H.—D

The concern of this study is with the seventeenth century rather than with the eighteenth, and these few isolated comments cannot, of course, be claimed to represent the whole of the eighteenth-century view of poetic style. They do, however, form a sufficiently consistent picture to be significant—notice that, coincidentally, of the four main passages quoted above, three repeat an identical phrase in speaking of poetry as having a style 'peculiar to itself': an indication perhaps that the idea had reached the stage of a literary cliché. Some of the outlines of this picture may be unchanged from the previous period, but the dominant colouring cannot be readily duplicated from the seventeenth century—nor for that matter from the sixteenth; and it is for this reason a picture that lends support to the suggestion made earlier that the eventual result of the seventeenth-century influences on discourse was a widening of the gap between poetry and prose, though this was to be an eighteenth- rather than a seventeenth-century phenomenon.

More, however, will have to be said of this matter in a later chapter, for the reason that changing concepts of style were only one aspect of a more fundamental change in theories of the nature and function of poetry in relation to other forms of discourse. Poetry as 'the language of the passions' implies more than a distinctive style; its full implications form part of the development of the concept of the creative imagination.

This survey has shown the beginnings of a systematic definition of the styles of poetry and prose in the later sixteenth century as having been strongly influenced by the importance given to the evolution of a formal literary type of prose. This emphasis caused prose to take on many of the characteristics usually associated with poetry; and, at the same time, poetic style itself was influenced by a similar striving after formal verbal qualities. The result was that during the sixteenth century the dominant literary style of prose had much in common with its contemporary poetry, and discussions of poetic style also tended to accept the relatively close relationship of poetry with oratorical prose. Only an occasional voice, such as

George Chapman's, was heard to stress the essential peculiarities of poetic style.

During the later seventeenth century the attitude of poets and critics of poetry appears not to have changed to any considerable extent; many of their statements regarding style echo very closely those of their predecessors of a century earlier. The most noticeable change, perhaps, is a growing consciousness of prose, but with the result that poetry tended to be drawn closer to prose as a 'norm' of style. Only in relation to the Pindaric ode is there any considerable stress laid on the extent of poetry's deviation from prose; but it is a tentative attitude, rather self-consciously aware of its own extravagance.

Those men who in the seventeenth century demanded a plainer style of prose were not especially interested in nor directly antagonistic to poetry. None the less their attitude certainly had its effect, both in the development of a greater awareness of prose, and through their attacks on the rhetorical eloquence with which poetry had been traditionally associated. Their most significant influence towards a distinction of poetry from prose came probably, however, from their readiness to equate poetry with those stylistic elements to which they objected in prose; and associated with this, in a manner which perhaps more than anything else in the seventeenth century looked forward to the future development of poetic theory, there was a tendency to regard the rhetoric of the Bible as the greatest poetry.

In the eighteenth century the emphasis changes. Poetry is now clearly seen as having a style 'peculiar to itself'. There is a consistent body of opinion showing no longer any desire, such as had been apparent in the sixteenth and seventeenth centuries, to equate poetry and prose: on the contrary, its whole aim seems to be to show how totally different they are.

One important effect of the seventeenth-century 'scientific' influence was undoubtedly to emphasize a new concept of 'utility' in relation to discourse, different from the kind of utility associated with words in the rhetorical tradition that was being displaced. In the next chapter this rhetorical tradition, which the seventeenth century inherited from the Renaissance, will be surveyed in order to learn more of the role given by it to poetry. The following chapter will then take up the problem of 'utility' as it might have been applied to discourse in the later seventeenth century.

CHAPTER TWO

Poetry and Rhetoric

ONE of the difficulties facing readers of the present day in their attempts to appreciate and understand the poetry of the seventeenth century is their lack of sympathy with the rhetorical tradition. C. S. Lewis has referred to this difficulty in his history of sixteenth-century English literature:

While Tudor education differed by its humanism from that of the Middle Ages, it differed far more widely from ours. Law and rhetoric were the chief sources of the difference . . . In rhetoric, more than in anything else, the continuity of the old European tradition was embodied. Older than the Church, older than Roman Law, older than all Latin literature, it descends from the age of the Greek Sophists. Like the Church and the law, it survives the fall of the empire, rides the *renascentia* and the Reformation like waves, and penetrates far into the eighteenth century . . . Nearly all our older poetry was written and read by men to whom the distinction between poetry and rhetoric, in its modern form, would have been meaningless. The 'beauties' which they chiefly regarded in every composition were those which we either dislike or simply do not notice. This change of taste makes an invisible wall between us and them . . . we must reconcile ourselves to the fact that of the praise and censure which we allot to medieval and Elizabethan poets only the smallest part would have seemed relevant to those poets themselves.[1]

What Lewis says here remains equally true for the seventeenth century.

Incidental references were made in the previous chapter to the close relationship between poetry and rhetoric. Such references were perhaps inevitable in a study of poetic style, because a concern

[1] C. S. Lewis, *English Literature in the Sixteenth Century, excluding Drama* (Oxford, 1954), pp. 60–61.

with style is something that poetry and rhetoric have always had in common. However, the connexion of poetry and rhetoric is more extensive, and goes deeper, than might perhaps be indicated by the presence of style as a common element; and poetry has at times also had connexions with the other parts of the trivium, as well as with theology and philosophy. At the purely educational level, for example, poetry and the parts of the trivium were very much intermingled during the sixteenth and seventeenth centuries. *Lily's Latin Grammar*,[1] which was compulsory for grammar schools in the seventeenth century, devotes twelve pages to *Prosodia*, while Grant's Greek Grammar[2] had thirty-three pages on the same subject. Similarly, perhaps the most popular textbook of rhetoric, Butler's edition (1598) of the rhetoric of Talaeus,[3] treats prosody in twenty pages, and Milton's schoolmaster, Dr. Gil,[4] gave twenty-two pages to prosody in his *Logonomia anglica* (1619). Milton himself, in his *Art of Logic* (1672) teaches logic by literary examples, on the assumption that orators and poets alike must make use of that art.[5]

Before this seventeenth-century position can be understood or examined further it will be desirable to trace the origins of this association of poetry with the subjects of the classical trivium.[6]

[1] The book that became famous as *Lily's Latin Grammar* was originally composed by William Lily and John Colet between 1510 and 1515, for use at the newly founded St. Paul's School.

[2] E. Grant, *Graecae linguae spicilegum* . . . (London, 1575).

[3] C. Butler, *Rhetorica libri duo* (London, 1598).

[4] A. Gil (the elder), *Logonomia anglica* (London, 1619).

[5] John Milton, *Art of Logic* (London, 1672); the reasons for the assumption of a common debt of poets and orators to logic will be discussed during the later treatment of Ramism (see below, pp. 108–19). Further attention will also be given in a later section of the present chapter to seventeenth-century rhetorical education.

[6] The relationship of poetry to the trivium in classical times and through the Middle Ages and Renaissance to the seventeenth century has been treated directly and indirectly in a number of works. None of these, however, provide an arrangement or interpretation of the material entirely satisfactory as a basis for the present study; hence the necessity for the survey that follows. The more important works with some bearing on the subject are listed below. This study is indebted to a greater or lesser extent to many of these; however, apart from this general listing acknowledgement will be

The association of poetry and rhetoric had very early beginnings, as Lewis has pointed out. Before Plato and Aristotle had distinguished poetry from other forms of discourse on philosophical grounds as an 'imitative' art, Gorgias (485–375 B.C.), the Sicilian Sophist, had given the art of oratory a new aspect by making the study of oratory

made only when direct reference is made. The list is not intended as a comprehensive survey of the literature, but of only those works serving to emphasize aspects of the rhetorical tradition that are important for this study:

J. W. H. Atkins, *Literary Criticism in Antiquity* (2 vols., London, 1952).

J. W. H. Atkins, *English Literary Criticism: The Medieval Phase* (Cambridge, 1943).

J. W. H. Atkins, *English Literary Criticism: The Renaissance* (London, 1947).

J. W. H. Atkins, *English Literary Criticism: 17th and 18th Centuries* (London, 1951).

C. S. Baldwin, *Ancient Rhetoric and Poetic* (New York, 1924).

C. S. Baldwin, *Medieval Rhetoric and Poetic* (New York, 1928).

C. S. Baldwin and D. L. Clark, *Renaissance Literary Theory and Practice* (New York, 1939).

T. W. Baldwin, *William Shakspere's Small Latin & Lesse Greeke* (2 vols. Urbana, 1944).

B. Chagnard, *Rhetoric and Poetry in the Renaissance* (New York, 1922).

D. L. Clark, *Milton at St. Paul's School* (New York, 1948).

D. L. Clark, *Rhetoric and Poetry in the Renaissance*, op. cit.

W. Crane, *Wit and Rhetoric in the Renaissance* (New York, 1946).

Hardin Craig, *The Enchanted Glass* (New York, 1935).

E. R. Curtius, *European Literature and the Latin Middle Ages* (London, 1953), trans. W. R. Trask; originally published as *Europäische Literatur und lateinische Mittelalter* (Berne, 1948).

W. S. Howell, *Logic and Rhetoric in England 1500–1700*, op. cit.

W. J. Ong, *Ramus, Method, and the Decay of Dialogue* (Camb., Mass., 1958).

G. Saintsbury, *History of Criticism and Literary Taste in Europe* (3 vols., London, 1900).

J. E. Spingarn, *A History of Literary Criticism in the Renaissance* (New York, 1899).

J. Sweeting, *Early Tudor Criticism* (Oxford, 1940).

Rosamund Tuve, *Elizabethan and Metaphysical Imagery* (Chicago, 1947).

K. R. Wallace, *Francis Bacon on Communication and Rhetoric*, op. cit.

Ruth Wallerstein, *Studies in Seventeenth Century Poetic*, op. cit.

Bernard Weinberg, *A History of Literary Criticism in the Italian Renaissance* (2 vols., Chicago, 1961).

In addition there are numerous articles related to the subject, including those of Feder, Howard, Howell, Hale, McKeon, Nelson, Duhamel, Ong, Smith, Thorne, Tuve, Paetow, Weinberg, and Williamson which will be found listed in the bibliography.

(or rhetoric) one of style, of literary technique. His use of what became known as the 'Gorgian figures', and particularly his use of poetic rhythms and rhyming words to achieve a musico-poetic effect, brought eloquence into conscious relationship with poetry.

Aristotle is at times quite definite in distinguishing between poetry and rhetoric, even in matters of style—for example, in the *Rhetoric*:

Now it was because poets seemed to win fame through their fine language when their thoughts were simple enough, that the language of oratorical prose at first took a poetical colour, e.g. that of Gorgias. Even now most uneducated people think that poetical language makes the finest discourses. That is not true: the language of prose is distinct from that of poetry. This is shown by the state of things today, when even the language of tragedy has altered its character. Just as iambics were adopted, instead of tetrameters, because they are the most prose-like of all meters, so tragedy has given up all those words, not used in ordinary talk, which decorated the early drama and are still used by writers of hexameter poems. It is therefore ridiculous to imitate a poetical manner which the poets themselves have dropped; and it is now plain that we have not to treat in detail the whole question of style, but may confine ourselves to that part of it which concerns our present subject, rhetoric. The other—the poetical—part of it has been discussed in the treatise on the *Art of Poetry*.[1]

On the other hand, however, Aristotle can state elsewhere, in the *Poetics*, that diction is in essence the same both in verse and prose: 'Fourth among the elements enumerated comes Diction; by which I mean, as has already been said, the expression of the meaning in words; and its essence is the same in both verse and prose.'[2]

In the passage of the *Poetics*[3] referred to by Aristotle at the end of the first of the passages quoted above, he discusses the various ways of achieving perfection of style, which is 'to be clear without being

---

[1] Aristotle, *Rhetoric*, III, i; *The Works of Aristotle translated into English* (11 vols., Oxford, 1924), v. xi.

[2] Aristotle, *Poetics*, VI, 18; ed. S. H. Butcher, *Aristotle's Theory of Poetry and Fine Art* (London, 1898), p. 29.

[3] Ibid., XX–XXII; pp. 71–87.

mean'. The ideal style of the orator is defined slightly differently: 'Style to be good must be clear, as is proved by the fact that speech which fails to convey a plain meaning will fail to do just what speech has to do. It must be appropriate, avoiding both meanness and undue elevation.'[1] For the poet the emphasis is on avoiding meanness, but for the orator undue elevation is equally dangerous. Thus 'poetical language is certainly free from meanness, but it is not appropriate to prose';[1] and in the subsequent discussion it appears that of the various devices of style available to the poet for the purpose of elevation, only metaphor can safely be used by the orator: 'In the language of prose, besides the regular and proper terms for things, metaphorical terms only can be used with advantage.'[1] This is the forerunner of many statements, continuing up to and beyond the seventeenth century, to the effect that prose is more circumscribed in its resources than poetry.

Something of the same distinction between poetry and prose continues throughout antiquity, though usually less clearly defined than it is by Aristotle. Thus Cicero considers the style of the orator and the poet to be similar but not identical;[2] they use the same methods of ornament,[3] and poets are nearest kin to the orators.[4] Quintilian advises students of rhetoric against imitating the style of the historians, because it is too much like that of the poets,[5] a criticism of the historians that is repeated by Lucian.[6] On the other hand, for Dionysius of Halicarnassus the best prose is that which resembles poetry though not entirely in metre, and the best poetry is that which resembles beautiful prose.[7] Only perhaps in 'Longinus' is the distinction given an emphasis that has already been seen as reappearing with the eighteenth-century writers like Trapp and Lowth. 'Longinus' distinguishes between 'sublimity' based on passion, and that which has no such basis; and, while the former is

---

[1] Aristotle, *Rhetoric*, III, ii; op. cit.
[2] Cicero, *Orator*, 66–68.
[3] Cicero, *De oratore*, I, 70.
[4] Ibid., III, 27.
[5] Quintilian, *De inst. orat.*, X, ii, 21.
[6] Lucian, *Quomodo historia conscribenda*, sit 8.
[7] Dionysius of Halicarnassus, *De compositione verborum*, xxv–xxvi.

attained by the orators and poets alike, the language used by
'Longinus' might suggest that it is more characteristic of the poets:

Among the orators, too, eulogies and ceremonial and occasional
addresses contain on every side examples of dignity and elevation, but
are for the most part void of passion. This is the reason why passionate
speakers are the worst eulogists, and why, on the other hand, those
who are apt in encomium are the least passionate. If, on the other
hand, Caecilius thought that passion never contributes at all to
sublimity, and it was for this reason that he did not deem it worthy of
mention, he is altogether deluded. I would affirm with confidence that
there is no tone so lofty as that of genuine passion, in its right place,
when it bursts out in a wild gust of mad enthusiasm and as it were
fills the speaker's words with frenzy.[1]

One further distinction made by 'Longinus' that is of interest for
later periods is that between intensity, which is typically associated
with sublimity, and amplification:

The point of distinction between them seems to me to be that sublimity consists in elevation, while amplification embraces a multitude
of details. Consequently, sublimity is often comprised in a single
thought, while amplification is universally associated with a certain
magnitude and abundance.[2]

He does not, however, associate 'intensity' with poetry and
'amplification' with oratory;[3] this is a much later development,
perhaps as late as the nineteenth century. In medieval times, and at
least until the end of the seventeenth century, rhetorical amplification continued to be closely associated with poetry, and degenerated
into a complicated means of rendering expression more luxuriant
and profuse; and, contrary to 'Longinus', it was thought of as perhaps the primary means of achieving 'elevation'.

If these distinctions of style between poetry and prose are less
than convincing, even as stated by Aristotle, the latter settles the

---

[1] 'Longinus', *On the Sublime*, viii; ed. W. R. Roberts (Cambridge, 1899),
p. 59.

[2] Ibid., xii; p. 77.

[3] As D. L. Clark, *Rhetoric and Poetry in the Renaissance*, op. cit., p. 17, claims
he does.

question more definitely in the *Poetics* when he makes poetry, as an art of imitation, basically independent of style. It is the imitation, and not the verse, that constitutes the poetry:

People do, indeed, add the word 'maker' or 'poet' to the name of the metre, and speak of elegiac poets, or epic (that is hexameter) poets, as if it were not the imitation that makes the poet, but the verse that entitles them all indiscriminately to the name. Even when a treatise on medicine or natural science is brought out in verse, the name of poet is by custom given to the author, and yet Homer and Empedocles have nothing in common but the metre, so that it would be right to call the one poet, the other physicist rather than poet.[1]

And again:

The poet and the historian differ not by writing in verse or prose. The work of Herodotus might be put into verse, and it would still be a species of history, with metre no less than without it. The true difference is that one relates what has happened, the other what may happen.[2]

This concept of poetry as imitation continued virtually unchallenged as the nominal basis of poetic theory until the eighteenth century; nevertheless the strength of the rhetorical tradition caused the concept, even in classical times, to be widely distorted, though lip-service may have been paid to it.[3] Firstly 'imitation' was popularly taken to include (as indeed it had done at least from the time of Isocrates) the imitation of good models. Cicero frequently recommends the practice, as does Quintilian.[4] Dionysius of Halicarnassus wrote a treatise *On imitation* with this application, and 'Longinus' also recommended imitation of past models as a means of achieving sublimity:

Accordingly it is well that we ourselves also, when elaborating anything which requires lofty expression and elevated conception, should

---

[1] Aristotle, *Poetics*, I, 7–8; op. cit., p. 9.

[2] Ibid., IX, 2; p. 35.

[3] For a full discussion of the changing concept of imitation in antiquity, see R. B. McKeon, 'Literary Criticism and Concept of Imitation in Antiquity', *MP*, xxxiv (1936), 1–35.

[4] See, for example, Quintilian, *De inst. orat.*, X, ii, 1–28.

shape some idea in our minds as to how perchance Homer would have said this very thing, or how it would have been raised to the sublime by Plato or Demosthenes or by the historian Thucydides. For those personages, presenting themselves to us and inflaming our ardour and as it were illuminating our path, will carry our minds in a mysterious way to the high standards of sublimity which are imaged within us.[1]

This interpretation of imitation, which was applied as it is by 'Longinus' to poetry and oratory alike, was to have a long history, particularly during the Renaissance, and lasting until at least the eighteenth century, when it was still possible for Pope to write:

> Learn hence for ancient rules a just esteem;
> To copy nature is to copy them.[2]

Another shift made in classical times from the position of Aristotle is of even more fundamental importance for English poetry of the sixteenth and seventeenth centuries; and this again was part of the dominance of poetry by an attitude that was essentially rhetorical rather than aesthetic. Concepts of poetry may, from one point of view, be classified according to whether the emphasis falls on the poet as creator of the poem, on the poem itself as an autonomous object, or on the effect which the poem has on its audience. Aristotle had sought to do the second of these things: he had emphasized 'poetics' as the objective analysis of the work of art. He did, of course, give some consideration to the pleasure derived by the audience from the drama, and the reasons for this pleasure: but the effect on the audience provided no actual criteria for judging the tragedy. These criteria were to be looked for within the work itself, in such elements as plot, character, and thought.[3] For rhetoric, on the other hand, the only interest can be in the reaction of the audience; and it is this effect on the audience that is made the centre of interest in one of the most influential of classical works on literary theory, the *Ars Poetica* of Horace, which though it purports to

---

[1] 'Longinus', xiv; op. cit., p. 83.
[2] Pope, *An Essay on Criticism* (1709), ll. 139–40.
[3] See *Poetics*, VI; op. cit., pp. 25–29.

follow Aristotle becomes a treatise on methods of pleasing and entertaining an audience:

The poet's aim is either to profit or to please, or to blend in one the delightful and the useful . . . Elder folk rail at what contains no serviceable lesson; our young aristocrats cannot away with grave verses; the man who mingles the useful with the sweet carries the day by charming his reader and at the same time instructing him.[1]

At this point poetry and rhetoric come together not only in matters of style but of aim and purpose as well; the aim of delightful teaching given to the poet by Horace is given to the orator by Cicero: the orator seeks 'docere, delectare et movere'—to prove, to delight and to move emotionally.[2] Similarly, although here the influence seems to move in the opposite direction, from poetry to oratory, Quintilian repeats for the orator what Aristotle had demanded of the poet, that he himself must feel strong emotion in order to be convincing.[3] Both poetry and oratory are seen as primarily seeking to win the approval of an audience. Only by 'Longinus' is this tie between poetry and 'persuasion' explicitly broken:

. . . sublimity is a certain distinction and excellence in expression, and . . . it is from no other source than this that the greatest poets and writers have derived their eminence and gained immortality of renown. The effect of elevated language upon an audience is not persuasion but transport.[4]

[1] Horace, *Ars Poetica*, ll. 333 ff; trans. A. H. Gilbert, *Literary Criticism—Plato to Dryden* (New York, 1940), p. 139. D. L. Clark (*Rhetoric and Poetry in the Renaissance*, op. cit., pp. 6–7) claims that 'not until the renaissance did critics define poetry as an art of imitation endeavouring to inculcate morality'. He maintains that for the classical period profit and delight were the purpose of the poet but not of poetry. However, whatever the validity or worth of this distinction, a reading of the *Poetics* and of the *Ars Poetica*, the two main treatises of antiquity on the subject, makes it clear that the author of the first is interested primarily in the nature of the work itself, and that of the second in its effect on an audience. This is all the point it is desired to make here—that in antiquity thinking about poetry became dominated by what were essentially rhetorical considerations.

[2] Cicero, *De optimo genere oratorium*, I, 3; also *Orator*, 69, and *De oratore*, II, 28.

[3] Quintilian, *De inst. orat.*, VI, ii, 25–36; and Aristotle, *Poetics*, XVII, 2.

[4] 'Longinus', i; op. cit., p. 43.

The emphasis on the audience, however, remains, and something of this common ground between poetry and rhetoric will remain for so long as the aim of poetry is accepted as being to teach and delight, or to do both together: that is, as with the idea of imitating the great models of the past, it remains until well into the eighteenth century. One of the eighteenth-century reforms of poetry that will be discussed later is the shift of interest from the audience to the poet himself.[1]

One final aspect of the poetry-rhetoric relationship in antiquity which was also to have a long history is suggested by Plato when he deals with rhetoric and poetics as arts that are both concerned with the construction of semblances of the truth; and since the semblance is most perfect when its maker is one who knows what the truth is, the ultimate questions of poetics and rhetoric transcend the limitations of these arts and become part of dialectic, since they involve knowledge, a problem that is properly treated only by the dialectician. Thus in the *Ion* the true poet, and in the *Phaedrus* the true rhetorician, are each ultimately the one who knows—i.e. the dialectician. And, of course, the reason for the banishment of the poets from Plato's ideal Republic is that they deal in matters at least two removes from the truth.

For Aristotle 'thought' is one of the constituent elements of tragedy, although it is more properly treated as part of rhetoric:

Third in order is Thought, that is, the faculty of saying what is possible and pertinent in given circumstances. In the case of oratory, this is the function of the political art and of the art of rhetoric: and so indeed the older poets make their characters speak the language of civic life; the poets of our time, the language of the rhetoricians . . . Thought . . . is found where something is proved to be or not to be, or a general maxim is enunciated.[2]

And later:

Concerning Thought, we may assume what is said in the *Rhetoric*, to which inquiry the subject more strictly belongs. Under thought is

[1] See below, pp. 177–94.
[2] Aristotle, *Poetics*, VI, 16–17; op. cit., p. 29.

included every effect which has to be produced by speech; in particular,—proof and refutation; the excitation of feelings, such as pity, fear, anger, and the like; the suggestion of importance or its opposite.[1]

Here the particular treatment given to 'thought' is obviously rhetorical in its emphasis on effects, and even for Aristotle it apparently served the same function in poetry as it did in oratory.

The metaphorical expression of thought, moreover, is seen as common to both poetry and oratory, though belonging more directly perhaps to poetry, since it is treated more fully in the *Poetics*, whence the reader of the *Rhetoric* is referred. 'Prose writers', Aristotle warns, 'must, however, pay specially careful attention to metaphor, because their own resources are scantier than those of the poets.'[2] But, apart from these more specific issues, Aristotle's whole theory of imitation depends on the concept of a special kind of poetic truth:

The poet being an imitator . . . must of necessity imitate one of three objects,—things as they were or are, things as they are said or thought to be . . . the standard of correctness is not the same in poetry and politics, any more than in poetry and any other art . . . If a poet has proposed to himself to imitate something, but has imitated it incorrectly through want of capacity, the error is inherent in the poetry. But if the failure is due to the thing he has proposed to do—if he has represented a horse as throwing out both his off legs at once . . . the error is not essential to the poetry.[3]

These Aristotelian concepts of thought and metaphor as common to poetry and oratory, and of poetry as dealing with the 'probable' or 'possible' rather than the actual, are brought together by 'Longinus' in his treatment of ideas and their expression in poetry and oratory:

Images, moreover, contribute greatly, my young friend, to dignity, elevation, and power as a pleader. In this sense some call them mental representations. In a general way the name *image* or *imagination* is

[1] Ibid., XIX, 1–2; pp. 69–70.
[2] Aristotle, *Rhetoric*, III, 2; op. cit.
[3] Aristotle, *Poetics*, XXXV, 1–4; op. cit., 97–99.

applied to every idea of the mind, in whatever form it presents itself, which gives birth to speech. But at the present day, the word is predominantly used in cases where, carried away by enthusiasm and passion, you think you see what you describe, and place it before the eyes of your hearers . . . Further, you will be aware of the fact that an image has one purpose with the orators and another with the poets, and that the design of the poetical image is enthralment, of the rhetorical—vivid description.[1]

And:

It is no doubt true that those images which are found in the poets contain, as I said, a tendency to exaggeration in the way of the fabulous and that they transcend in every way the credible, but in oratorical imagery the best feature is always its reality and truth.[2]

The distinction made here between the imagery of poetry and that of oratory is largely peculiar to 'Longinus' himself; but in various forms the idea of poetry as being concerned with the less or other than immediately true, and in particular as being concerned with matters further removed from actual truth than those dealt with by rhetoric and dialectic, persisted throughout the Middle Ages and the Renaissance, and perhaps was only finally supplanted by the development of the concept of the creative imagination.

These then were the directions which the rhetorical domination of poetic theory took in classical times. Against the attempt of Aristotle to build a distinctly aesthetic theory of poetry with imitation, in the sense of 'fiction' or 'fable', as its essential element, there is firstly the didactic, moralistic emphasis of Horace's *Ars Poetica* which brought poetry into relationship with rhetoric by making the effect on an audience instead of the poem itself the centre of interest. Then there was the dialectical emphasis of Plato which served to link poetics with rhetoric and logic as a means of 'knowing', and which turned both the poet and the rhetorician into inferior dialecticians. Finally there was the overall rhetorical colouring given to poetry by its stylistic links with oratory, which tended

[1] 'Longinus', xv; op. cit., pp. 83–84.
[2] Ibid., p. 89.

to bring into prominence the concept of imitation as the copying of good models of style.

This situation carried over into the post-classical and medieval periods, with the difference that the one purely aesthetic influence, that of Aristotle's *Poetics*, was lost. In the complicated intellectual tradition of the Middle Ages that centred around the study of the trivium and quadrivium (the seven liberal arts), rhetoric became even more deeply embedded than it had previously been. The role of poetry in this tradition was both more closely integrated and less straightforward than it had been in that of the classical period. As an independent subject of study, medieval interest in poetics was generally slight; it was treated instead either as metrics, in which case it was regarded as part of grammar, or as a form of argument when it was associated with dialectic and rhetoric. In the later medieval period, when the tendency was towards the development of rhetoric as a discipline of words, independent of philosophy or dialectic, the connexion of poetry as a form of composition shifted from grammar to rhetoric. But no matter what particular position was assigned to poetry the Middle Ages were not inclined to concern themselves with the manner in which the particular formal qualities of poetry enabled it to deal with its subject-matter.[1]

Only with the rediscovery of Aristotle's *Poetics* at the end of the fifteenth century was something of his aesthetic position recovered; but the association with rhetoric had been so firmly established that even then a strong rhetorical flavour remained and was to remain until well into the eighteenth century. The remainder of the present chapter will be concerned to examine the details of the Renaissance synthesis of these various elements of its classical literary heritage.

Before the full effect of the rediscovery of Aristotle's *Poetics* was felt in the sixteenth century, an earlier movement, which has become

---

[1] For a detailed study of rhetoric, and its relation to poetry, in the medieval period see R. B. McKeon, 'Rhetoric in the Middle Ages', *Speculum*, xvii (1942), 1–32; and R. B. McKeon, 'Poetry and Philosophy in the Twelfth Century: The Renaissance of Rhetoric', *MP*, xliii (1946), 217–34.

known generally as 'humanism', played an important role in determining the relationship of poetry and rhetoric, especially on the
stylistic level. In particular, humanism brought to the fore the concept of imitation in the sense of the imitation of good models, which
it will be remembered had been one of the ways in which Aristotle's
concept of poetry as an art of imitation had been varied in the
direction of rhetoric during classical times.

Humanism, in the sense of a resurgence of interest in classical
literature, was to some extent heralded during the medieval period
in the writings of such men as John of Salisbury (1110–1180), Roger
Bacon (1214–1294), and Richard of Bury (1281–1345). It reached its
full fruition, however, in fifteenth-century Italy. Its effect was to
make literature, and particularly classical literature, the centre of
the world of learning. Vergerius, for example, one of the earliest
of the Italian humanists, in his *De ingenuis moribus* (*c.* 1404), thinks of
the art of letters as vital both to the discovery of new knowledge
and to the application of knowledge already existing:

The Art of Letters, however, rests upon a different footing. It is a
study adapted at all times and to all circumstances, to the investigation of fresh knowledge, or to the recasting and application of old.
Hence the importance of grammar and of the rules of composition
must be recognized at the outset, as the foundation on which the
whole study of Literature must rest: and closely associated with these
rudiments, the art of Disputation or Logical argument. The function
of this is to enable us to discern fallacy from truth in discussion.
Logic, indeed, as setting forth the true method of learning, is the
guide to the acquisition of knowledge in whatever subject. Rhetoric
comes next, and is strictly speaking the formal study by which we
attain the art of eloquence.[1]

Poetry was generally distinguished by the humanists from other
forms of discourse only by reason of its harmony, although there
is no emphasis on the Platonic idea of harmony as revealing an

[1] Vergerius, *De ingenuis moribus* (*c.* 1404); passage quoted is from the
English version in W. H. Woodward, *Vittorina da Feltre and Other Educators*
(Cambridge, 1897), p. 107.

deal order. L. Bruni d'Arrezzo, in his *De studiis et literis* (*c.* 1405), writes:

We know, however, that in certain quarters—where all knowledge and appreciation of Letters is wanting—this whole branch of Literature, marked as it is by something of the Divine, and fit, therefore, for the highest place, is decried as unworthy of study. But when we remember the value of the best poetry, its charm of form and the variety and interest of its subject-matter, when we consider the ease with which from our childhood up it can be committed to memory, when we recall the peculiar affinity of rhythm and metre to our emotions and our intelligence, we must conclude that Nature herself is against such headlong critics . . . Hence I hold my conviction to be soundly based; namely that Poetry has, by our very constitution, a stronger attraction for us than any other forms of discourse. . . .[1]

This in a way may be reminiscent of Aristotle, but the limitation of the humanists' attitude appears a little later, when Bruni says that 'when I read the loves of Aeneas and Dido in the *Aeneid* I pay my tribute of admiration to the genius of the poet, but the matter itself I know to be a fiction and thus it leaves no moral impression'.[2] Out of context these words might be taken as evidence of an aesthetic approach to poetry; within the essentially didactic and utilitarian context of humanist writing, however, they are no more than an indication of an absorption with style.

There were a number of reasons why the humanists' interests in literary matters should have been primarily rhetorical, and have tended above all towards considerations of style. Firstly the early humanists were almost all practical educationists, and their ideas were presented mainly through educational treatises.[3] For this reason, they looked at literature from a didactic, moral, and utilitarian point of view, though with an emphasis different from that

[1] L. Bruni d'Arrezzo, *De studiis et literis* (*c.* 1405); trans. W. H. Woodward, op. cit., pp. 130–1.
[2] Ibid.; p. 132.
[3] In addition to those of Vergerius and Bruni, the principal humanistic treatises of the period were Aeneas Sylvius, *De liberorum educatione* (1450); L. Valla, *Elegantiae linguae latinae* (*c.* 1345); and B. Guarino, *De ordine docendi et studendi* (1459).

derived from Horace. As J. W. H. Atkins has said of the humanistic movement:

Literature was valued not so much for its aesthetic and artistic qualities as for its practical uses, for its influence on character, its ability to train a man for his part in active life, or again, as providing models of expression; and these tests remained characteristic of Humanistic criticism to the end.[1]

Thus literature became linked with rhetoric through its didactic purpose, as an educational discipline, just as poetry as a form of moral entertainment was to be linked with rhetoric by Castelvetro and his fellow theorists of the following century.

The second influence towards a rhetorical orientation of humanism was the selection of classical literature on which it chanced to be originally based. The main inspiration came from Cicero's works on rhetoric, and from the *De institutione oratoria* of Quintilian, the latter being perhaps the most influential of all on humanistic attitudes to literature. Aristotle's *Rhetoric* was well known, but the first modern edition of the *Poetics* did not appear until almost the end of the fifteenth century.[2] The predominantly educational interests of the early humanists were in this way reinforced by the rhetorical character of the literature that influenced them most strongly.

The humanists' pedagogical interests, and the interest in oratory which was aroused by the nature of the material they studied, both tended to lead to a preoccupation with style. 'Literature indeed exhibits not facts alone', declared Vergerius: '. . . but thoughts and their expression. Provided such thoughts be worthy and worthily expressed we feel assured that they will not die: although I do not think that thoughts without style will be likely to attract much notice or secure a sure survival.'[3] In consequence, the tendency of medieval times for rhetoric to become a discipline of words was

[1] Atkins, *English Literary Criticism: The Renascence*, op. cit., p. 15.
[2] The Averroës paraphrase of the *Poetics* appeared in a Latin translation in 1481, the Giorgio Valla translation into Latin in 1498, and the *editio princeps* of the Greek text in 1508. The first commentary was that of Robortello, published in 1548.
[3] Vergerius, op. cit., p. 105.

strongly accelerated and extended to the study of literature generally. Grammar was greatly raised in status, and the study of logic and rhetoric came to be regarded chiefly as valuable aids to the acquirement of an effective style. The function of grammar, according to Aeneas Sylvius, was 'to order . . . expression', that of dialectic 'to give it point', of rhetoric 'to illustrate it', and of philosophy 'to perfect it'.[1] And a little later the same writer shows how poet and historian alike are dependent on rhetoric:

> Between Grammar and Rhetoric there is of necessity the closest connection; for it is by means of Rhetoric that the author, whether historian or poet, displays his literary style and artifice, and derives the form in which he casts his judgements of men and things, or the Orator exhibits his appeals and his conclusions. Both poet and historian have habitual recourse to the rules of Rhetoric, for which you will do wisely to betake yourself exclusively to the great authorities, to Cicero, Quintilian and Aristotle, whose *Rhetoric* has lately appeared in a translation . . .
>
> Nor can you neglect Dialectic, which in its turn has so near a relation with Rhetoric; for both alike aim at convincing the reason. Logic, indeed, has no profit except it serve as a direct aid to clear and precise thinking and expression, enabling us to recognize in our reasonings the fundamental difference between certain, probable and manifestly false steps in argument.[2]

The learning of the humanists thus became not only centred on literature as the source of knowledge, but also to a large extent confined to the study of literary style.

The result in classical times of a predominantly rhetorical and stylistic interest in literature had been the study of the great works of literature, including both poetry and oratory, for the purpose of imitation. Now again, associated with the humanists' pedagogical and rhetorical interest in style, there arises the doctrine of classicism, the idea that authority in literary matters is vested in the great works of antiquity. Valla lays down the principle: *Ego pro lege accipio*

[1] Aeneas Sylvius, *De liberorum educatione* (1450); trans. W. H. Woodward, op. cit., p. 144.
[2] Ibid., pp. 154–5.

quidquid magnis auctoribus placuit.[1] Even as early as 1450 the cult of imitation had grown to the point where Aeneas Sylvius warned against 'the forced imitation of an older style', and also against the introduction 'of words and phrases, now obsolete, into speech whose cast is of today'; writers, he believes, should copy the virtues of the great men of old and let their archaisms die with them.[2] Politian expressed himself more strongly on the subject:

Nor are those who are thought to have held the first rank of eloquence like one another, as has been remarked by Seneca. Quintilian laughs at those who shall think themselves cousins of Cicero because they conclude a period with *esse videatur* . . . Certainly they who compose only by imitation seem to me like parrots or magpies uttering what they do not understand. For what they write lacks force and life, lacks impulse, lacks emotion, lacks individuality, lies down, sleeps, snores. Nothing true there, nothing solid, nothing effective. But are you not, some one asks, expressing Cicero? What of it? I am not Cicero. I am expressing, I think, myself.[3]

The prose of Cicero was, of course, the principal object of imitation and despite the efforts of Valla and Politian the cult of Ciceronianism, which was to play such an important part in the English literary scene, both in itself and through the reactions to it, was firmly established.

The influence of the fifteenth-century Italian humanists appears, therefore, on a number of counts, to have been firmly on the side of rhetoric against the establishment of an independent poetic theory. J. W. H. Atkins believes that the stylistic, rhetorical movement, which in England reached its peak in the later sixteenth century, was an aberration of the earlier humanism, which had failed to fulfil its earlier promise.[4] However, it is difficult to see how humanism could have developed other than as it did. The interests of the

[1] L. Valla, *Elegantiae linguae latinae*, III, 17.

[2] Aeneas Sylvius, op. cit., pp. 147–8; also p. 158.

[3] Letter to Paolo Cortesi, in *Politiani Opera*, ed. Gryphius (Lyon, 1537–9), i, 251; quoted from Baldwin, *Renaissance Literary Theory and Practice*, op. cit., p. 48.

[4] Atkins, *English Literary Criticism: The Renascence*, op. cit., p. 20; also Chap. IV.

humanists were from the start didactic and pedagogical; their prophets were the great rhetoricians of the past; they accepted the high place awarded to eloquence by Cicero, and as a consequence concentrated much of their attention on style; and their acceptance of the classical standard, coupled with their interest in style, seemed certain to lead to the imitation of classical models. The most recent study of humanism, that of H. A. Mason, finds that:

> . . . two consequences of this Roman bias are: a crudely utilitarian view of the function of literature and a merely external account of style. The Humanists had never known a world in which the command of speech could sway the fortunes of a powerful state. When they tried to wear the Roman clothes, they could only wear them with a medieval air. Consequently, their utilitarian view of literature, when it was not totally unreal, was far cruder than the Roman view.
>
> Put shortly, roughly, and not allowing for brilliant exceptions, we may say that the Humanists' *impasse* was that they could find no justification for literature other than its moral instructiveness . . .[1]

But despite their limitations, and perhaps because they were practical educationists, the influence of the humanists on the literary scene was eventually much greater overall than was that of the more directly literary and more philosophical treatises of their sixteenth-century successors. In sixteenth-century England certainly, the vital influence on literary theory and practice was not that of contemporary Italian theorists but of the humanists of the fifteenth century.

The humanists, moreover, made a further contribution to the Renaissance literary heritage, at least equal in importance to their emphasis on rhetorical style. Though learning throughout the medieval period had been predominantly verbal it could not have been truly described as literary; the humanists' exaltation of literature, however, to a central position in education gave a special meaning and substance to the long-accepted interdependence of wisdom and eloquence. The tradition that developed from the humanists serves to accentuate the contrast between the position of literature at the close of the sixteenth century, when the humanist

[1] H. A. Mason, *Humanism and Poetry in the Early Tudor Period* (London, 1959), p. 66.

ideal of the art of letters could still be held valid, and its position a
century later when the learning based on the new science was
asserting its complete independence of words.

The influence of the fifteenth century had worked towards relating
poetry to rhetoric mainly in matters of style. The rediscovery of the
Poetics of Aristotle led in the sixteenth century to the development
of new relationships based on moralistic, didactic considerations of a
different, and generally more philosophic, nature.

Knowledge of the *Poetics* did not, at least at first, alter the position of poetry in relation to truth that it had occupied in medieval
times. Robortello, whose edition of the *Poetics* published in 1548 was
the first attempt actually to expound Aristotle's meaning, begins
his Prologue by establishing a descending hierarchy from the true to
the false, and places the five arts in relation to it. Poetics comes even
lower on the scale than it had done in St. Thomas's somewhat
similar scheme:

demonstratoria	: verum
dialectice	: probabile
rhetorice	: suasorium
sophistice	: specimen probabilis, sed verisimilis
poëtice	: falsum, sed fabulosum.[1]

[1] *Francisci Robortelli Utinensis in librum Aristotelis de arte poetica explicationes*
(Florence, 1548), p. 1. All passages from this text are repeated from Weinberg,
'Robortello on the *Poetics*' in *Critics and Criticism*, ed. R. S. Crane (Chicago,
1952), pp. 319–48. Robortello's scheme may be compared with that of St.
Thomas Aquinas (*In libros posteriorum analyticorum Aristotelis expositio*, lectio
prima; *Opera Omnia iussi impensaque Leonis XIII. P.M. edita* 12 vols., Rome,
1882–1906, i, 139–40: "*Per huiusmodi enim processum, quandoque quidem, etsi non
fiat scientia, fit tamen fides vel opinio propter probabiltatem propositionum ex quibus
proceditur; quia ratio totaliter declinat in unam partem contradictionis, licet cum
formidine alterius, et ad hoc ordinatur* Topica sive Dialectica. *Nan syllogismus
dialecticus ex probabilibus est, de quo agit Aristotelis in libro* Topicorum.—*Quandoque vero, non fit complete fides vel opinio, sed* suspicio *quaedam, quia non totaliter
declinatur ad unam partem contradictionis licet magis inclinetur in hanc quam in illam.
Et ad hoc ordinatur* Rhetorica.—*Quandoque vero sola existimatio declinat in aliquam
partem contradictionis propter aliquam repraesentationem, ad modum quo fit homini
abominatio alicuius cibi, si repraesentetur ei sub similitudine alicuius abominabilis. Et ad
hoc ordinatur* Poetica; *nam poetae est inducere ad aliquod virtuosum per aliquam
decentem repraesentationem.*"

The reason for placing poetics below even sophistics is that for Robortello poetry differs from the other arts in that it *intentionally and openly* takes for its subject-matter things that are not true. The whole function of poetry depends on the 'imitation' of things other than as they actually are, and this emphasis on imitation gives a special significance to poetry's lack of truth:

Since, then, poetics has as its subject matter fictitious and fictional discourse, it is clear that the function of poetics is to invent in a proper way its fiction and its untruth; to no other art is it more fitting than to this one to intermingle lies . . . In the lies used by the poetic art, false elements are taken as true, and from them true conclusions are derived.[1]

'*The function of poetics is to invent in a proper way its fiction and its untruth*' — this means that poetry has a special form and method associated with its fictional nature, and these special characteristics should be open to analysis after the manner of Aristotle.

However, whereas for Aristotle the main purpose of poetics had been to perform such an analysis, in Robortello's exposition imitation is combined with the Horatian aims of pleasure and moral utility. (The *Ars Poetica* had, of course, remained known throughout the Middle Ages.) Poetry, Robortello declares: '. . . if we consider it carefully, bends all its efforts towards delighting, although it also does profit.'[1] And again: 'Poetry thus sets a double end for itself, one of which is prior to the other; the prior end is to imitate, the other to delight.'[2] Further to this, it is clear that imitation is an intermediate end only, towards the more fundamental ends of delight and utility:

There is, indeed, for men no greater pleasure, truly worthy of a man of refinement, than that which is perceived by the mind and by thought; it frequently happens that things which arouse horror and terror in men as long as they are in their own nature, once they are taken out of nature and represented in some form resembling nature, give great pleasure . . . What other end, therefore, can we say that the poetic faculty has than to delight through the representation,

[1] Ibid., p. 2.   [2] Ibid., p. 30.

description, and imitation of every human action, every emotion, every thing animate as well as inanimate.[1]

And:

. . . just as poetic readings and imitations are of various kinds, so they bring to man a multiple utility. If, on the one hand, the reading (or performance) and imitation consist in the virtue and the praise of some excellent man, people are incited to virtue; if, on the other hand, vices are represented, people are strongly deterred from those vices, and they are driven away from them with much greater force than if you were to use any other form of persuasion.[2]

Thus despite his return to the Aristotelian concept of poetry as imitation, the emphasis given to the *Poetics* as it is interpreted by Robortello remains less on the analysis of the elements of poetry than on the pleasure or utility to be derived from those elements.

Robortello himself sees poetics and rhetoric as exactly similar in all things save one: '. . . they agree on almost all things; they differ in this only, that the latter [poetics] uses meters, the former [rhetoric] prose discourse'.[3] And Weinberg, in his discussion of Robortello's exposition, stresses its essentially rhetorical nature:

Persuasion, effect upon the audience, moral betterment, pleasurable sensations—I choose a few terms which seem to summarize the major tendencies of Robortello's system as we have seen it so far. If these be indeed the ends proposed for his system, then it becomes strikingly different from Aristotle's system in the text which Robortello is expounding. How different, and in what measure, will perhaps best be discovered by an investigation of this problem: To what extent is his system a rhetorical system rather than a poetic system in the Aristotelian sense? By 'rhetorical system' I mean, of course, one in which a specific effect of persuasion is produced upon a specified audience by

---

[1] *Francisci Robortelli Utinensis in librum Aristotelis de arte poetica explicationes*, p. 2. It might be noted in passing that, contrary to Aristotle, Robortello allows for the imitation not only of 'men in action', but of 'every human action, every emotion, everything animate as well as inanimate'.

[2] Ibid., pp. 3–4.

[3] Ibid., p. 66.

using the character of the audience, the character of the speaker, and the arguments of the speech as the means to persuasion.[1]

Weinberg's answer to the question he asks is that the only thing lacking to make Robortello's system a fully rhetorical one is the role of the character of the poet as an element of persuasion. 'The poet, for Robortello', he says, 'is merely a man capable of imitating, through gifts of nature and the acquired rules of art, the objects which he uses in his poems . . . To this extent only is the rhetorical system of Robortello incomplete and the distinctly poetic orientation of Aristotle's system respected.'[2]

This dominance of poetry by rhetoric has already been noted as the inevitable outcome of the original Horatian variation of Aristotle. So long as the ultimate emphasis is given to the poem's effect on its audience rather than to its own qualities as a poem, the primary interest in it will be rhetorical. Nevertheless, the revival of the concept of imitation in something of the Aristotelian sense gives poetry a special kind of subject-matter, and thus at least provides material for the sort of distinctly poetic analysis that Aristotle had attempted in the *Poetics*—material which had been largely lacking in the medieval treatment of poetry. Not imitation itself but only its effects can be discussed in purely rhetorical terms; as was apparently realized by Robortello himself, despite his virtual identification of poetics and rhetoric. In his discussion of imitation he makes a distinction other than that between metre and prose to separate the language of poetry from that of rhetoric: 'And since this imitation or representation is produced by means of discourse, we may say that the end of poetry is language which imitates, just as that of rhetoric is language which persuades.'[3] This, however, is not apparently a distinction that Robortello is interested to develop.

The rhetorical tendencies of Robortello are carried to what may be regarded as their culmination in the *Poetica d'Aristotele vulgarizzata et sposta* (1570) of Lodovico Castelvetro. For Castelvetro, nevertheless, poetry is closest not to rhetoric but to history:

[1] Weinberg, 'Robortello on the *Poetics*', op. cit., p. 343.
[2] Ibid., p. 346.
[3] Robortello, op. cit., p. 2.

Poetry is the similitude or likeness of history. Just as history is divided into matter and words, so poetry is divided into two principle parts, which are likewise matter and words, but in these two parts history and poetry differ from each other, because history does not have matter that is given to it by the abilities of the historian . . . The matter of poetry is found and imagined by the ability of the poet . . .[1]

For this reason, perhaps, Castelvetro gives no attention directly to the relationship between poetry and rhetoric. None the less his interpretation of Aristotle, which often indeed amounts to an actual rewriting, is even more specifically rhetorical than Robortello's, in the sense of seeing all things from the point of view of their effect on an audience. Thus he declares that 'poetry has been discovered solely to delight and to recreate, I say to delight and to recreate the minds of the crude multitude and of the common people',[2] and the material and methods of poetry are therefore determined not by any internal demands, but by considerations of what will, in fact, delight such an audience. It is, indeed, from just such considerations as these that there developed the notorious pseudo-Aristotelian unities of place, time, and action, for which Castelvetro is now primarily remembered. An extreme example of how such considerations could affect poetic theory is provided by his remarks on the need for 'unity of time' in the drama:

. . . the restricted time is that during which the spectators can comfortably remain seated in the theatre, which, as far as I can see, cannot exceed the revolution of the sun, as Aristotle says, that is, twelve hours [!]; for because of the necessities of the body, such as eating, drinking, excreting the superfluous burdens of the belly and the bladder, sleeping, and because of other necessities, the people cannot continue its stay in the theatre beyond the aforementioned time.[3]

Few literary theories can have had more mundane origins.

[1] Castelvetro, *Poetica d'Aristotele vulgarizzata et sposta* (Vienna, 1570), 28.20; ref. is to the page and line of a second edition (Basle, 1576), and the translation is that of A. H. Gilbert, *Literary Criticism, Plato to Dryden*, op. cit. pp. 304–57.
[2] Ibid., 29.36.
[3] Ibid., 109.21.

Robortello and Castelvetro will thus serve to illustrate the Renaissance development of one of the main influences that had been operating since classical times towards the close association of poetics and rhetoric. In the same period, however, there were other theorists who sought to develop concepts that would allow for a more distinctively poetic system.

Alessandro Lionardi's *Dialogi della inventione poetica* (1554)[1] is one work which shows well both the rhetorical and the poetic influences. Lionardi has the humanists' utilitarian view of literature. 'Two things', he says, are 'especially necessary to human life—speech and action', and:

. . . neither one nor the other of these activities can be properly fulfilled without the knowledge of history, orations, and poems—as things which teach us to do, say, and decide what is required in this life, in every estate, age, and condition, showing us in actions and in discussions what must be imitated and avoided.[2]

'It is proper', he says, following Horace, 'for the poet to delight and edify.'[3] On the other hand, his central interest is in the nature of poetic invention, which he believes to be more important than the other parts of the poetic art, 'disposition' and 'elocution'. Invention alone 'is the reason why man better expresses his ideas, because the abundance and richness of invention enables one to deal properly and easily with any matter to the full'.[4] Verse is one of the distinctive elements of poetry, but the essential element is the imitation—which for the poet is virtually synonymous with invention.[5] This is

[1] No translation or modern edition of these *Dialogues* is at present available. A translation and commentary by the present author, in collaboration with C. A. McCormick, is in course of preparation. Passages quoted are from the draft of this translation, and references are to the original edition of 1554. I am indebted to Ruth Wallerstein (*Studies in Seventeenth Century Poetic*, op. cit., pp. 16–19) for introducing me to this very interesting work.

[2] *Dialogi di Messer Alessandro Lionardi, della inventione poetica* (Venice, 1554), p. 13.

[3] Ibid., p. 46.   [4] Ibid., p. 11.

[5] The historian like the poet is also dependent on invention. His invention, however, is of what is true or factual, and therefore is not imitation. The poet invents things that are verisimilar rather than true—that is, he 'imitates the truth'.

so both because Aristotle said so and because 'the ability to speak reasonably and copiously in every subject seems to me to come first from invention, and afterwards from the words used as an organic instrument animated by [the invention]'. The poet, like the orator, is dependent on invention 'because his concepts and words are true or probable when the things are such . . . Delight and emotion are found in comparisons, in similes, and examples, in virtues and vices, which are not words but things well expressed and represented . . .'[1] Words are less important than things 'because they are only an artificial instrument, produced by the intellect, to declare the being and nature of things.'[2]

Lionardi distinguishes between the embellishment of the subject-matter through style, and that adornment and enrichment that is part of the invention:

. . . just as knowing art and the manner in which things must be said and ordered [that is, elocution and disposition] is of great importance, so it is also necessary to believe that not only is all this necessary to invention; but we must have another greater and more useful knowledge—in what manner it [invention] may be adorned and enriched.[3]

For poetry this adornment and enrichment is achieved through the 'fable'—the elaboration of detail; detail of place, of time, of cause, of passion. And it is this that enables the poet to develop his subject as the painter's colours develop his design. 'The shadow or image of truth is that fable called poetic imitation, that is, narration or exposition of probable things. And the tragic or heroic poem consists of what is true and what is possible together, and the latter colours and enriches the former.'[4]

Something of the rhetorical influence is seen when Lionardi treats the delineation of passion by the poet as important both for the imitation and for its effect on the reader. For the imitation, the passions and the accidental causes that arouse them are part of the

---

[1] *Dialogi di Messer Alessandro Lionardi, della inventione poetica* (Venice, 1554), p. 13.
[2] Ibid., p. 12.
[3] Ibid., p.9.
[4] Ibid., p. 63.

detail by which the poet's invention is developed. But they are also the principal source of that delight in the reader that it is the function of poetry to create. Metaphors, similes, epithets, and the rest are important in giving life to the subject; but they are also important to some extent extrinsically, as sources of feeling in the reader. But despite this intrusion of a more narrowly rhetorical concept of poetry, the main emphasis of Lionardi's *Dialogues*, unlike the commentaries of Robortello and Castelvetro, remains on the essential imitation.

A little more naïve, perhaps, than Lionardi, but also more widely representative of the various attitudes and theories of his time, is Giraloma Fracastoro, whose *Navgerivs, sive de poetica dialogvs* appeared in 1555, the year following Lionardi's work. Fracastoro concludes his *Dialogue* with a definition that indicates the scope of his treatment, in which imitation, instruction, and aesthetic pleasure all have their place: '. . . we should say that the aim of the poet is to please and to instruct, by imitating in every individual object the most excellent and most beautiful elements, in a style which is appropriate and simply beautiful.'[1]

Fracastoro accepts imitation as the basis of poetry, but is thoroughly rhetorical in his insistence on its didactic function. To him the poet is a master of eloquence, who uses imitation, not as Aristotle would have it as a means of idealization, but for instruction. This rhetorical purpose, however, is seen as achieved in a manner that is distinctively poetic. The poet is not alone in teaching through imitation, but his imitation is different:

After all, if we should grant you everything, that the purpose of the poet is to teach through imitation, not even then should we have described what is peculiarly the poet's, what makes him different from the others. For the others do this same thing, the historian for instance . . . It seems to me beyond doubt that the style peculiar to the poet ought to be found in him alone, and that no subject matter is prescribed unless perhaps in general it should be what can be adorned in the treatment . . . Every subject is proper for the poet so

---

[1] *Girolamo Fracastoro Navgerivs, sive de poetica dialogvs* (1555); trans. R. Kelso, *Univ. of Ill. St. in Lang. & Lit.*, ix (1924), no. 3, pp. 87–88.

long as he can adorn it; but his method of treatment differs greatly from the others.[1]

Ornamentation is thus the special function of the poet and the means whereby his eloquence surpasses all others:

Certainly all who have the gift of eloquence say well and appropriately whatever is theirs to say, but this differentiates them, that except for the poet, no one expresses himself merely well and appropriately, but each limits himself to the purpose set for him in his own particular field, one to teaching, another to persuading, and so on. But the poet as a poet is inspired by no other aim than simply to express himself well about anything that proposes itself to him. He indeed wishes also to teach and persuade and speak of other things, but, restricted as it were by his aim, he does not develop the matter enough to explain it, but making a different idea for himself, of untrammeled and universal beauty, seeks all the adornments of speech, all the beauties which can be given to it.[2]

Ornamentation is also the end of the poet's imitation, and is what links the Aristotelian concept of imitation with Fracastoro's didactic purpose: 'They [i.e. all others who strive for eloquence] imitate the particular, that is the object exactly as it is. The poet imitates not the particular but the simple idea clothed in its own beauties, which Aristotle calls the universal.'[2]

The 'beauties' of its own, in which the poet clothes his simple ideas, are the ornaments of poetry. And in his treatment of ornament as the poet's special means of teaching Fracastoro makes of it something much closer to the imaginative observation of experience than would be required for the merely extrinsic adornment of subject matter:

. . . But when I speak of simply beautiful language I wish to be understood in this way: that this beauty harmonizes with the subject under discussion and is appropriate to it and its different attributes, and is not merely beautiful in and for itself.[3]

[1] *Girolamo Fracastoro Navgerivs, sive de poetica dialogvs* (1555); trans. R. Kelso, *Univ. of Ill. St. in Lang. & Lit.*, ix (1924), no. 3, pp. 58.
[2] Ibid., p. 60.
[3] Ibid., p. 64.

And again:

> . . . no one else gifted with the art of eloquence can equal the poet since all the others speak well and appropriately indeed but not simply . . . the poet alone speaks simply. Therefore he who wishes to be called poet, however he may conceive his subject, whatever the subject he proposes, must know all the ornaments, all the beauties which are in any way appropriate to it. Such knowledge is necessary to him; otherwise he will never be able to select the greatest and most beautiful. This ability the poet must have: since he is not a poet who employs the commonplace.[1]

The ornaments are, indeed, for Fracastoro the very life and truth of the subject-matter with which the poet deals:

> . . . For if you mean whatever is added to the bare object, certainly it will be enough to use ordinary speech in explaining things, for the other refinements are not necessary. And similarly, if columns and peristyles and other things are added to houses, they will be extraneous, for the barest structure will serve the purpose of a house, which is to protect us from storm and cold. But, indeed, if we consider objects as they should be, and look for perfection, these additions will not only not be extraneous but essential. Or ought we to think splendid garments extraneous because poor ones are sufficient. Do you not see that just as perfection and ornament are a real part of the things which nature produces, so they are of the things which art produces? What perfection and beauty are, only the greatest artists know. And if you take them away from the subject, assuredly you have somehow taken away life itself. Therefore what the painters and the poets add to things for perfection is not extraneous, if we mean by 'thing' not the bare object such as common artificers, or those who are controlled and restricted by some purpose, make, but the object perfected and given life.[2]

Finally, in a manner rather untypical of his age, Fracastoro denies the Platonic idea, accepted throughout the Middle Ages, of the possession of the poet by a sort of divine frenzy or madness, and finds his inspiration to come instead from within the poetry itself:

[1] Ibid., pp. 65–66.   [2] Ibid., p. 68.
T.H.—F

As soon as he [the poet] had joined all the beauties of language and subject and spoken them, he felt a certain wonderful and almost divine harmony steal into him, to which no other was equal . . .

Hence, O friends, that Platonic madness (in the *Ion*) which Socrates thought heaven-sent. God is not the cause, but music itself, full of a great exalting wonder which makes the pulse beat with a rhythm as if stirred by some violent frenzy . . .[1]

Apart perhaps from this last point, Fracastoro's *Dialogue* is not out of its time. It belongs to the Renaissance, and with an immediately attractive clarity and simplicity reveals the possibilities for a vital, dynamic theory of poetry inherent in Renaissance ideas. Above all, it demonstrates how the concept of poetic ornament could transcend the idea of ornament merely for its own sake which it had tended to become by the later seventeenth century.

Julius Caesar Scaliger, whose *Poetices libri septem* was published in 1561, is immediately notable for the fact that, with the exception of his professed disciple Pontanus, and also Dante, he is the only notable theorist before the eighteenth century who asserted quite definitely against Aristotle that verse was what constituted poetry. This he applies both ways: only discourse that is in verse is poetry, and also any discourse in verse must necessarily be poetry. Thus he claims that if the History of Herodotus were versified it would no longer be history, but historical poetry instead, and he dismisses the usual argument that Lucan was an historian rather than a poet.[2]

Scaliger is therefore unusual in providing a completely clear-cut answer to the central problem of this study. There are, however, other things in his *Poetics* which are equally important and interesting. For Scaliger goes even further than either Robortello or Castelvetro in replacing the poetic system of Aristotle with one based primarily on an interest in the audience; at the same time, however, his emphasis on the essential role of verse, and particularly the

---

[1] *Girolamo Fracastoro Navgerivs, sive de poetica dialogvs* (1555); trans. R. Kelso, *Univ. of Ill. St. in Lang. & Lit.*, ix (1924), no. 3, p. 65.

[2] Julius Caesar Scaliger, *Poetices libri septem* (1561), p. 1; translations of this work are from B. Weinberg, 'Scaliger versus Aristotle on Poetics', *MP*, xxxix (1942), 337–60.

manner in which he relates this to the Platonic concept of order, leads to a more distinctively poetic theory than was achieved by either Robortello or Castelvetro.

Perhaps the principal determinant of Scaliger's system is the concept he holds of poetry as language, and of language as standing in a dual relationship, related on the one side to the things signified by it, and on the other to the audience for whom the signification is intended. The effects of these relationships are maintained with Scaliger's characteristic logicality throughout his work. They exist, he claims, in all forms of discourse, in logic, in rhetoric, and in history, as well as in poetry, and in consequence poetry will be like other forms of discourse in certain respects. In all discourse words are related to things by a process of imitation, in the Platonic sense of the term. The word imitates the thing, just as the thing imitates the 'idea' of the thing:

For Plato establishes the order of things thus: the unchanging separately-existing Idea; the changing visible thing derived from it, which exists as an image of the Idea itself; in the third place a picture or a speech, related indeed in the same way . . . I believe that one can in no wise disagree with this opinion.[1]

In this sense at least, therefore, imitation has no special application for poetry as compared with other forms of discourse, and poetry differs from those other forms only by being in verse, and by the imitation of fictional rather than true objects. To the latter of these distinctions, however, Scaliger pays very little attention.

Scaliger also rejects, as a proper basis for poetry, imitation in what he takes to be the sense of the term as Aristotle used it:

Since all these things ['actions' and 'circumstances'] are represented in the works of the poet, Aristotle asserted that his whole end was imitation, which he attributed to man alone as peculiar to him of all living beings. So in truth this idea once expressed and frequently repeated he kept alive perpetually, and misled us into two absurdities.[2]

[1] Ibid., p. 55.
[2] Ibid., pp. 346–7.

The two 'absurdities' arising from Aristotle's theory are that poetry would have to include certain imitations that are not poems— Scaliger apparently overlooked the logical fallacy in this argument —and that all works in verse are not necessarily poems, which is absurd to Scaliger because for him verse is what constitutes poetry. Thus for Scaliger lyric and several other forms of poetry are not imitations at all,[1] and are poetry simply because they are in verse. Apart from these 'absurdities', however, Scaliger has necessarily to reject imitation as an ultimate end for poetry because of his view that poetry consists of words and words have significance only in relation to an audience; Aristotle's concept, on the contrary, required the poet to strive to create a work which would have its own independent form and existence.

In this view imitation ceases to be an end in itself, and where it exists at all becomes only a means to the end of teaching with pleasure, as it had been conceived of also by Robortello:

The end of poetry is not imitation, but rather delightful instruction by which the habits of men's minds are brought to right reason, so that through them man may achieve perfect action, which is called Beatitude . . . [Poetry is distinguished] not by imitation, for every poem is not an imitation, and every man who imitates is not a poet; not by the use of fiction or lying, for poetry does not lie, or rather that poetry which lies, lies constantly and would therefore be that kind of poetry, and not poetry in general. Finally there is imitation in all speech, since words are images of things. The end of the poet is to teach with pleasure.[2]

However, whereas with Robortello and Castelvetro the emphasis on delight and utility had turned their theories virtually into systems of rhetoric, the manner in which Scaliger derives these ends from his concept of verse as being what constitutes poetry enables him to avoid this subordination of poetry to rhetoric.

[1] Cf. Francis Bacon (*De dignitate et augmentis scientiarum*, op. cit., iv. 315), who does not recognize such forms as satires, elegies, sonnets, and other lyrical forms as poetry, on the ground that they are not imitations, and makes them instead part of rhetoric or philosophy. See below, pp. 131–2.

[2] Scaliger, op. cit., pp. 346–7.

Primarily Scaliger accepts the identification of poetry and verse on historical grounds:

The name of poet therefore did not come from his 'feigning' as some thought because he used feigned objects; but in the beginning was derived from the making of verse. That is, this rhythmical power by which verses are expressed came into being at the same time as human nature itself.[1]

Poetry at the outset was exclusively pleasurable, and it continues to differ from other forms of discourse in that it presents its lessons through the medium of pleasure. For this reason there can be no poetry without verse. However, pleasure has now become only an intermediate and not a final end:

Wherefore it should be said that the end of the poet is to teach with pleasure, and that poetry indeed is a part of politics which is contained (although different in aspect and appearance) under the power of the legislator. For those things which are decreed in the laws, which are subjects of exhortation for the orator and the governor of the people; these things, which are the definite and distinct subjects of poetry are combined with certain pleasurable accompaniments for the instruction of the citizenry.[2]

This transition from pleasure to moral instruction seems to be accomplished by means of Plato's concept of order. Song is order, Scaliger tells his son in the Preface to the *Poetics*, and is thus the special element of order in poetry. Poetry delights not only by the order of its verse, but by presenting through this order a picture to the mind of that perfect moral order which supplies the will with an object worthy of her contemplation. Through verse the reader is given an immediate intuition of beauty and thereby of goodness.

In Scaliger's theory words can have no intrinsic importance, but are significant only in so far as they reflect things and are directed to an audience; and in his strictly logical system the same must be true of poems. 'Poetry must of necessity be useful', he says, 'for there is no imitation for its own sake, for indeed every art envisages that outside of itself which can be advantageous to somebody.'[3] On this basis there can be no independent science of poetics. None the

[1] Ibid., p. 3.   [2] Ibid., p. 347.   [3] Ibid., p. 346.

less, Scaliger remains of great importance for this study in that he combined a wholeheartedly didactic approach to poetry with a more sophisticated aesthetic system than had been attempted since Horace added utility and delight to Aristotle's concept of imitation. His work stresses the relationship of poetry to other forms of discourse, and by emphasizing the role of the audience draws it closer to rhetoric. Against this, the function he gives to verse as the revelation of an ideal order lifts his aesthetic theory clear of the domain of rhetoric. The way was now open for Sir Philip Sidney to attempt the synthesis of imitation and the Platonic elements to be found in Scaliger.

It now remains to examine the problem of poetry and the trivium as it relates specifically to England up to the beginning of the seventeenth century. This can be done quite briefly, partly because little that was new was added by English theorists to the general picture already outlined in this chapter, and also because the relationship of poetry to the other disciplines having been predominantly one of style, much of the material has already been covered in the previous chapter.

Rhetoric in medieval England, instead of being concerned only with prose oratory, as it had been originally, became merged with *poetria* and *dictamen*, the medieval arts of poetry and letter writing respectively. John of Garland, for example, writing in the early fourteenth century, thought that rhetorical ornament was as necessary in metre as in prose. In the Preface to his *Poetria* (*c.* 1300–1350) he wrote:

Presentis tractatus septem suberunt particule. Primo tradetur doctrina inveniendi, deinde docebitur, de modo eligendi materiam, postea de dispositione et de modo ornandi materiam deinde de partibus dictaminis postea de vicis vitandis in quolibet genere dictandi; consequenter constituitur tractatus de rhetorica ornatu, necessario tam in metro quam in prosa, utpote de coloribus materiam abbreviantibus et ampliantibus ad scribentis electionem. Septimo et ultimo subiciuntur exempla literarum curialium et dictaminum scolasticorum et versuum et rithmorum ornate compositorum et diversorum metrorum.[1]

[1] John of Garland, *Poetria magistri Johannis anglici de arte prosayca metrica et rithmica;* ed. G. Mari, *RF*, xiii (1902), 885–6.

The seventh section it will be noted is to contain 'examples of courtly correspondence and scholastic dictamen, pleasantly composed in verse and rhythms, and in diverse metres'.

Rhetorical and poetic ornament come to mean the same thing. Chaucer has the Clerk in the Prologue to his Tale praise Petrarch for his rhetoric:

> Fraunceys Petrark, the laureat poet,
> Highte this clerk, whos rethoryke sweete
> Enlumined al Itaille of poetrye, &c.[1]

And a similar identification of poetry and oratory is implied in James I of Scotland's *Kingis Quair* (1423), where both Gower and Chaucer are found sitting among the orators on the steps of rhetoric.[2] Lydgate, in the Prologue to his *Historye, Sege, and destrucyon of Troye* (1413) says of his translation that 'it stumbleth aye for faute of eloquence', and of Guido that he:

> This noble storye with many freshe coloure
> Of Rhethoryk and many ryche floure
> Of Eloquence to make it sounde the bette, &c.[3]

Also the author of *The Court of Sapience*, probably of the late fourteenth century (it has been attributed by Stephen Hawes to Lydgate), says of 'Dame Rethoryke':

> In prose and metre of all kynde ywys
> This lady blyssed had lust for to playe.[4]

The Court of Sapience confines its treatment of rhetoric wholly to matters of style, and it is probably true that at this period rhetoric,

---

[1] Chaucer, *The Clerk's Prologue* (CT, E, 31–33). J. M. Manly, 'Chaucer and the Rhetoricians', *Proc. of Brit. Acad.* (1926), pp. 95–113, discusses how much Chaucer was influenced by the medieval rhetoricians, and gives some evidence of how widespread the use of rhetoric was at this period and what great value was placed on it.

[2] James I of Scotland, *Kingis Quair*, cxcvii.

[3] John Lydgate, *Historye, sege and destrucyon of Troye*.

[4] *The Court of Sapience* (c. 1400?); from the text printed by Wynkyn de Worde in 1510; passage quoted from D. L. Clark, *Rhetoric and Poetry in the Renaissance*, op. cit., p. 49, to whom I am indebted for pointing out several of these references.

whether applied to poetry or to prose, was generally reduced to a concern with style. However, it should be remembered also that the emphasis of Horace on moral teaching, which had brought poetry and rhetoric closer together in classical times, continued to be strongly present throughout the whole of the medieval period. John Gower, for example, in the *Prologus* to his *Confessio Amantis* (1390) declares:

> I wolde go the middel weie
> And wryte a bok betwen the tweie
> Somewhat of lust, somewhat of lore, &c.[1]

That is, in the critical language to become familiar in the sixteenth and seventeenth centuries, he would combine delight with profit. Chaucer, too, makes frequent reference to the moral purpose of his poetry; his tales are to be 'of best sentence and most solas',[2] and Pandarus tells Criseyde that:

> . . . some men hem delyte
> With subtil art hir tales for to endyte,
> Yet for al that, in hir entencioun,
> Hir tale is al for som conclusioun.[3]

In addition, therefore, to common factors of style, poetry and rhetoric in the medieval period also shared a common aim to be persuasive or instructive. Poetry was already being seen as a peculiarly delightful form of rhetoric, and this attitude was to persist until the end of the seventeenth century and beyond.

The *Pastime of Pleasure* (1509) of Stephen Hawes is another of the didactic allegories, very similar to *The Court of Sapience*. It thus brings the medieval treatment of rhetoric into the sixteenth century, and at the same time introduces for the first time into English the terms of Ciceronian rhetoric. In the *Pastime* the seven liberal arts are introduced in a course of training intended as proper for the education of an ideal knight, and to this end the rhetoric of Cicero is

[1] Gower, *Confessio Amantis*, 'Incipit Prologus', ll. 17–19; ed. G. C. Macauley (2 vols., Oxford, 1901), i, 2; see also 'Liber septem', ll. 1507–1640.
[2] Chaucer, 'The Prologue' (*CT*, A, 800).
[3] Chaucer, *Troilus and Criseyde*, Bk. II, ll. 256–9.

converted to the uses of poetry. In particular, 'invencyon' becomes a theory of poetic composition and an explanation of the allegorical concept of poetry.

There is in the *Pastime*, in fact, less of an identification of poetics and rhetoric than a simple transfer of terminology from one to the other. 'Invencyon', to which Hawes devotes 119 of the 644 lines given to rhetoric, is seen as the product of 'comyn witte', 'ymagynacion', 'fantasy', 'good estymacion', and 'retentyfe memory',[1] and the whole treatment bears little relation to the 'invention' of the Ciceronian rhetorical system. In the latter it is defined as 'the discovery of valid or seemingly valid arguments to render one's cause plausible',[2] but the knight of the *Pastime* seeks from 'Dame Rethoryke' not plausible arguments but the talents of a poet. He would have her paint his tongue with her royal flowers, so that he may succeed in delighting his hearers, and:

> . . . with thy power that thou me endue
> To moralyse thy lytterall censes trewe
> And clense awaye the myst of ygnoraunce
> With depured beames of goodly ordynaunce.[3]

Here again, though the treatment is primarily one of style, there is the emphasis on the moral function of poetry.

The remaining four of the five parts of rhetoric, as they are treated in the *Pastime*, follow only a little more closely on the classical system, and in so far as they do the result is only to combine the terms and methods of classical rhetoric with the needs of the poet. Hawes confines himself almost entirely to poetry, Cicero, the only orator mentioned, having to share a single line with Virgil.

The great names of the earlier sixteenth century in England are not those of poetic theorists or rhetoricians, but of educationists and reformers, like the fifteenth-century Italian from whom they drew their inspiration. They are such men as John Colet, Sir Thomas More, Sir Thomas Elyot, and Roger Ascham, together with

[1] Stephen Hawes, *The Pastime of Pleasure* (1509), ll. 701–820; ed. W. E. Mead, EETS, 173 (1928), pp. 33–37.

[2] Cicero, *De inventione*, I, vii, 9.

[3] Hawes, ll. 676–9; op. cit., p. 31.

Erasmus and Juan Luis Vives, who though they were not English-men exerted a great influence on the literary and intellectual life of sixteenth-century England. The comments of these men on litera-ture are to be found incidentally, in works concerned primarily with religious, political, or pedagogical matters, and like their Italian predecessors their interest was almost exclusively practical and utilitarian rather than aesthetic. They attached the greatest sig-nificance to oratory, and went a long way towards rescuing the classical tradition of rhetoric from its medieval state of confusion. Above all they reasserted the importance of eloquence by insisting with Cicero on its essential relationship to wisdom.[1]

Thus Erasmus declares in his *De copia verborum* (1511): 'If the former [thought] is the first in importance, the latter [style] is acquired first in order of time . . . for ideas are only intelligible by means of the words that describe them.'[2] And while Roger Ascham could assert that in ancient literature 'we finde alwayes wisdom and eloquence, good matter and good utterance never or seldom asunder', and declare that 'ye know not what hurt ye do to learning, that care not for wordes but matter',[3] he could also show that it was a balance of matter and words, and not an undue emphasis on words that he wanted, by his plea for a middle style:

. . . he that wyll wryte in any tongue, muste folowe thys councel of Aristotle, to speake as the comon people do, to thinke as wyse men do: and so shoulde euery man understande hym, and the iudgement

---

[1] Most noteworthy of the works of these humanists are: Colet's *Lectures on St. Paul's Epistles*, delivered at Oxford (1497–8); Sir Thomas More's *Utopia* (1516); Erasmus's *Moriae encomium* (1509), *De ratione studii* (1511), *De copia verborum* (1511), *De conscribendis epistolis* (1521), and *Ciceronianus* (1528); Vives's *De corruptis artibus* (1531); *De ratione studii* (1523); *De ratione dicendi* (1533); and *De tradendis disciplinis* (1531); Elyot's *The Boke named the Governour* (1531); and Ascham's *Scholemaster* (1570) and *Toxophilus* (1545). For a largely unfavour-able assessment of the effects of humanism on literary development see C. S. Lewis, *English Literature in the Sixteenth Century*, op. cit., Chap. 1. A recent study of English humanism in relation to poetry is that of H. A. Mason, *Humanism and Poetry in the Early Tudor Period*, op. cit.

[2] Erasmus, *De copia verborum* (1511); trans. W. H. Woodward, *Erasmus concerning Education* (Cambridge, 1904), p. 162.

[3] Roger Ascham, *The Scholemaster*, op. cit., p. 265.

of wyse men alowe hym. Many English writers haue not done so, but vsinge straunge wordes as latin, french and Italian, do make all thinges darke and harde. Ones I communed with a man whiche reasoned the englyshe tongue to be enryched and encreased thereby, sayinge: Who wyll not prayse that feaste, where a man shall drinke at a diner, bothe wyne, ale and beere? Truely, quod I, they be all good, euery one taken by hym selfe alone, but if you putte Maluesye and sacke, reade wyn and white, ale and beere, and al in one pot, you shall make a drynke, neyther easie to be knowen, nor yet holsom for the bodye . . .[1]

For Vives rhetoric was the most powerful of the arts, and eloquence a mighty instrument of society, by which men in all ages have acquired power and authority.[2]

In matters relating directly to poetry the English humanists showed either a lack of interest, such as was later to be characteristic of Francis Bacon, or a tendency (also to be reflected in Bacon) to borrow ideas from medieval or classical sources. Vives is typical in his refusal to allow poetry any serious role in life: '. . . we must not ignore the fact, that poetry is to be relegated "to the leisure hours of life". It is not to be consumed as if it were nourishment, but is to be treated as a spice.'[3] Something of the pervasiveness of this view of poetry may be gauged from the fact that it had been expressed by Vergerius at the beginning of the fifteenth century: 'After Eloquence we place Poetry and the Poetic Art, which though not without value in daily life and as an aid to oratory, have nevertheless their main concern for the leisure side of existence.'[4] And by Bacon two centuries later, in concluding his discussion of poetry: 'But we stay too long in the theatre; let us now pass to the palace of the mind, which we are to approach and enter with more reverence and attention.'[5]

Poetry for these humanists of the English Renaissance was

---

[1] Ascham, 'To all Gentle Men and Yomen of England', prefixed to *Toxophilus: The Schole of shooting conteyned in two books* (London, 1545); ed. A. M. Wright, op. cit., p. xiv.
[2] Vives, *De tradendis disciplinis* (1531); trans. F. Watson, *Vives on Education* (Cambridge, 1904), pp. 180 ff.
[3] Ibid., p. 138.
[4] Vergerius, *De ingenuis moribus*, op. cit., pp. 107–8.
[5] Bacon, *De augmentis scientiarum*, op. cit., iv, 335.

primarily an object for discussion in stylistic terms, a model of expression, or a source of instructive subject matter. Their importance for this study lies in their establishment in England of the classical ideal of eloquence, freed from most of the earlier confusion with poetics, and in the emphasis they gave to rhetorical considerations of style.

Strangely enough, too, through their insistence on a classical balance of matter and style, the early humanists were also the precursors of the revolt against the extreme elaboration of style which gathered momentum in the later sixteenth century. This is particularly true of Erasmus, whose *Ciceronianus* (1528) marks the beginning of the anti-Ciceronian movement. This movement, having as its target the elimination, not only of Ciceronian imitation, but of all the extreme forms of ornate style that grew out of the rhetorical emphasis of humanism, connects through Bacon with the 'plain' style in prose of the later seventeenth century.

Apart from the treatment given to Ciceronian rhetoric in *The Pastime of Pleasure*, Cicero's five terms were discussed in Caxton's *Mirrour of the World* (first published around 1481, although it was not until the third edition of around 1527 that all five classical terms were included), and in Leonard Cox's *The Arte or Crafte of Rhethoryke* (*c.* 1530). The latter was the first published textbook on rhetoric, and like the texts that followed until the coming of the Ramists it was concerned wholly with prose oratory.

The last, most important, and only really complete Ciceronian rhetoric to appear in English before the arrival of the English Ramists (after whom Ciceronian rhetoric never fully recovered its original form) was Thomas Wilson's *The Arte of Rhetorique* (1553). This, however, was in the tradition of classical rhetoric, and consequently dealt almost entirely with prose oratory; its few brief comments on poetry, following the manner of the humanists, are of a purely medieval kind, treating it as an essentially allegorical and esoteric art. Of more interest, particularly in view of the later agitation for a plainer style of preaching, is Wilson's disapproval of the intrusion of poetic techniques, particularly rhyme, into the prose of sermons:

I heard a preacher deliting much in this kind of composition, who vsed so often to ende his sentences with wordes vnto that which went before, that in my judgement there was not half a dozen sentences in his whole sermon, but they ended all in Rime for the most parte. Some not best disposed, wished the Preacher a Lute, that with his rimed sermon he might vse some pleasant melody, and so the people might take pleasure diuers waies, and dance if they list.[1]

Compared with a work such as Puttenham's *Arte of Englishe Poesie*, Wilson's *Rhetorique* represents a relatively clear distinction of oratory from poetry. It would seem, indeed, a significant fact that the sixteenth century as a whole found it more possible to think of oratory without reference to poetry than to write of poetry without using the machinery and concepts of oratory.

The sixteenth-century rhetorical tradition petered out after Wilson in a series of school manuals, such as Rainolde's *Foundacion of Rhetorike* (1563), Peacham's *Garden of Eloquence* (1577), Abraham Fraunce's *Arcadian Rhetorick* (1584), in which the principles of rhetoric were illustrated from Sidney's *Arcadia*, as well as from a variety of other sources, prose and verse, Greek, Latin and Italian in addition to English, and the same author's *Lawyier's Logike* (1588), which used *The Shepheardes Calendar*, as well as law, for the same purpose in relation to logic. Of these, the earlier textbooks like Rainolde's were based not on Cicero, Quintilian, or the other classical rhetoricians, but on later Greek writers such as Hermogenes (second century) and Apthonius (fourth century), who confined themselves much more to the mechanical rules of eloquent expression. The principal object of these texts was to promote a copious style, by providing an abundance of material for amplifying a theme or for encouraging a varied and lively diction; and, though they made no contribution to theory, the systematic training in rhetoric they gave deeply influenced Elizabethan prose style.[2]

---

[1] Thomas Wilson, *The Arte of Rhetorique, for the use of all such as are Studious of Eloquence* (London, 1553); ed. G. H. Mair (Oxford, 1909), p. 168.

[2] Richard Rainolde's *A book called the Foundacion of Rhetorike* (London, 1563), for example, is an English adaptation of Apthonius's *Progymnasmata*. A detailed study of the contents of these rhetorical texts is provided by F. Johnson, 'Two Renaissance Textbooks of Rhetoric', *HLQ*, vi (1942/3) 427–44.

In the later years of the sixteenth century the rhetorical texts were almost without exception adaptations from or translations of the new rhetoric of Peter Ramus, and what significance they have will be discussed in a later section devoted to the influence of Ramism.

Opposition to rhetorical extravagance in the sixteenth century, apart from that of the humanists which was discussed earlier, is represented by such men as Nashe, whose views on fine writing were mentioned in the earlier chapter on style, and particularly by John Jewel, Praelector of Humanity at Oxford, in his *Oratio contra rhetoricum* (1548). This oration, as the title suggests, attacks not only the cult of Ciceronian imitation, but the whole rhetorical tradition from which it sprang. In the manner to become common a century later, Jewel argues that because man speaks to be understood there can be no better way than that of plain utterance:

Truth, indeed, is clear and simple; it has small need of the armament of the tongue or of eloquence. If it is perspicuous and plain, it has enough support in itself; it does not require flowers of artful speech. If it is obscured and unpropitious, it will not be brought to light in vociferation and flow of words.[1]

Jewel's disquisition apparently had little influence, but despite its extravagance it remains interesting, as Atkins says, as 'a plea . . . for that plain unadorned speech which has been intermittently advocated by English writers from the time of Bede onwards'.

Sir Philip Sidney's *An Apologie for Poetrie* (*c.* 1583) represents the philosophic aspect of English Renaissance poetic theory, in contrast to the purely stylistic or practical treatment deriving from the rhetorical orientation of humanism. At least for English poetic theory the *Apologie* provides the culmination of the movement associated with the Renaissance rediscovery of Aristotle's *Poetics* and studied earlier in this chapter in the work of Robortello, Castelvetro, and the other sixteenth-century Italian theorists. In this defence of the poetic art Sidney finally established the Renaissance

---

[1] John Jewel, *Oratio contra rhetoricum* (London, 1584); trans. H. H. Hudson, 'Jewel's Oration against Rhetoric', *QJS*, xiv (1928), 374–92.

victory of poetry over philosophy, and as far as possible within a moralistic-didactic, and therefore essentially rhetorical system, the art of poetry achieved its independence to a degree not realized since the time of Aristotle.

The *Apologie* is far too well known to require any detailed analysis here. A few reminders are all that is necessary to show how it draws together almost all the main strands of classical and Renaissance poetic theory. Poetry is defined by Sidney as: '. . . an arte of imitation, for so *Aristotle* termeth it in his word *Mimesis*, that is to say, a representing, counterfetting, or figuring foorth: to speak metaphorically, a speaking picture: with this end, to teach and delight.'[1] Sidney thus accepts the Aristotelian theory of poetry as imitation, with the usual Renaissance addition, inherited from Horace, that its end is to teach and delight. His working out of the concept of imitation is not greatly at variance with that of Aristotle: much less so, indeed, than had been the case with Robortello, Castelvetro, or Scaliger. His departures from Aristotle, however, are like theirs the result primarily of his didactic leanings, which cause him to deal almost exclusively with 'things as they ought to be'. He omits any consideration of 'things as they were or are, and as they are said or thought to be', all of which were included within the scope of poetry's imitation by Aristotle, for whom the poet 'must of necessity imitate one of three objects—things as they were or are, things as they are said or thought to be, or things as they ought to be'.[2] In keeping with the general lack of any strong moral emphasis, Aristotle does not place any special stress on the last of these alternatives. Sidney, on the contrary, of those whom he describes as 'right Poets'—as distinct from poets who deal with

---

[1] Sidney, *An Apologie for Poetrie* (c. 1583); ed. G. G. Smith, op. cit., i, 158. The idea of poetry as a 'speaking picture' was derived originally from Plutarch (*De audendis poetis*, III): '. . . poetry is vocal painting, and painting silent poetry.' The analogy, which remained a commonplace throughout the seventeenth century and until refuted by Lessing in his *Laokoon* (1766), ignored the element of action which was an essential part of Aristotle's theory —the object of tragedy is 'men in action', portrayed in a plot which must have a beginning, a middle, and an end.

[2] Aristotle, *Poetics*, XXV, 1; op. cit., p. 97.

'matters philosophical'—writes: 'For these third be they which most properly do imitate to teach and delight, and to imitate borrow nothing of what is, hath been, or shall be; but range, onely rayned with learned discretion, into the diuine consideration of what may be, and should be.'[1]

The Platonic colouring that is evident throughout his work causes Sidney to see imitation as a means whereby the poet can obtain glimpses of a perfect world:

> Onely the Poet, disdayning to be tied to any such subiection, lifted vp with the vigor of his owne inuention, dooth growe in effect another nature, in making things either better then Nature bringeth forth, or, quite a newe, formes such as neuer were in Nature . . .
> Nature neuer set forth the earth in so rich tapistry as diuers Poets haue done, neither with plesant riuers, fruitful trees, sweet smelling flowers, nor whatsoeuer els may make the too loued earth more louely. Her world is brasen, the Poets onely deliuer a golden.[2]

The emphasis here on 'invention', which is virtually identified (as it had been by Hawes) with the poetic imagination, may be seen as deriving from the rhetorical influence. Aristotle had seen the task of the poet as being that of taking a philosophical rather than a practical view of things as they are, in order to arrive at an understanding of the universal through the particular; Sidney, by contrast, sees the poet as transcending the individual species in nature. For both, however, what raises poetry above factual discourse is that it is not tied to the immediate and accidental circumstances of everyday life.

Scaliger had seen verse as the essential element in poetry that would reconcile delight and moral utility in a poetic system based on the beauty of order. Sidney's concept of poetry has much in common with this. Though he accepts Aristotle in agreeing that verse is 'an ornament and no cause to poetry', and that 'it is not rhyming and versing that maketh a poet',[3] elsewhere he comes close to Scaliger in allowing that 'the exquisite obseruing of number and

---

[1] Sidney, op. cit., i, 159.
[2] Ibid., i, 156.   [3] Ibid., i, 159–60.

measure in words . . . did seeme to haue some dyuine force in it'.[1]
And again, there is this most memorable passage from the *Apologie*,
when the tone perhaps indicates better than anything where his
true feelings lay:

. . . hee cometh to you with words sent in a delightfull proportion,
either accompanied with, or prepared for, the well inchaunting skill of
Musicke; and with a tale foorsooth he commeth vnto you, with a tale
which holdeth children from play, and old men from the chimney
corner.[2]

But it is not primarily the qualities lent to it by verse but imitation
that Sidney sees as giving poetry its power of delightful teaching;
this power, which Scaliger had found in verse and which he saw as
enabling poetry to provide a glimpse of ideal perfection, lay for
Sidney in poetry's transcendence through imitation of the ordinary
world. For him, however, as for Scaliger, it was the special virtue of
this power of poetry that it could lead to delight, and through
delight to moral teaching.

Sidney may thus be allowed to represent the philosophical aspects
of that inheritance which the long-standing relationship of poetry
and rhetoric bequeathed to the seventeenth century. An amalgam
primarily of the ideas of Plato, Aristotle, and Horace, it had been
developed during the Renaissance into a fully fledged didactic
theory of poetry, capable of a relatively autonomous existence, independent of the subjects of the trivium which had, alternately or
simultaneously, tended to nurse or to strangle it since birth. What
the seventeenth century did with this inheritance is the subject of
the succeeding chapter. In the meantime, however, it will be
desirable to look briefly at the purely educational role of rhetoric
during the earlier seventeenth century, because of its formative
influence on the writers and critics of the later period with which
this study is primarily concerned.

Popular attitudes towards rhetoric in the seventeenth century have
already received considerable attention in the earlier chapter con-

[1] Ibid., i, 154. Cf. passage quoted from Fracastoro above, p. 74.
[2] Ibid., i, 172.
T.H.—G

cerned with style, and the more important aspects of rhetoric's relationship to poetry during this period will be the main part of the subjects dealt with in the chapter to follow. All that is intended here is a very brief glance at the place given to poetry by the seventeenth-century formal training in rhetoric.[1]

Of the close relationship of poetry and the trivium in the seventeenth-century educational pattern no document is more revealing than John Milton's *Art of Logic, arranged after the method of Peter Ramus* (1672).[2] In the 'Life of Peter Ramus', which Milton adapted from the study by John Thomas Fregius and appended to his own work, he writes of Ramus:

In the thirty-first year of his age he delivered an oration recommending the union of the studies of philosophy and eloquence; with his brother Talon (for this he always called him) he so divided the parts of the profession that Talon in the morning could teach philosophy and he himself in the afternoon could teach eloquence. He demonstrated the service of dialectic in explaining the poets, orators, philosophers and authors of all sorts.[3]

And throughout the *Art of Logic* Milton draws on poets and orators alike to exemplify his precepts. For example, his treatment of similitudes:

A similitude is disjunct when the four terms or things *are distinguished in fact*, that is, when the two terms or distinct things in the propositions

---

[1] For more detailed discussions of this subject see D. L. Clark, *Milton at St. Paul's School*, op. cit.; T. W. Baldwin, *Shakspere's Small Latin & Lesse Greek*, op. cit., and R. Barker, *Memoir of Richard Busby D.D. 1606–1695* (London, 1895), especially pp. 77–82 referring to Dryden at Westminster School. Much valuable primary material is also available in John Brinsley's *Ludus literarius*, op. cit., and in Charles Hoole's *A new discovery of the old art of teaching school, in four small treatises* (London, 1660, probably written *c.* 1637); ed. E. T. Campagnac (Liverpool, 1913).

[2] For a discussion of the relationship of rhetoric to logic and dialectic, and of poetry to all three, in the system of Peter Ramus and his followers, see below, pp. 108–19.

[3] John Milton, 'The Life of Peter Ramus', appended to *A fuller institution of the Art of Logic arranged after the method of Peter Ramus* (London, 1672); ed. F. A. Patterson et al., *The Works of John Milton* (18 vols., New York, 1931–8), xi, 501–3.

are compared with two terms or distinct things in the reddition. This form also occurs with signs or without signs. The signs are *such as . . . so*, the first the sign of the proposition, the second of the reddition. Likewise signs of the proposition are *in whatever way, as, just as*, to which answer *so, in the same way, similarly* in the reddition. Examples follow.

Eclogues 5 : What thing that sleep and rest on grass
          To weary men appear,
        The same to me of thy sweet verse
          The melody so clear.

Poetry is to the hearer as sleep to the tired: the four terms are distinct. *Ad fratrem* I : 'As the best governors of ships oftentimes may not overcome the strength and rage of the tempest, so the most wise man may not always vanquish the invasion and violence of fortune.' Here there also are four terms for as the pilot is to the tempest so is the wise man to fortune. *Tristia* I :

        As tawny gold is tried in fire
        In time of need must faith be tested.

Cicero (*Philippics* 2): 'But even as those . . . &c.'[1]

In this mixing of examples from poetry and rhetoric Milton is following the example of Abraham Fraunce and other Ramist rhetoricians and logicians, for whom no distinction between poetry and oratory is necessary, in so far as the use of logic is concerned, since both poets and orators must make use of it.[2] On the other hand, his practice is in contrast with that of the earlier classical rhetoricians such as Thomas Wilson, and also that of textbooks like Rainolde's *A booke called the foundacion of Rhetorike* (1563), which are confined to the consideration of prose oratory; as are also the foremost rhetorical works of Milton's own time, Thomas Blount's *The Academie of Eloquence* (1654) and John Smith's *The Mysterie of*

---

[1] Ibid., xi, 197 and 199.
[2] L. Howard, 'The *Invention* of Milton's *Great Argument*: A Study of the logic of *God's Way's to Men*', HLQ (1946), 149, makes use of Ramean logic, as interpreted by Milton himself in the *Art of Logic*, to explain Milton's ideas of causation in *Paradise Lost*.

Rhetorique Unveil'd (1657). These latter works, however, were not school texts, which field was almost entirely occupied by the Ramists, notably Charles Butler, whose various editions of Ramist rhetoric were the most widely used in the schools.

Nevertheless the close association of poetry and prose oratory within the purely educational tradition was not simply a matter of Ramist influence, but one that went back to classical times: the practice of paraphrase, for example, is at least as old as Quintilian, who recommends it as part of the training of orators,[1] and St. Augustine records having had to paraphrase passages from the *Aeneid* while at school.[2] The immediate origin of much seventeenth-century educational practice, however, at least in the schools, was sixteenth-century humanism; and here, as was discussed earlier in this chapter, literature, including poetry, was valued mainly for its educational role. Thus Erasmus, the founder along with John Colet and William Lily of the famous St. Paul's School in London, in his *De ratione studii* (1511) recommended not only the turning of prose into poetry and of poetry into prose, but also the turning of poetry out of one metre into another. Roger Ascham, who expressed disapproval of paraphrasing, nevertheless grudgingly admits that paraphrase from prose into verse, or verse into prose, has classical sanction and is better than paraphrase from one prose version to another.[3]

The continuance of this kind of practice into the seventeenth century may be attested from one of the most influential school-teaching manuals of the time, Charles Hoole's *A new discovery of the old art of teaching school* (c. 1637):

As they read this Author, you may cause them sometimes to relate a pleasing story in good English prose, and to try who can soonest turn it into elegant Latine, or into some other kinde of verses which you please for the present to appoint them, either English or Latine, or both.[4]

[1] Quintilian, *De inst. orat.*, X, v, 4–8.
[2] Saint Augustine, *Confessions*, I, xvii, 27.
[3] Ascham, *The Scholemaster*, op. cit., pp. 246–7.
[4] Hoole, *A new discovery of the old art of teaching school*, op. cit., p. 180.

Or again, this time from John Brinsley's equally popular *Ludus literarius* (1612), on the subject of the teaching of versifying:

To look that they be able in good manner to write true Latine, and a good phrase in prose, before they begin to meddle with making a verse . . .

I find this a most easie and pleasant way to enter them; that for all the first books of Poetry which they learn in the beginning, they use to reade them dayly out of the Grammaticall translations: first resolving every verse into the Grammaticall order, like as it is in the translation; after into the Poeticall, turning it into verse, as the words are in the Poet: according as I shewed the manner before, in the benefit and use of the translations. For the making of a verse, is nothing but the turning of words forth of the Grammaticall order, into the Rhetoricall, in some kind of metre; which we call verses . . .

For this practice of reading their Poetry, out of the translations into verse, a little triall will soone shew you, that very young children will doe it as fast as into prose: and by the use of it, continually turning prose into verse, they will be in a good way towards the making of a Verse, before they have learned any rules thereof.[1]

Even from this brief survey it becomes obvious that for poets such as Milton or Dryden who experienced it, the seventeenth-century rhetorical education could not have failed to influence them towards a view of poetry as differing from prose only by virtue of its different way of manipulating or organizing words. Within this educational system poetry tended to be reduced to *elocutio*, the art of clothing thoughts and feelings in language that is correct, appropriate, and pleasing, which had a common reference to both poetry and prose. At the same time it was an education wholly rhetorical in emphasis, its aim being the training of the whole man for public affairs; and in this aim poetry was seen as playing its part, receiving inevitably in return a strong rhetorical colouring. It was in the light of this rhetorical education that Milton wrote his own *Treatise on Education* and later set out to write a poem 'doctrinal and exemplary to a nation'.

[1] Brinsley, *Ludus literarius*, op. cit., p. 192.

The aim of this chapter has been to provide a background survey that would establish the position of poetry in the pattern of discourse as it was at the beginning of the seventeenth century; and from the very tangled skein that has been revealed several reasonably firm threads of fact may be withdrawn. Firstly, the seventeenth century inherited a tradition in which poetry was closely associated with, if not wholly dominated by, considerations that were essentially rhetorical. Then, either as a result or a cause of this association, poetry was seen as having a didactic, moral purpose which in its turn focused the attention of critics ultimately on the poet's audience, rather than on the poet himself or on his poem. Thirdly, because rhetoric is primarily a matter of an effective style, so discussion of poetry tended to revolve around style; which, however, at its highest level, with, for example, a Lionardi or a Fracastoro, could encompass a doctrine which sees 'poetic ornament' as giving the very life and truth to the subject-matter of poetry.

These things are found to have had two important consequences: because it is related to a moral purpose outside itself, an independent science or art of poetry, such as Aristotle originally envisaged, becomes difficult to formulate; and in the tradition in which eloquence is seen as an indispensable part of knowledge, and in which all learning is centred on literature, poetry's association with rhetoric gives it a high place in the scheme of things, so that Sidney is able to declare without incongruity that the poet is 'of all our Sciences . . . the Monarch'. It should now be possible, by examining what happened to the rhetorical tradition during the seventeenth century, to assess the effects on men's concepts of poetry of the changes that took place.

CHAPTER THREE

Concepts of Utility in Poetry and Prose

THE discussion in an earlier chapter of 'plain' style in later seventeenth-century prose has already provided some evidence of what might be described as a utilitarian attitude towards prose discourse. There was also some suggestion that this emphasis on utilitarian prose was opposed to the rhetorical, eloquent use of language with which poetry tended to be traditionally associated. The present chapter will examine in more detail the problem of the extent to which prose had, in the later seventeenth century, come to be thought of as a primarily utilitarian form of discourse, and also the meaning of this development for attitudes towards discourse in general and towards poetry in particular.

In modern usage, 'utilitarian' discourse would be that existing for some end or purpose outside itself, and of no value except in relation to that purpose; and it would be contrasted with what might be termed 'creative' or perhaps 'imaginative' writing which would be seen as in some measure its own justification for existence. How far would these or similar concepts have been understood or applied in the seventeenth century? Part of the answer might be supplied from such a work as John Webster's *Academarium Examen* (1653):

Lastly, for *Rhetorick*, or *Oratory*, Poesie, and the like, which serve for adornation, and are as it were the outward dress, and attire of more solid sciences; first they might tolerably pass, if there were not too much affectation towards them, and too much pretious time spent about them, while more excellent and necessary learning lies neglected and passed by: for we do in these ornamental arts, as people usually do in the world, who take more care often time about the goods of fortune, than about the good of the body, and more nice and precise solicitousness about fashions and garbs, than either about the body it self or the goods of the mind, regarding the shell more than the kernal, and the shadow more than the substance.[1]

Webster serves to illustrate both the dichotomy of verbal eloquence and utility, and also the identification of poetry with the former of these. His attitude to poetry is not, of course, dissimilar to that of the humanists, but, whereas they had reserved this attitude for poetry as distinct from eloquence in general, Webster extends it to include 'Rhetorick, or Oratory . . . and the like'—apparently, perhaps, the art of letters in general. The *Academarium Examen* is, in fact, a direct and overall rejection of the literary values of Renaissance humanism.

Webster's attitude is strictly utilitarian, but he represents the Puritan, anti-scholastic, anti-rationalist side of the movement associated with the utilitarianism of Bacon. He is not a scientist. Bishop Sprat, however, in his *History of the Royal Society* (1667), is even more explicit than Webster in the distinction he makes, and his application of it is made more directly to the scientific and literary uses of language respectively. After enlarging on the 'close, naked, natural way of speaking' as the style proper to scientific inquiry, he goes on to defend the activities of the Royal Society as being 'inoffensive to all the various wayes of Living, already in use':

First then I will make no scruple to acquit *Experimental Philosophy*, from having any ill effects, on the usual *Arts*, whereby we are taught the Purity and Elegance of *Languages*. Whatever discoveries shall appear to us afresh, out of the hidden things of *Nature*, the same words, and the same waies of Expression will remain. Or if perhaps by this means, any change shall be made herein; it can be only for the better; by supplying mens Tongues, with very many *new things*, to be nam'd, and adorn'd, and describ'd in their discourse.[2]

Nothing could be more revealing of the scientist's attitude to the literary use of language. Experimental philosophy is alone concerned with the exploration and discovery of nature that is man's primary

[1] John Webster, *Academarium Examen* (London, 1653), p. 88.
[2] Sprat, *History of the Royal Society*, op. cit., p. 324.

interest. The new philosophical style may be associated with it, but only as an ancillary, something subsequent to it—not, that is, as an integral part of experimental science, as the earlier philosophical style had been part of the philosophy with which it had been associated in the classical and humanistic organization of learning. In the central part of the new learning words have no part. The 'usual arts'—the literary uses of language, including presumably poetry—are unaffected only because they are unconcerned, except for the new material that is condescendingly thrown to them by science, 'to be nam'd, and adorn'd, and describ'd in their discourse'.

The same attitude, this time applied explicitly to poetry, is apparent when Sprat later in the *History* enlarges on the benefits that experimental science will confer on 'our wits and Writers'. After examining the basis of poetic wit, which following Hobbes he finds to consist in striking resemblances between things, he concludes that the traditional sources of imagery tend to have been worked out, and that:

It is now therefore seasonable for *Natural Knowledge* to come forth, and to give us the understanding of new *Virtues* and *Qualities* of things; which may relieve their fellow creatures, that have long born the burden alone, and have long bin vex'd by the imaginations of Poets. This charitable assistance Experiments will soon bestow.[1]

And, perhaps rather strangely, Francis Bacon is cited as an example of a writer who has received this 'charitable assistance', although in his case it has been as a result of his own scientific activities:

The use of *Experiments* to this purpose is evident, by the wonderful advantage that my Lord Bacon receiv'd from them. This excellent Writer was abundantly recompenc'd for his Noble Labors in that *Philosophy* by a vast Treasure of admirable *Imaginations* which it afforded him, wherewith to express and adorn his thoughts about other matters.[2]

[1] Ibid., p. 416.
[2] Ibid. It is, I presume, Francis and not Roger Bacon who is being referred to, although the apparent reference to experiments might seem to fit the latter more accurately. Sprat's ideas on poetic imagery are discussed by A. Rosenberg, 'Bishop Sprat on Science and Imagery', *Isis*, xl (1952), 220–2.

Sprat shows clearly that he held a concept of language usage that could be described as utilitarian, in the modern sense of the word, and that he differentiated this usage from another which might be vaguely termed literary but which is much less clearly defined. The idea of a strictly utilitarian use of language was, of course, not new; it had been held, for instance, by Wiclif in the fourteenth century. But for reasons that were discussed in a previous chapter, it had never before in England received such authoritative support, nor aroused such widespread interest, as it did in the later seventeenth century. And at the same time as defining the scientific use of language, Sprat completely reverses the relationship between poetry and philosophy that had enabled Sidney to claim for poetry its high position: instead of being a vehicle for the highest kind of knowledge, higher than either philosophy or history, poetry is made dependent on science for the very materials it works with.

However, despite this acceptance of a utilitarian function for language as it is related to science, and the consequent definition of the position of 'literary' discourse in relation to scientific learning, there is no evidence from what Sprat has to say of any new concept of 'creative' writing. The uses of language which the Royal Society opposed to their own work, the 'usual Arts', were by Sprat's own statement part of the 'various waies of Living, already in use', and it must be concluded that the dichotomy was to him one between the new scientific or 'utilitarian' use of language, and the older rhetorical or 'eloquent' usage. Any concept which Sprat had of 'literary' discourse would be very likely little different from those discussed in the previous chapter as part of the rhetorical tradition, despite the different role he was prepared to give to literature in the world of learning.

What seems to be a typical account of poetry from a seventeenth-century scientist might be provided from Sir Kenelm Digby's *Treatise of Mans Soul* (1657). Digby was the author of another Treatise, *On Bodies* (1644), and in 1661 he is recorded as having lectured to the Royal Society on the vegetation of plants. He is also the man most likely to have introduced the writings of Descartes to England. This passage comes from the chapter *Of discoursing*, and it follows sections dealing in turn with logic, rhetoric, and grammar:

Poetry, is not a governour of our Actions, but by advantagious expressing of some eminent ones, is becometh a useful directour to us; and therefore challengeth a place here. The design of it is, by representing humane actions in a more august and admirable hew, then in themselves they usually have: to frame specious Ideas, in which the people may see, what is well done, what amisse, what should be done, and what by errour is wont to be done: and to imprint in mens mindes a deep conceit of the goods and evils, that follow their vertuous and vitious comportment of their lives.

If those who assume the title of *Poets*, did aim at this end, and would hold themselves strictly to it, they would prove as profitable instruments as any the commonwealth had: for the delightfulness and blithness of their compositions, inviteth most men to be frequently conversant with them; (either in songs, or upon the Stage or in other Poems) while the sober aspect and severity of bare precepts, deturneth many from lending a pleased ear to their wholesome doctrine . . . But unto such a Poet as would aim at those noble effects, no knowledge of *Morality*, nor the nature and course of humane actions and accidents must be wanting: he must be well versed in *History;* he must be acquainted with the progress of nature, in what she bringeth to passe; he must be deficient in no part of *Logick, Rhetorick* or *Grammar:* in a word he must be consummate in all Arts and Sciences, if he will be excellent in this way.[1]

The whole treatment here is rhetorical in a narrowly didactic, moralistic, direction.

This change of emphasis in the seventeenth century from the eloquent to the utilitarian function of language froms a main part of the thesis of the latest and most extensive work of Professor R. F. Jones, *The Triumph of the English Language* (1953): 'The insistence upon usefulness plays somewhat the same part in determining linguistic attitudes in the seventeenth century that the emphasis

[1] Sir Kenelm Digby, 'A Treatise of Mans Soul', p. 35, in *Two Treatises: in the one of which, the Nature of Bodies: In the other the Nature of Mans Soul is looked into* . . . (London, 1658).

upon eloquence played in the sixteenth.'[1] There is, however, a difficulty here, arising from the implied contrast of eloquence and utility. The seventeenth-century emphasis on utility can be substantiated from Sprat, as well as from innumerable seventeenth-century writers associated either with the new science or with the demand for a plainer style of preaching; and the sixteenth-century emphasis on florid eloquence is equally a commonplace of literary history. But Jones's thesis implies not only an emphasis on utility at the expense of eloquence in the seventeenth century, which seems not open to dispute, but also a sixteenth-century emphasis on eloquence at the expense of utility, which is rather more questionable.

This latter implication, while it may reflect much of the practice of the sixteenth century, when the extravagance of eloquence led to widespread protests, is yet not true of the original, basic intentions or theory of rhetorical eloquence. Classical rhetoric, from which sixteenth-century eloquence orginated, was essentially utilitarian in aim: it was primarily an art of persuasion, and by Cicero's dictum was as necessary to wisdom as wisdom was to it; its greatest benefits were practical ones, associated with the welfare of the State. And for the humanists, both in Italy and later in England, who were the men primarily responsible for the sixteenth-century rhetorical tradition, eloquence was an instrument of practical education—indeed, the humanists' limited appreciation of literature has been repeatedly blamed on their utilitarian bias.[2]

The fundamental change from the sixteenth to the seventeenth century, then, is less one of a change from an emphasis on eloquence to an emphasis on utility than one of a change in attitude towards the utilitarian value of eloquence and of words in general. It is a change which might well be illustrated by reference to variations in the meaning of the word 'ornament', as shown by the Oxford Dictionary. In the fifteenth century the hand could be described as a 'great help and ornament to the body', and in the sixteenth century

---

[1] R. F. Jones, *The Triumph of the English Language*, op. cit., p. 300.
[2] See above, pp. 38–64 and 81–84, particularly the passage from H. A. Mason, quoted on p. 63.

the tackling was part of the 'ornament of a ship'.[1] Throughout this same period, and indeed from classical times, reference is made to figures, tropes, metaphors, etc., as the ornaments of discourse. Poetry is seen as matter in language richly ornamented, and though there are wide differences as to the nature of the ornaments, there is consistently this same idea of them as essential to the proper functioning of the thing ornamented. By the seventeenth century 'rhetorical flourishes' were still regarded as the 'ornaments' of discourse, but the word had taken on much more of its modern meaning of something wholly additional and incidental, as is illustrated by the passage quoted above from Webster's *Academarium Examen*, when he likens oratory and poetry, as 'ornamental arts', to 'fashions and garbs' as distinguished from the body itself which wears them. A similar change in the attitude to language can be seen in the *Anacrisis* (1634?) of Sir William Alexander, in which he refers to language as 'but the Apparel of Poesy', and declares that 'I value Language as a Conduit, the Variety thereof the several Shapes, and adorned Truth or witty Inventions that which it should deliver'.[2] Alexander's purpose is to maintain the Aristotelian view of poetry by which the imitation or 'fiction' is its essential part and which allows fiction even when in prose to be poetry; but the degree of separation of the imitation from the words in which it is expressed (implied especially by his use of the word 'but') is quite un-Aristotelian and a long way from Sir Philip Sidney's statement of the concept.

Prior to the seventeenth century language had, of course, commonly been used for what would now be regarded as purely utilitarian purposes, without any thought for or interest in formal eloquence. However, the association in the humanistic tradition of wisdom and eloquence, and the predominantly verbal nature of learning, meant that this unselfconscious use of language tended not to go beyond the level of the ordinary affairs of everyday life. In the

---

[1] John Trevisa, *De proprietatibus rerum*, V, xxviii (1945); and T. Cooper, *Thesaurus amphistre* (c. 1565–73); both as cited by the *OED*.

[2] Sir William Alexander, Earl of Stirling, *Anacrisis* (London, 1634); ed. Spingarn, op. cit., i, 182.

more serious pursuits as much attention was to be paid to the words used as to the matter expressed: 'Ye know not what hurt ye do to learning, who search more after matter than words', Ascham had declared. The development of scientific learning, primarily experimental rather than verbal, meant a change in this situation, and part of this change was that 'eloquence' and 'utility' when applied to language could be much more widely and clearly seen as contrary terms.

For R. F. Jones this change is largely, if not entirely, a seventeenth-century phenomenon. The 'plain' style of the later seventeenth century can, he believes, be satisfactorily accounted for in terms of the influence of the new science and of the activities of the Royal Society in particular. However, he pays no attention to the origins of this influence itself—that is, to the origins of the scientific movement, confining himself to the linguistic effects resulting from its influence.[1] This restricted treatment, however, may not be altogether valid, in so far as the new scientific attitude was itself one part of a change in the position of language—the change from a way of thinking that was primarily a matter of manipulation of words to one which was basically mechanistic and spatial in its methods. The utilitarian attitude to language, or at least the particular form of utility allowed to language in the later seventeenth century, was, as Jones claims, associated with the rise of the new science, but the association was more complex than that of a simple influence of the one on the other, and the nature of this association may prove to have a more fundamental importance for the present study than might at first appear from Jones's thesis.

G. E. Williamson, in his study of developments in seventeenth-century prose style, *The Senecan Amble* (1951), sees the plain style of the scientists as having deeper roots than those suggested by Jones:

In the *History of the Royal Society* there are two sharply contrasted attitudes towards eloquence, of which no one is more aware than

---

[1] The principal treatment of this subject by Jones is in his 'Science and English Prose Style in the Third Quarter of the Seventeenth Century', op. cit.

Sprat. These attitudes may represent his dual role as a member of the Royal Society and of its committee for improving the English tongue. But in a larger way they represent two different ambitions of his time, literary and scientific, relative to different ends of writing.[1]

The uses of language are thus seen as being distinguished according to the ends they are expected to serve. 'These ends', says Williamson, 'are old, and have old associations; for style they may still be distinguished as the philosophical and rhetorical.' Here 'philosophical' and 'rhetorical', as they would have been used by Sprat and also by previous centuries, are apparently being treated as interchangeable with 'scientific' and 'literary' respectively, as these terms would have been understood by the Royal Society. In so far as the new science went under the title of experimental philosophy it would have been appropriate to term its style 'philosophical', and it is plainly distinguished by Sprat and others from rhetorical style. However, to identify this philosophical style with the older philosophical style, or to see it as bearing the same relationship to 'literary' style as the older philosophical style had to rhetorical style, is rather less easy to justify.

From classical times a distinction had been recognized between philosophical and rhetorical styles; that is, a distinction had been made between the styles appropriate to logical and rhetorical argument respectively. The most common distinction, and one which appears continually in the logical and rhetorical treatises of the English Renaissance, is expressed by the metaphor borrowed from Zeno through Cicero and Quintilian of the closed fist of logic and the open palm of rhetoric, exemplifying the preoccupation of logic with the tight discourses of the philosopher and that of rhetoric with the more open discourses of the public orator. Logical style was concerned with communication within the world of learning, and rhetoric with that between the learned and the lay world, or between expert and layman. Again, the distinction was made between logic as appropriate for dealing with strict truth and rhetoric for dealing with matters whose truth could be regarded as no more

[1] Williamson, *The Senecan Amble*, op. cit., p. 275.

than probable. Thus far the parallel with the seventeenth-century situation seems to be maintained: there remains, nevertheless, a fundamental source of difference.

The interest of the seventeenth century was in scientific investigation, and only incidentally in the means of communication of their findings. Attention was focused on things, on concrete objects and forces, not on words. For the Renaissance, on the other hand, logic stood at the centre of the world of philosophical learning, and was first and foremost an art of discourse or statement rather than of thought—or rather, in so far as it was an art of thought it identified thought with words, so that thought and its verbal communication or statement were virtually one and the same thing. The distinction which W. S. Howell makes between Renaissance and modern logic could also hold as between the predominant attitudes of the sixteenth and seventeenth centuries, even though in the seventeenth century logic itself still retained much of its traditional form and function:

Logic, conceived today as the science of the validity of thought, and as the term for the canons and criteria that explain trustworthy inferences, was in the English Renaissance a theory not so much of thought as of statement. For all practical purposes, the distinction between thoughts and statements is not a very real distinction, since the latter are merely the reflection of the former, and the former cannot be examined without recourse to the latter. But what distinction there is consists in a differentiation between mental phenomena and linguistic phenomena, the assumption being that the thing to which either set of phenomena refers is reality itself. Logicians of the twentieth century are primarily interested in mental phenomena as an interpretation of the realities of man's environment, and in that part of the mental phenomena which we call valid or invalid inference. Logicians of the English Renaissance were primarily interested in statements as a reflection of man's inferences, and in the problem of valid and invalid statement. Thus Renaissance logic concerned itself chiefly with the statements made by men in their efforts to achieve a valid verbalization of reality . . .[1]

---

[1] Howell, *Logic and Rhetoric in England 1500–1700*, op. cit., p. 3.

Put briefly, the 'scientific' style of the later seventeenth century attempted to communicate through words knowledge achieved by non-verbal methods; the earlier 'philosophic' style was primarily an attempt to arrive at knowledge through words.

Alongside his attempt to link scientific style with the older philosophic style, Williamson also sees the former as a continuation of the anti-Ciceronian movement that had served to replace the florid, extravagant, eloquence of sixteenth-century prose with the curt, brief, 'Senecan' style associated particularly with Bacon. Again this linking may serve to blur a real difference in attitude. Erasmus and Bacon, Williamson writes:

. . . had been confronted by the conflict between scholastic and Ciceronian style—varieties of the philosophic and the rhetorical—and to Bacon the former was plainly less of a hindrance to the advancement of learning. If the Royal Society, as represented by Sprat, rejected the scholastic style, it did not reject a philosophical style, for it was most vehement against the rhetoric which had been associated with Ciceronianism. The Anti-Ciceronian style, on the other hand, rejected not only the rhetoric of the Ciceronian, but the logic of the scholastic, which became its most reprehensible feature. As it was the Anti-Ciceronian style that Bacon advanced, so it is the Anti-Ciceronian style from which the Royal Society programme derived.[1]

There are a number of difficulties here. Firstly, anti-Ciceronian style, at least in its early stages, rejected not the rhetoric of Cicero but the abuse of it. Erasmus, with whom as Bacon (and following him Williamson) suggests, the study of anti-Ciceronianism must begin, was first and foremost a humanist, with the humanists' rhetorical approach to life—the approach of Isocrates, Cicero, and Quintilian, in which words, and particularly the spoken word, are the medium in which the human mind and sensibility lives. As a humanist Erasmus is no more anti-rhetorical than he is anti-logical; he is opposed to excess, whether it be of words as with the Ciceronians, or of the triviata of thought associated with scholasticism. And as with Erasmus, anti-Ciceronianism as a whole was not in itself a

[1] Williamson, op. cit., p. 276.

movement against rhetoric, and the various forms of anti-Ciceronian style remain essentially rhetorical forms of style closely related to classical forms, a point to which Williamson himself devotes a complete chapter.[1]

The second difficulty raised by Williamson's statement is the one which has already been discussed concerning the nature of the philosophical style which it is claimed the Royal Society inherited from the anti-Ciceronians. Humanism, in which it is agreed anti-Ciceronianism had its origins, attacked medieval scholasticism because of its aridity, its difficulty, its attention to minute detail, its highly technical vocabulary, its concern with real or apparent difficulties. Its opposition was not to traditional logic as such: not to logic, that is, as a theory of statement, as an art by which man sought to achieve a valid verbalization of reality. It was not a movement towards inductive as opposed to deductive logic, any more than it was a movement seeking to replace rhetorical discourse with one that was non-rhetorical, or utilitarian in the sense that Sprat would have used the term. It certainly did not represent an opposition to either logic or rhetoric having much in common with the Royal Society's distrust of words, as expressed by Sprat:

The ill effects of this superfluity of talking, have already overwhelm'd most other *Arts* and *Professions*; insomuch, that when I consider the means of *happy living*, and the causes of their corruption, I can hardly forbear recanting what I said before, and concluding, that *eloquence* ought to be banish'd out of all *civil Societies*, as a thing fatal to Peace and good Manners.[2]

[1] Ibid., pp. 32 ff. M. W. Croll ('Attic Prose in the Seventeenth Century, op. cit., 80) makes a similar point: 'One of the objections to the term anti-Ciceronianism is that it may be taken as describing a hostility to Cicero himself, in the opinion of the new leaders, instead of his sixteenth-century "apes", whereas in fact the supreme *rhetorical* excellence of Cicero was constantly affirmed by them.' Cf. also Cowley's inclusion of Senecan style among the varieties of false wit in his *Ode: Of Wit*:

'Nor a Tall *Metaphor* in the *Bombast way*,
Nor the dry chips of short lung'd *Seneca*.'

[2] Sprat, op. cit., p. 111.

The style sought by the scientists may have had something in common with that of the anti-Ciceronians, but not the attitude towards words that lay behind it.

This attitude probably did not originate wholly with the Royal Society, and its earlier beginnings will be discussed in the next section of this chapter. The important point to be stressed here is that the anti-humanist character of the Royal Society should not be blurred by any apparent similarity between its ideal of style and that of the humanists. For the Royal Society was indeed anti-humanist, in so far as the humanists recognized wisdom and eloquence as equally indispensable parts of learning and the new scientists did not. And this perhaps is the most important contribution of the later seventeenth-century scientific attitude to the difficult position that poetry found itself in a the end of the seventeenth century compared with its position a hundred years earlier. For the status of poetry in the Renaissance world depended ultimately on the high place given to words as a means to knowledge.

R. F. Jones attributes the later seventeenth-century 'plain' style directly to the influence of the new science. Williamson sees it as the culmination of a process that began with the anti-Ciceronianism of Erasmus and led through the Senecan movement of the earlier seventeenth century to the 'close, naked, natural way of speaking' demanded by the Royal Society of its members.[1] While each of these accounts is without doubt at least partly accurate, both have the disadvantage that they leave too much unexplained. In particular they do not reveal anything of the profound changes in linguistic attitudes involved in the emergence of modern science. A third explanation, and one that may prove more suggestive for this study,

---

[1] A further account is provided by H. Fisch, 'The Puritans and the Reform of Prose Style', *ELH*, xix (1952), 229-48. This account has much in common with Jones's thesis as stated in *The Triumph of the English Language*, which however, does not seem entirely consistent with Jones's earlier writings in laying emphasis on the effect of Puritanism on style in the earlier sixteenth century. The picture is further complicated by Wallerstein (*Studies in Seventeenth Century Poetic*, op. cit., p. 55) who connects the impulse to Senecan style with Augustinian neo-Platonism.

is provided by the researches of W. J. Ong, who places the beginnings of 'plain' style in the milieu of the Ramist 'reformation' of
traditional logic and rhetoric.[1] The manner in which this connexion
is made by Ong provides a link between 'utilitarian' prose and the
origins of the scientific attitude itself, at a much more fundamental
level than that suggested by either Jones or Williamson.

Pierre de la Ramée (1515–72), or Peter Ramus as he is more commonly known, has occupied perhaps more than his proper share of
attention among literary historians during the past twenty-five
years, and in the process has aroused a good deal of difference of
opinion as to his importance and influence.[2] Concerning the man
himself opinions range from that of Professor Hardin Craig, for
whom he was a great intellectual force in a period of great thinkers,[3]
to that of N. E. Nelson, who sees him as 'a bold and clever ignora-
mus'.[4] Claims as to his real influence on the literature of the seventeenth century are equally varied. Rosamund Tuve, for example,
sees Ramism as having heightened the prestige of logic, particularly

---

[1] W. J. Ong, *Ramus, Method, and the Decay of Dialogue*, op. cit., pp. 283–4.

[2] The first appearance of Ramus's logic in English was in the work of
Roland MacIlmaine, who produced both an English translation of the
Dialectic and a Latin edition in 1574. The Ramist rhetoric appeared first in
1584 in Dudley Fenner's *The Arte of Logike and Rhetorike*. Some indication of
the impact of Ramism can be gained from the fact that only one edition of
Wilson's *Rule of Reason* appeared after 1574. His *Arte of Rhetorique* appeared
three times in the 1580s, but thereafter ceased to have any influence. On the
other hand, in addition to those of MacIlmaine, Fenner and Fraunce, three
further translations of Ramus's *Dialectic* appeared—those of Wotton (1626),
Spencer (1628) and Fage (1632). In addition, during the period 1574–1674 at
least eleven Latin editions appeared, including Milton's *Art of Logic* (1672).
The *Rhetoric* also appeared in numerous editions, both of Charles Butler's
Latin version, *Oratoriae libri duo* (1629) and also the same author's edition of
the rhetoric of Ramus's collaborator, Talaeus, which appeared first in 1597
and continued to hold its popularity for the next half-century. The orbit of
the Ramist rhetoric was the public school. Thus Brinsley wrote in 1612
(*Ludus literarius*, op. cit., p. 203): "For answering the questions of Rhetoricke,
you may if you please, make them perfect in Talaeus Rhetoricke, which I take
to be the most vsed in the best Schooles."

[3] Hardin Craig, *The Enchanted Glass*, op. cit., pp. 139–59.

[4] N. E. Nelson, 'Peter Ramus and the Confusion of Logic, Rhetoric and
Poetry', *Univ. of Mich. Contrib. in Mod. Phil.*, ii (1947), 2.

in poetry, thereby accelerating the development of 'wit' at the expense of traditional poetic ornament, and consequently as being a primary influence on the development of metaphysical poetry.[1] On the other hand, her claims for Ramism have been more or less hotly disputed by such writers as N. E. Nelson and A. J. Smith.[2] For Ong, however, Ramus's importance is not primarily a matter of his own originality or genius, or even of his unique influence. He sees him as important because he provides the most overt and clearly defined expression of a movement in the history of ideas that begins much earlier than Ramus and culminates in the emergence of the modern world.

As Regius Professor of Eloquence and Philosophy in the College de France from 1551 until his death at the hands of the mob in the St. Bartholomew's Day massacre of 1572, the world in which Ramus sought to carry through his reforms of traditional logic and rhetoric was that of Valla, Erasmus, Vives, and their fellow humanists, whose influence on English poetic theory is discussed in the previous chapter. And although more famous, or notorious, for his attack on Aristotelianism,[3] Ramus also shared the prevailing anti-scholasticism of the humanists. According to Ong, however, this anti-scholasticism was a complex attitude, because in spite of it the influence of scholasticism, inherited from the medieval universities,[4] still played an important part in shaping the humanist ways of thinking:

Indeed, humanism, with its program calling for a controlled vocabulary and a carefully policed classical style, is a product of scholastic scientism almost as much as a reaction against it. No one can mistake

---

[1] Rosamund Tuve, *Elizabethan and Metaphysical Imagery*, op. cit.; also her 'Imagery and Logic: Ramus and Metaphysical Poetics', *JHI* (1942), 365–400.

[2] Nelson, op. cit.; and A. J. Smith, 'An Examination of some Claims for Ramism', *RES*, vii (1956), 348–59.

[3] '*Quaecumque ab Aristotele dica essent, commentitia esse?*' This is the title of the thesis with which Ramus reputedly began his career. For a discussion of the authenticity and importance of the thesis see Ong, *Ramus, Method, and the Decay of Dialogue*, op. cit., pp. 37–41; and for an examination of the proper English translation of the thesis see P. H. Duhamel, 'Milton's Alleged Ramism', *PMLA*, lxvii (1952), 1036.

[4] One important part of Ong's whole argument depends on what is understood by scholasticism. 'Despite the prevailing impression,' he writes,

the different accent when the same ground is covered by these professed devotees of the classical rhetoricians, who foreswear scholasticism with bell, book, and candle, and the classical rhetoricians
themselves. The Renaissance rhetoricians, almost to a man, have a
pronounced dialectical twang which contrasts with the smoother,
more random, and often inconsistent observations of Cicero.[1]

The influence of scholasticism on the reforms that Ramus sought
to achieve is to be seen particularly in the manner in which the emphasis on logic is carried further into the humanist educational
scheme. Speaking of his early plans as a teacher he writes:

After my regular three and a half years of scholastic philosophy,
mostly the *Organon* of Aristotle's logical works, terminating with the
conferring of my master's degree, I began to consider how I should
put the logical arts to use. But they had left me no better off in history,
antiquity, rhetoric, or poetry.

Thus, I went back to my study of rhetoric, ended when I began my
philosophy course four years before. My aim was to put the logical
books of the *Organon* to the service of erudition.[2]

Ramus here proposes to apply to *eruditio* (that is, to the material of
history, antiquity, rhetoric, and poetry) the rules of logic. This may
in one way be interpreted as an attack on the scholastic organization

'scholasticism as a whole has not been studied exhaustively over the past few
decades. What has been studied is a certain kind of scholasticism, the scholasticism of theologians, and of a select group of theologians at that. Very few
"scholastics", if by that we mean teachers of philosophy in the period called
scholastic, were theologians. Still fewer of the students of this period ever
studied any theology at all. They studied mostly the scholasticism of the arts
course. The scholasticism which most students knew has never appeared in
modern editions.
'. . . All in all, perhaps three-fourths of the scholasticism of the Middle
Ages and the Renaissance was studied in the arts faculty.
'This arts scholasticism was almost entirely logic and physics. Of metaphysics there was almost none—at least as prescribed in the arts curricula and
studied directly . . .' ('Ramus: Rhetoric and the Pre-Newtonian Mind', in
English Institute Essays, ed. A. S. Downer, New York, 1952, pp. 142–3).
  [1] Ong, Ramus: 'Rhetoric and the Pre-Newtonian Mind', op. cit., p. 155.
  [2] Ramus, 'Scholae dialecticae', lib. iv, in *Scholae in liberales artes* (1569), cols.
155–6; trans. Ong, *Ramus Method, and the Decay of Dialogue*, op. cit., p. 41.

of education, but at the same time it served to extend the influence of scholastic logic throughout the curriculum, from its lowest levels in the humanities to its highest in philosophy.

Another and perhaps more far-reaching aspect of Ramus's reform of the curriculum also had its origins in the scholasticism of the medieval arts course in which he was trained. This was his determination to distinguish each of the arts and sciences from each other, and in distinguishing within these arts and sciences to define their separate parts. This preoccupation with sorting out the arts and sciences, which was what perhaps concerned Ramus most deeply, was something that had been going on since the beginning of the medieval study of Aristotle's *Organon*.[1] The advance, if it was an advance, made by Ramus was that his divisions were much more rigid than any that had been made previously. The analogy he used was that of 'Solon's Law', which had regulated building developments in ancient Athens, and which by requiring a foot's margin for a wall, two feet for a house, and so on, ensured that each building was kept within its allotted area. Just as this law was designed to keep buildings from encroaching on neighbouring land, so Ramus's aim was to provide a rigid definition of the arts, without any overlapping or encroachment on each other's territory.

The importance of this part of Ramus's reform of the curriculum for the present study is that at the centre of his system there is a rigid separation of logic from rhetoric. As has been stressed on a number of occasions previously, in the tradition that the Renaissance inherited from the Middle Ages logic and rhetoric were both alike in being primarily arts of discourse. These two arts had their different methods appropriate to their different aims, but the

---

[1] This movement towards the classification of knowledge was one which also affected Bacon, and may account at least in part for his treatment of poetry—particularly his banishment of lyric and reflective poetry to the 'arts of speech'. On the other hand, Bacon was very likely referring to the Ramists when he spoke of 'men of this sort', who 'press matters by the laws of their method, and when a thing does not aptly fall into those dichotomies, either pass it by or force it out of its natural shape, the effect of their proceeding . . . being this,—the kernels and grains of the sciences leap out, and they are left with nothing in their grasp but the dry and barren husks'. (*De augmentis scientiarum*, op. cit., iv, 448.)

amount of overlap that remained was sufficient to offend the pedagogical instincts of Ramus. His chief objection was to their common
possession of 'invention' and 'disposition'; as a teacher he probably
thought it a waster of time for students to learn invention and disposition twice over, once in their course in rhetoric and again in
logic. Thus he sought to reorganize the two disciplines, confining
invention and disposition to dialectic (which following the general
practice of scholasticism he did not distinguish from logic), and
style and delivery to rhetoric. 'Memory', the fifth part of classical
rhetoric, was detached from rhetoric and associated with dialectical
disposition. A convenient short summary of this rearrangement of
the materials of logic and rhetoric is provided by Omar Talon,
Ramus's collaborator and the man largely responsible for the
detailed working out in relation to rhetoric of his programme of
reform:

Peter Ramus cleaned up the theory of invention, arrangement, and
memory, and returned these subjects to logic, where they properly
belong. Then, assisted indeed by his lectures and opinions, I recalled
rhetoric to style and delivery (since these are the only parts proper to
it); and I explained it by genus and species, (which method was
previously allowed to me); and I illustrated it with examples drawn
from both oratory and poetry. Thus these present precepts are almost
wholly in words drawn from those authors; but as this first and rude
outline has unfolded, the precepts have been tested by the judgement
of both of us, and disposed in order, and ornamented and treated by
kind.[1]

The effect of this was to open the way for a separation of thought
and discourse; to a habit of treating thought as something independent of words. For in the Ramist scheme logic can no longer be
regarded as an art of discourse, nor can rhetoric be seen as having in
itself anything to do with the processes of thought.

Further evidence of this same movement towards a breaking
down of the traditional attitude to logic as a mode of communication

[1] Omar Talon, Preface (dated Paris, 1544) to *Petri Rami Professoris Regii, &*
Audomari Talaei Collectaneae Praefationes, Epistolae, Orationes (Marburg, 1599);
trans. Howell, *Logic and Rhetoric in England*, op. cit., pp. 148–9.

is to be found in the writings of Francis Bacon—though Bacon was
no Ramist and with him the movement takes a somewhat different
form. Whereas in the classical system both logic and rhetoric had
been seen as concerned primarily with communication, logic in the
learned and rhetoric in the popular field, Bacon sought to extend the
sphere of rhetoric to include communication in the field of learning,
in order to fill the gap caused by his tendency to withdraw logic into
the field of inquiry. There are, he believed, two kinds of 'invention',
one of which is concerned with words and another which is not,
and only the latter is valuable towards the advance of knowledge:

The invention of arguments is not properly an invention, for to invent
is to discover that we know not, not to recover or resummon that
which we already know. Now the use and office of this invention is
no other than out of the mass of knowledge which is collected and
laid up in the mind to draw forth readily that which may be pertinent
to the matter or question which is under consideration . . . So (as I
have said) this kind of invention is not properly an invention, but a
remembrance or suggestion with an application . . . But not to be
too nice about words, let it be clearly understood that the scope and
end of this invention is readiness and present use of our knowledge,
rather than an addition or amplification thereof.[1]

There is thus to be a clear distinction between discourse, particularly
eloquent discourse—which serves only for communication or for
the rediscovery of something previously known and temporarily
forgotten—and true learning understood as the discovery of things
previously unknown, in which words have no part.

Ong claims, however, that the tendencies towards this change
were already strongly entrenched in the scholasticism of the medieval universities; and, indeed, that such a profound change in the
organization of thought should have resulted from the accident of
Ramus's attempt to tidy up the school curriculum does not seem,
on the face of it, historically plausible. Ong explains the nature of the
link thus:

As the art of discourse or speaking, or of teaching, dialectic or logic
had a definite connection with the audile and with words as sounds,

[1] Bacon, *De augmentis scientiarum*, op. cit., iv, 421–2.

with the definite personalist and existentialist implications which attach to a world of voices. Ramus arrives on the scene at the time when this dialectic is being 'simplified' in an operation which is among the most complicated and critical and central in the whole history of the human mind and out of which grows preoccupation with method and the whole mechanistic-minded world . . . This simplification of logic is connected with the humanists' determination to provide something adapted to the capacities of children . . . But the simplification is even more deeply related to a widespread and mysterious shift from the audile to the visile in the whole way of thinking about cognition and the nature of man . . .

'It is within this shift', says Ong, 'that Ramus turns up . . .':

As one observes Ramism in its historical unfolding, beginning with Rudolph Agricola and his replacement of the old Scholastic logic or logistic with a logic of 'places' (commonplaces or loci) even more mechanistic in implication, and developing through Ramus himself and into German philosophic 'systems' conceived by analogy with Copernican space and into English 'methodism' it becomes possible to assign what, I believe, is the central significance of Ramus and Ramism, at least for our own age.

Ramism is above all, although not exclusively, a manifestation of the subtle and apparently irresistible shift sacrificing auditorily oriented concepts for visually oriented ones which sets in with medieval scholasticism and on which most of the characteristic manifestations of the modern as against the ancient world depend. This shift is intimately connected with the scholastic emphasis on a logic which, as against more purely Aristotelian logic, was a kind of logistic, and on physics—a bad physics, but physics nevertheless, taught to millions of schoolboys from the thirteenth to the sixteenth century . . .[1]

[1] Ong, 'Ramus and the Transit to the Modern Mind', *Mod. Sch.*, xxxi (1955), 307–9. The connexion between scholasticism, Ramism, and 'plain' style had previously been suggested, as Ong himself points out, by Professor Perry Miller in *The New England Mind: The Seventeenth Century* (New York, 1939), one of the first major studies of the influence of Ramism. Miller lays special emphasis on the connexion between Ramism and the Puritan obsession for logic and distaste for symbolism.

Ong's evaluation of scholastic logic may be substantiated from such a work as P. Boehner, *Medieval Logic* (Manchester, 1952), especially pp. 19–75.

The study of Ramism, Ong claims, shows the inadequacy of regarding Bacon or Descartes as the originators of an interest in method. They are not the beginning but the culmination of what he describes as:

. . . the struggle between sound and sight, between habits of thinking based on listening to voices and habits of thinking based on looking at surfaces, between living in a world inhabited by persons who talked back and living in a world occupied by passive objects scattered in 'systems' through the new Copernican space.[1]

Seen against this background Ramism may be claimed to have provided not only the actual mechanics, through its separation of logic and rhetoric, of the seventeenth-century divorce of thought and discourse as revealed by the Royal Society's distrust of words, but also the direct link with the origins of the non-verbal modes of thought that lay behind the divorce. In particular, Ramism may serve to indicate the extent to which the new attitude to words was not a simple result of the new scientific methods, but rather a vital part of the whole process by which those methods came into existence; and by so doing it may reveal something of the fundamental nature of the changes in the pattern of discourse which were taking overt shape in the seventeenth century. Even though perhaps it may be accepted only as a hypothesis, Ong's treatment of Ramism is a more satisfactory explanation of these changes, because it goes deeper, than those of either Jones or Williamson; and its importance for an understanding of the history of poetic theory may ultimately be greater than suggested by those studies, such as Rosamund Tuve's which have sought to reveal the immediate influence of Ramism on the poetry of the seventeenth century.

A study of the actual Ramist treatment of poetry, indeed, leads to doubt as to whether this immediate or direct influence could, in fact, be expected to have had any lasting effect on poetry. With

The standard account of the pre-Ramist University educational tradition is that of H. Rashdall, *The Universities of Europe in the Middle Ages*, new edition by F. M. Powicke and A. B. Emden (3 vols., Oxford, 1936).

[1] Ibid., 310.

dialectic separated off from rhetoric and become what might be described as a kind of intellectual diagrammatics based on mechanical and spatial rather than linguistically framed analogies, rhetoric is left in absolute control of the world of words, as words. In these circumstances Ramism, because of the manner in which it separated logical thought from words, could possibly have been expected to provide the impulse to new movements in non-logical verbal expression, such as it has been a large part of the endeavour of poets of the present century to explore. The importance in the development of metaphysical poetry that Professor Tuve gives to Ramism might at first glance seem to suggest such a movement. However, her actual thesis, in fact, points in just the opposite direction. Because invention and disposition have become the sole property of dialectic, orator and poet alike must go to dialectic for these essential parts of their work, and thus the barriers between logic and rhetoric, and particularly those between logic and poetry, are broken down:

This [Ramus's separation of logic and rhetoric] does not mean that orators and poets no longer were supposed to invent and dispose matter. It meant that they were to learn to do this from the discipline to which Ramus said it properly belonged: *dialectica*. Awareness of the process might vary, but, given the structure of man's mind, there was but one way to 'invent' or think out what one wished to say—logically, and but one way to dispose thought—reasonably.[1]

And thus:

. . . the connection between poetry and dialectic is not only something praiseworthy though occasional: it is inevitable, not necessarily planned out, but in any case the natural mark of the poet as a reasonable creature. What poet will not note with pleasure the natural logic of his own images when such doctrines become the fashion of the day, screwing up their unavoidable logical relevance with an additional witty twist? So far, however, we have simply to notice: that such general conceptions take hold much more easily than special points of doctrine; that no denizen of the cultivated world of the

---

[1] Tuve, *Elizabethan and Metaphysical Imagery*, op. cit., p. 340.

1590's and early 1600's could escape knowing about them or miss the excitement caused by the Ramist idea of a unity of all the arts of thought, past and present; and that imagery is bound to be written differently by a man who makes no basic separation between poet and dialectician.[1]

Some measure of confirmation for Tuve's argument may be provided from an essay in the *Philosophia libera* (1662), by Nathaniel Carpenter, which sets out to demonstrate that logical discourse is not necessarily compact, and rhetorical discourse not necessarily diffuse, and in the process maintains that 'amplification' (which was the main basis of the poetic as well as of the rhetorical mode of expression) is the work of logic:

Moreover, since three things are required for the fulness of a speech, namely invention of the subject matter, arrangement of arguments, and adornment, it is obvious that the first is supplied from the various fields of knowledge conformably to the speaker's end and purpose, the second from logic, and the third from rhetoric. Accordingly it follows that the various fields of knowledge contribute substance or content, logic the tying together and arrangement of arguments, and rhetoric merely the flower and spice of speech. But no sane person denies that the faculty of amplification is based upon the faculty of arranging arguments.[2]

Carpenter was not a Ramist, so that the emphasis given to logic in seventeenth-century poetry may not have been always the result of Ramist influence. No matter what its origin, however, this emphasis on logic—at least as it is seen by Tuve—could not have led poetry to the new mode of existence that it would ultimately need to counter the scientific domination of logical thought and discourse. In fact, it could serve only to put poetry in competition with science. And indeed, an examination of the textbooks compiled on the subject of rhetoric by the disciples of Ramus and Talon will

[1] Ibid., pp. 338–9.
[2] Nathaniel Carpenter, 'Logica pugno, Rhetorica palmae, non recte a Zenone comparatur', in *Philosophia Libera* (Oxford, 1622), pp. 158–61; trans. W. S. Howell, 'Nathaniel Carpenter's Place in the Controversy between Dialectic and Rhetoric', *Speech Monographs*, i (1934), 20–41.

show their extremely mechanical conception of poetry: '*Poetica est ars bene versificandi*'; '*Quid est poetic? Est facultas bene scribendi versus*'.[1] These are typical definitions of the Ramists, and more perhaps than anything else their accounts of the nature of poetry revealed the changed conception of poetic ornament that was discussed earlier as being reflected in the changed connotations of the word 'ornament' itself. Following their master Ramus, the Ramist rhetoricians were mainly concerned to get things straightened out. Here is the opening of an early Ramist rhetoric, a French translation of Talon's *Rhetorica* made by Antoine Foclin in 1555:

Definition of Rhetoric.
Rhetoric is the art of speaking well and elegantly.

The parts of Rhetoric.
Rhetoric has two parts, style and delivery.

Style and its species.
Style is not anything but the ornamenting and enriching of speech and discourse; the which has two species, the one being called trope, the other figure.

Trope.
Trope is a style by means of which the proper and natural meaning of the word is changed to another, as is indicated by the word trope, which in French means interchange.

The species of Trope.
There are four sorts of trope: metonymy, irony, metaphor, and synedoche.[2]

It is highly unlikely that this kind of mechanical enumeration could lead to any advance on the vital, dynamic treatment of poetic ornament by, say, Fracastoro, as the essence of poetic thought and expression. Style, for example, is conceived by the Ramists as '*not any thing but* the ornamenting and enriching of speech'. Much of the

[1] Johann Thomas Freige, *Pedagogus* (1582), p. 131; and Johann Bilsten *Syntagma Philippo-Ramaeum* (1596), p. 271. Cf. Bilsten, op. cit., p. 261: *Rhetorica est ars ornate dicendi*'.
[2] Antoine Foclin, *La Rhetorique D'Antoine Foclin de Chauny en Vermandois* (Paris, 1555), pp. 1–2; trans. W. S. Howell, *Logic and Rhetoric in England*, op. cit., p. 168.

Ramist treatment of poetry, in fact, as distinct from rhetoric, was confined to a consideration of 'numbers' or 'dimensions' (i.e. length of lines and kinds of feet), and as Ong sums it up: '. . . if all Ramist rhetoric was appliqué work, poetry was appliqué work of the worst mechanical sort, for as Ramus occasionally hints, the rules which govern it belong less perhaps to rhetoric than to arithmetic.'[1]

If Ramism did indeed help towards the establishment of a new concept of the utilitarian use of language through its part in the divorce of thought and words, it provided no new horizons for poetry—except perhaps that suggested by Tuve. Its dialectical bent, however, important as it may have been in influencing the nature of early seventeenth-century poetry, could provide no lasting determinant of poetic method. It could, in fact, only serve to give poetry the role envisaged for it by Sprat—that of using the materials offered to it by science for the purpose of witty expression. The importance of Ramism for poetry is primarily an indirect one, arising from its relationship to deeply rooted changes in linguistic attitudes.

Any distinction based on 'utility' that may be made between the poetry and prose of the later seventeenth century must, in view of the previous discussion, take account of whether the utility is what might be described as of a 'primary' or 'secondary' nature: that is, whether the utility is thought of as resting primarily in the words themselves, or is only given to the words through their relationship to some exterior, non-verbal system, such as the experimental data of science. And further, forms of discourse that serve either of these ends might be contrasted with those that are independent of utility, having no purpose beyond their own existence.

The influences so far discussed in this chapter appear to have led to the development in the seventeenth century of an emphasis on 'secondary' utility in relation to words, and to the particular association of prose with this kind of utility; and this emphasis may be contrasted with the humanistic view of the art of letters, both prose and poetry, as being in itself valuable, in a directly utilitarian way.

[1] Ong, *Ramus, Method, and the Decay of Dialogue*, op. cit., p. 282.

For the humanists, knowledge was to be gained immediately through words; for the men of the Royal Society words were only of a very secondary importance in the pursuit of knowledge. There has, however, as yet been no real evidence of any consequent change in the attitude to poetry from that associated with the rhetorical tradition, which determined that poetry should be either simply entertaining or that it should use its delightfulness to be utilitarian in a didactic or moral way; in particular there has been no evidence of a change in the direction of a more 'creative' view of poetry as independent of utility altogether. The task of the remainder of this chapter will be to seek some such evidence of poetry's position in relation to this new emphasis on 'secondary' verbal utility: and whereas the centre of attention so far in this chapter has tended to be prose, the main interest henceforward will be in poetry.

A beginning might be made with a 'character' of a Poet that appeared in 1670, from the pen of Sir Richard Graham:

Some have turn'd that which us'd to charme our thoughtful heads, and perswade our distemper'd spirits into gentle slumbers, by easie and natural softness, into a rough Mystery and Art; they strive to bring wit, which is of so unknown a Nature, that like wind no one knoweth whence it is, under logical Notions; arguing syllogistically and troubling the world with Volumes of what is impertinent to it; that they may achieve their own names, so turning our delight into trouble.[1]

Here is contemporary evidence of that craze for logic in poetry that has caused Professor Tuve to link metaphysical wit with the effects of Ramism; and the evidence is given by one who obviously preferred the older 'delightfulness' of the poetry belonging to a time when logical hair-splitting kept to its own sphere of disputation, and did not invade that of poetry and rhetoric.

Sir Richard has no doubts as to what causes poets to write in this annoying manner—it is 'that they may achieve their own names'. His attack is probably aimed at the more extravagant of the later metaphysical poets, and his cynical opinion may possibly have been

[1] Sir Richard Graham, *Angliae Speculum Morale* (London, 1670) pp. 65–66.

justified. However, while most of the poets of the later seventeenth century avoided these extravagances of the metaphysical poets in favour of a less obtrusive form of wit, they could still be interested in arguing 'syllogistically'. Dryden, for example, while he rebukes Donne because he 'perplexes the minds of the fair sex with nice speculations of philosophy', provides in his own *Religio Laici* (1682) an obvious instance of the use of poetry for what at least has the appearance of logical argument; and it would therefore be interesting to know what was Dryden's purpose in writing this poem, and how his choice of poetry as a medium was related to this purpose. Why should he choose poetry for *Religio Laici* and prose for, say, *An Essay of Dramatic Poesy* (1668). An answer to this question might reveal something of his concept of the nature and function of poetry and of how it was to be distinguished in these respects from prose.

To begin with, Dryden has some remarks to make on the place of poetry in relation to prose in his 'Defence of an Essay of Dramatic Poesy' (1668). He is replying to Sir Robert Howard, who mainly on the grounds of the unnaturalness of rhyme, had attacked the argument for it put forward by Dryden in *An Essay of Dramatic Poesy*. After first dismissing the greater naturalness of prose as no good reason for its use in the drama, Dryden writes:

. . . 'tis enough for me that he acknowledges he had rather read good verse than prose; for if all the enemies of verse will confess as much, I shall not need to prove that it is natural. I am satisfied if it cause delight; for delight is the chief, if not the only end of poesy: instruction can be admitted but in the second place, for poesy only instructs as it delights.[1]

This is, of course, but another statement of the traditional function of poetry derived from Aristotle by way of Horace and the sixteenth-century Italian theorists and given its classic expression in English by Sidney: poetry has a didactic function, but one which it achieves only through its ability to give delight, and therefore the first aim of the poet must be to please.

[1] Dryden, 'A Defence of an Essay of Dramatic Poesie'; op. cit., i, 113.

Later in the *Defence* Dryden answers the charge levelled at him by Howard of being 'magesterial':

. . . in vindication of myself, I must crave leave to say that my whole discourse was sceptical, according to that way of reasoning which was used by Socrates, Plato, and all the Academies of old, which Tully and the best of the Ancients followed, and which is imitated by the modest inquisitions of the Royal Society. That it is so, not only the name will show, which is an *Essay*, but the frame and composition of the work. You see it is a dialogue sustained by persons of several opinions, all of them left doubtful, to be determined by the readers in general . . .[1]

Thus the object claimed for the *Essay* (though not perhaps with entire sincerity) is not that it is to teach, and therefore it need not seek to delight: its object is rather to place the facts before the reader for his own judgement, in a manner, as he says, that is 'imitated by the modest inquisitions of the Royal Society'. In writing prose, Dryden claimed to be using words with all the care of the scientist to ensure that they did not exceed their proper function by obtruding themselves between the reader and the facts. This claim may not be altogether true; but the desire at least to give this *impression* of disinterested scepticism could have been sufficient to influence Dryden's choice of prose as a medium. Under the influence of the Royal Society's attitude to elaborate, artificial, or formal discourse of any kind, he would very likely have seen this impression of judicial detachment as difficult to achieve in verse.

By contrast, the didactic purpose of *Religio Laici* is freely admitted by Dryden in the closing paragraph of the Preface to the poem:

If anyone be so lamentable a critic as to require the smoothness, the numbers, and the turn of heroic poetry in this poem, I must tell him that, if he has not read Horace, I have studied him, and hope the style of his *Epistles* is not ill imitated here. The expressions of a poem design'd purely for instruction ought to be plain and natural, and yet majestic; for here the poet is presum'd to be a kind of lawgiver, and those three qualities I have nam'd are proper to the legislative style.

---

[1] Dryden, 'A Defence of an Essay of Dramatic Poesie'; op. cit., i, 124.

The florid, elevated and figurative way is for the passions; for love and hatred, fear and anger, are begotten in the soul by shewing their objects out of their true proportion, either greater than the life or less, but instruction is to be given by shewing them what they naturally are. A man is to be cheated into passion, but to be reason'd into truth.[1]

Notice the difference between this statement and that last quoted from Dryden's reply to Howard. Where in the latter he had denied that he was being 'magesterial', here Dryden sees himself as a 'kind of lawgiver'. And again, earlier in the Preface, he allows that it is his own faith he is professing, by contrast with the disinterestedness he had claimed for *An Essay of Dramatic Poesy*: '. . . but in the due sense of my own weakness and want of learning, I plead not this; I pretend not to make myself a judge of faith in others, but only to make a confession of my own.'[2] There is perhaps some inconsistency with the rest of the Preface here, but at least the moral and didactic purpose of the poem is clear. And consequently, though the style is to have the 'plainness and naturalness' which Sprat required of scientific prose—

> . . . this unpolish'd, rugged verse, I chose,
> As fittest for discourse, and nearest prose;[3]

it must be 'yet majestic', in order that it may succeed in its aim of persuading men to truth. The inculcation of truth through its special power to move and delight still appears as a primary function of poetry for Dryden as it had for Sidney: poetry remains close to rhetoric as an art of persuasion, and, significantly, it is apparently to be preferred to prose for this purpose.

Dryden's stress on the poet's ability to appeal to the 'reason' of his audience is also of interest. It indicates no emphasis on the attempt to find a new field for poetry, independent of man's rational processes. This matter, however, can be discussed more conveniently later, in relation to the link between poetry and the imagination.

[1] Dryden, Preface to *Religio Laici; or, A Layman's Faith* (1682); ed. G. R. Noyes, *The Poetical Works of John Dryden* (Cambridge, Mass., 1909), p. 162.
[2] Ibid., p. 157.
[3] *Religio Laici*, ll. 453–4.

Some further light on Dryden's attitude to this question is provided by another phase of the rhyme versus blank verse controversy. *The Rival Ladies* (1663?) was probably the first play in which Dryden used the new fashion for rhymed verse.[1] Rhyme, however, is used in the play for only a few passages, the remainder being in a very ordinary kind of blank verse, to which Dryden's own description of blank verse as 'measured prose' might well be applied: there is practically no difference between it and prose except for its metrical regularity. In fact, at this stage of his work Dryden regarded blank verse as very little different from prose. Thus in the Epistle Dedicatory to *The Rival Ladies* he writes:

Shakespeare . . . was the first who, to shun the pains of continual rhyming, invented that kind of writing which we call blank verse, but the French, more properly, *prose mesurée*; into which the English tongue so naturally slides, that in writing prose, it is hardly to be avoided.[2]

And blank verse, though its has the naturalness which Dryden often sought, was also like prose in lacking the 'majesty' of which poetry

---

[1] Dryden's *The Indian Queen*, which also uses rhyme, appeared at about the same time and may possibly have been written first. Internal evidence, however, points to *The Rival Ladies* as the earlier composition.

[2] Dryden, Epistle Dedicatory to *The Rival Ladies*, op. cit., i, 6. This virtual identification of prose and blank verse occurs in various places in essays written by Dryden at this time: e.g. *An Essay of Dramatic Poesy* (op. cit., i, 96–97): 'As for that place of Aristotle, where he says plays should be writ in that kind of verse which is nearest prose, it makes little for you; blank verse being properly but measured prose. Now measure alone, in any modern language, does not constitute verse . . . Therefore, at most 'tis but a poetic prose, a *sermo pedestris*; and as such, most fit for comedies . . .

And again, in the 'Defence of an Essay of Dramatic Poesy' (op. cit., i, 115): 'Thus prose, though the rightful Prince, yet is by common consent deposed, as too weak for the government of serious plays: and he falling, there now start up two competitors: one, the nearer in blood, which is Blank Verse; the other, more fit for the ends of government, which is Rhyme. Blank Verse is, indeed, the nearer Prose, but is blemished with the weakness of his predecessor.'

The fact that Dryden's assessment of the poetic qualities of blank verse may have been quite inadequate—something which he himself later admitted by turning to blank verse for his later plays—does not affect the present issue.

was capable: 'Blank verse is acknowledged to be too low for a poem, nay more, for a paper of verses . . .'[1]

The relationship between the rhymed passages and the remaining blank verse then, to Dryden's way of thinking, is very close to the one between poetry and prose. Of *The Rival Ladies*, for instance, although it contains no scenes in actual prose, he tells of 'writing scenes in verse', obviously referring to the scenes where rhyme is used as distinct from those in blank verse,[2] and in the early folios the former were generally distinguished by being printed in italics. For this reason it is interesting to notice the particular passages that Dryden considered suitable for rhyme.

The rhymed passages seem to be of two distinct kinds. Firstly there are those such as the lyrical monologue spoken by Angelica as she wanders alone in the deserted twilight. Here verse is used for conventional poetic description:

> Silence and Solitude dwell everywhere:
> Doggs cease to bark; the Waves more faintly roar,
> And rowl themselves asleep upon the Shore:
> No noise but what my Footsteps make, and they
> Sound dreadfully, and Louder than by Day:
> They double too, and every step I take
> Sounds thick me-thinks, and more than one could make.[3]

The second kind of rhymed passage, however, is more distinctive of the heroic play, and also more interesting for the present purpose. In these passages rhyme is apparently used to give sharpness and point to dramatic argument, something that Dryden dearly loved: 'For I am of opinion', he once declared, 'that they cannot be good poets, who are not accustomed to argue well.'[4] The longest of these

---

[1] Dryden, *An Essay of Dramatic Poesy*, op. cit., i, 101.

[2] 'But I fear lest, defending the received words, I shall be accused for following the new way; I mean of writing scenes in verse.' (Epistle Dedicatory to *The Rival Ladies*, op. cit., i, 5.)

[3] *The Rival Ladies; A Tragi-Comedy* (1663?), Act I, Sc. 3; references to the plays are from Montagu Summers (ed.) Dryden, *The Dramatic Works* (6 vols., London, 1931).

[4] Dryden, 'Defence of an Essay of Dramatic Poesy', op. cit., i, 121.

passages in *The Rival Ladies* is one in which Julia, the heroine, finding herself in the difficult position of being left by her father in the power of her rejected suitor Gonsalvo, resorts to an appeal to his honour in order to extricate herself. There develops then one of the interminable debates on issues of love and honour, derived largely from the French prose romance and typical of the heroic play; and the arrival of the rhyme signals the beginning of the debate, just as its departure does the conclusion:

GONS: There's something more than ordinary in this:
Go Amideo, quickly follow him,
And bring me word which way he takes.
AMID: I go, Sir. (Exit Amideo.)
GONS: Madam, when you implore the Pow'rs divine,
You have no Pray'rs in which I would not joyn
Though made against myself. (Kneels with her.)
JUL: . . . In vain I sue
Unless my Vows may be Conveigh'd by you.
GONS: Conveigh'd by me! . . . My ill success in love
Shews me too sure I have few friends above.
How can you fear your just desires to want?
When the Gods pray, they both request and grant.
JUL: Heav'n has resign'd my Fortune to your hand,
If you, like Heav'n the Afflicted understand.
GONS: The Language of the Afflicted is not new;
Too well I learnt it when I first saw you.
JUL: In spight of me, you now command my Fate
And yet the vanquish'd seeks the Victors hate.
Ev'n in this low Submission, I declare,
That had I pow'r, I would renew the Warr.
I'm forced to stoop, and 'twere too great a blow
To bend my Pride, and to deny me too. &c.[1]

And so it goes on for ninety lines or more until Julia has made her point and the tone can again be safely lowered to that of prosaic blank verse.

The form of the heroic couplet is found here to be as well suited

---

[1] *The Rival Ladies*, Act IV, Sc. I.

to the parry and thrust of dramatic argument as Dryden was later to find it in *Religio Laici* for the enumeration of the propositions of logical argument;[1] and Dryden's realization of this is part of his reason for using it, as he indicates in the Epistle Dedicatory to the play:

But as the best medicines may lose their virtue by being ill applied, so it is with verse, if a fit subject be not chosen for it. Neither must the argument alone, but the characters and persons be great and noble; otherwise (as Scaliger says of Claudian) the poet will be *ignobiliore materia depressus*. The scenes which in my opinion most commend it, are those of argumentation and discourse, on the result of which the doing or not doing some considerable action should depend.[2]

And further:

. . . in the quickness of reparties (which in discoursive scenes fall very often), it has so particular a grace, and is so aptly suited to them, that the sudden smartness of the answer, and the sweetness of the rhyme, set off the beauty of each other.[3]

The precepts stated here are illustrated again by Dryden's use of rhyme in his *Marriage à la Mode* (1672), in which there is both prose for the comic scenes and blank verse for the serious passages, as well as two passages of rhymed verse, one a love scene and the other a long amatory debate concerned with whether or not there should be an armed uprising to dethrone Polydamas, the father of the heroine Palmyra—a debate which involves the latter in the usual conflict of the claims of love and honour, and which is a clear example of 'a discourse, on the result of which the doing or not doing some considerable action should depend'.

---

[1] The rhetorical qualities of the heroic couplet have been analysed by Ruth Wallerstein, 'The Development of the Rhetoric and Metre of the Heroic Couplet, especially 1625–1645', *PMLA*, L (1935), 166–210; G. E. Williamson, 'The Rhetorical Pattern of Neo-Classic Wit', op. cit.; and W. C. Brown, *The Triumph of Form* (Chapel Hill, 1948). For a detailed study of the use of the couplet for the purpose of argument in the heroic drama, see C. V. Deane, *Dramatic Theory and the Rhymed Heroic Play* (Oxford, 1931).

[2] Dryden, Epistle Dedicatory to *The Rival Ladies*, op. cit., i, 8–9.

[3] Ibid., i, 7–8.

Thus once again the great virtue of poetry over prose (or at least of rhyme over blank verse, which for Dryden is apparently much the same thing) is its ability to move men to action through appeal to their reason. And closely allied to this is that other virtue of verse which is also suggested in the Preface to *Religio Laici*: '. . . prose is not to be used in serious plays . . . because it is too near the nature of converse: there may be too great a likeness; as the most skilled painters affirm, that there may be too near a resemblance in a picture.'[1] Verse, while it may lack the immediate realism of prose:

. . . is the nearest the nature of a serious play; this last is indeed the representation of Nature, but 'tis Nature wrought up to a higher pitch. The plot, the characters, the wit, the passions, the descriptions, are all exalted above the level of common converse, as high as the imagination of the poet can carry them, with proportion to verisimility.[2]

The 'heightening' function of verse mentioned here is similar to that sought by Dryden through the 'plain, natural and yet majestic' style of *Religio Laici*, and though he nominally accepts the Aristotelian concept of poetry as imitation and does not explicitly identify 'verse' and poetry, it is none the less clear that this function of verse is closely related to what he sees as the ultimate purpose of poetry. He writes, as he says, firstly to entertain, but he also clearly regards poetry as having a public, and a moral function. Of his life-long desire to write an epic poem he declared: 'This, too, I had intended chiefly for the honour of my native country, to which a poet is particularly obliged.'[3] And he speaks of 'that kind of poetry which excites to virtue the greatest of men' as being 'of the greatest use to human kind'.[4] Poetry, he says, 'must resemble natural truth,

---

[1] Dryden, 'Defence of an Essay of Dramatic Poesy', op. cit., i, 114.

[2] Dryden, *An Essay of Dramatic Poesy*, op. cit., i, 100–1.

[3] Dryden, *A Discourse concerning the Original and Progress of Satire* (London, 1693); op. cit., ii, 38.

[4] Dryden, Epistle Dedicatory to the Duke of York, prefixed to *Almanzor and Almahide; or, The Conquest of Granada*; ed. Sir Walter Scott and G. Saintsbury, *The Works of John Dryden* (18 vols., London, 1882–92), iv. 9.

but it must be ethical'.[1] Dryden, in fact, regarded himself as in the role of the public orator, 'armed with the power of verse';[2] as being one who is skilled in what Quintilian describes as *ars bene dicendi*, the art of speaking well in a moral as well as a technical sense. Verse, and indeed all the ornaments of poetry, are ultimately means to this end.

Dryden's attitude to the basic nature and function of poetry, then, seems to bear the same close relationship to sixteenth-century concepts as his ideas on the proper style of poetry, as distinguished from prose, were earlier found to have. The new influences resulting from science and the Royal Society, with which Dryden is known to have been, for a time at least, closely associated,[3] and which probably had a considerable effect on his attitude to prose, do not appear to have influenced his fundamental attitude to poetry sufficiently to have turned it away from the tradition which as a poet he had inherited from the Renaissance and in which his rhetorical education had trained him.

And the same appears to have been true of Dryden's age generally, for whom Sir Richard Blackmore may be accepted as having spoken towards the end of the century, when he wrote in the Preface to his poem *Prince Arthur* (1695):

To what ill purpose soever Poetry has been abus'd its true and genuine End is by universal Confession the Instruction of our Minds and Regulation of our Manners, for which 'tis furnished with so many excellent Advantages. The Delicacy of its Strains, the Sweetness and Harmony of its Numbers, the lively and admirable manner of its Painting or Representation, and the wonderful Force of its Eloquence, cannot but open the Passages to our Breasts, and triumph over our

[1] Dryden, 'Defence of an Essay of Dramatic Poesy', op. cit., i, 12.

[2] Dryden, *Original and Progress of Satire*, op. cit., ii, 22. Evidence of the influence of rhetoric on Dryden's work is provided by Lilian Feder, 'Dryden's Use of Classical Rhetoric', *PMLA*, lxix (1954), 1258–78.

[3] For discussions of Dryden's membership of and connexion with the Royal Society see L. Bredvold, *The Milieu of John Dryden* (Ann Arbor, 1934); also the same author's 'Dryden, Hobbes, and the Royal Society', *MP*, xxv (1928), 417–38, and C. Lloyd, 'John Dryden and the Royal Society', *PMLA*, xlv (1930), 967–76; also answers to the last named by Bredvold, Riske, and Stroup, *PMLA*, xlvi (1931), 951–61.

Passions, and leave behind them very deep Impressions. 'Tis in the power of Poetry to insinuate into the inmost Recesses of the Mind, to touch any Spring that moves the Heart, to agitate the Soul with any sort of Affection, and transform it into any Shape or Posture it thinks fit.

. . . A Poet should imploy all his Judgement and Wit, exhaust all the Riches of his Fancy, and abound in Beautiful and Noble Expression, to divert and entertain others; but then it must be with this prospect, that he may hereby engage their Attention, insinuate more easily into their Minds and more effectually convey to them wise Instructions . . .[1]

In substance this is virtually what Puttenham had said of poetry more than a century earlier.

The kind of utilitarian discourse recognized by the experimental scientists of the seventeenth century was that which played its proper part towards a greater understanding of reality. Sixteenth-century literary theory, however, at least at its highest levels, had claimed a similar role for poetry. Poetry, by its ability to idealize, to escape beyond the accidents of every day existence, could open the way to knowledge of a higher kind than that to be reached by any other of the profane arts.

This claim to the revelation of 'universal' knowledge was, of course, derived originally by poetry from the Aristotelian concept of poetry as an art of imitation, by which it was freed from any necessary concern with the immediate and actual. In the sixteenth century, it will be recalled, imitation in something of the Aristotelian sense was accepted by literary theorists, including Sidney but with Scaliger as an important exception, as the essential element of poetry. Generally these theorists (especially Robortello and Sidney, though for different reasons) went further than Aristotle in excluding 'things as they are or were' from the material of poetry, thus identifying imitation even more closely with 'fable' or 'fiction'. At the same time their emphasis on the delightful teaching achieved

---

[1] Sir Richard Blackmore, Preface to *Prince Arthur; An Heroick Poem in Ten Books* (London, 1695); ed. Spingarn, op. cit., iii, 227–9.

by poetry caused them to lay considerable emphasis on the role of style and poetic ornament, which, however, could themselves be seen as serving to enable the creation of the fable.

Against this background, the seventeenth-century association of prose with the new emphasis on an exact, scientific correspondence between words and actual concrete objects or forces might be seen as placing prose in clearer opposition to poetry with its 'fictional' basis, thereby contributing something to the development of a sharper distinction of the two forms. Further, as a reaction to the new kind of utilitarian forces affecting prose, new ideas as to the special kind of utility achieved by poetry might possibly be expected to have emerged, in the form perhaps of a revitalized concept of imitation.

At the beginning of the seventeenth century Francis Bacon had stated the concept of poetry as 'fable' in an extreme form:

I now come to Poesy, which is a part of learning in measure of words for the most part restrained, but in all other points extremely free and licensed; and therefore (as I said at first) it is referred to the Imagination, which may at pleasure make unlawful matches and divorces of things. Now Poesy (as I have already observed) is taken in two senses; in respect of words or matter. In the first sense it is but a character of speech; for verse is only a kind of style and a certain form of elocution, and has nothing to do with the matter; for both true history may be written in verse and feigned history in prose. But in the latter sense, I have set it down from the first as one of the principal branches of learning, and placed it by the side of history; being indeed nothing else but an imitation of history at pleasure. And therefore, endeavouring as I do in these divisions to trace out and pursue the true veins of learning, without (in many points) following custom and the divisions which are received, I dismiss from the present discourse Satires, Elegies, Epigrams, Odes, and the like; and refer them to philosophy and arts of speech. And under the name of Poesy I treat only of feigned history.[1]

This statement shows some of the same desire to classify the parts of learning as characterized Ramism, but in its basic attitude to

[1] Bacon, *De augmentis scientiarum*, op. cit., iv, 314–15.

poetry it is ultimately within the tradition of poetic theory culminating in Sidney's *Apologie*. Style, ornament, form, and the rest, necessary as their delightfulness may be to poetry, have no essential connexion with poetry as such, which consists wholly in the 'fiction': except that in the case of Bacon this has been carried to the point where all forms of reflective poetry (satires, elegies, and other lyrical forms), because they contain no 'feigned history', are not considered as poetry at all.

The aim of this feigned history for Bacon is significantly not an understanding of truth or reality beyond that offered by philosophy or history, as it had been for Sidney: instead it is seen as providing a more complete mental satisfaction than is available from the actual 'nature of things'. The scientifically minded Bacon is obviously less impressed with the power of poetry than Sidney had been:

The use of this Feigned History hath been to give some shadow of satisfaction to the mind of man in those points wherein the nature of things doth deny it: the world being in proportion inferior to the soul: by reason whereof there is agreeable to the spirit of man a more ample greatness, a more exact goodness, and a more absolute variety than can be found in the nature of things.[1]

Taken out of their context like this, Bacon's statements on poetic fiction may sometimes be thought of as placing him in the line of development that was ultimately to identify poetry with the creative imagination. This matter will be dealt with in greater detail in the following chapter: for the present it is sufficient to point to the difficulty of sustaining this view of Bacon's ideas when his few pages on poetry are seen to play the minor role they actually do in the whole pattern of his work. Elsewhere he speaks of poetry as 'rather a pleasure or play of imagination, than a work or duty thereof',[2] and indeed his interests, like those of the scientists whose prophet he was, lay in prose, and his advances in the theory of communication were centred there. His ideas on poetry continued to be largely those of the previous century; he introduced no new

---

[1] Bacon, *The Advancement of Learning*, op. cit., iii, 343.
[2] Ibid., iii, 382.

notions, and in conceiving of the imagination as 'being not tied to the laws of matter' he was merely accepting a Renaissance commonplace. Compare, for example, Puttenham's view of the functions of the imagination in poetry: 'By it, as by a glasse, or mirrour are represented unto the soul all manner of bewtiful visions, whereby the inventive part of the mynde is so much holpen as without it no man could devise any new or rare thing.'[1]

Indeed, as was suggested above, Bacon's concept of poetic imitation was more restricted than that of the previous century. The particular emphasis given to this concept by his scientific leanings did not lead him to any exalted view of poetic fiction. He has no conviction of the divine nature of poetry, as had Sidney. 'Poesy is a dream of learning', he declared, 'a thing sweet and varied, and that would be thought to have in it something divine; a character which dreams likewise affect. But now it is time for me to awake, and rising above the earth, to wing my way through the clear air of Philosophy and the Sciences.'[2] Poetry is only a delusion of knowledge, like a dream—a thing that 'would be thought divine'. Nowhere can the position given to poetry by Sidney be seen so clearly as lost in the face of the scientific attitude.

Ben Jonson was equally traditional in his attitude, as might be expected from so confirmed a classicist. His main critical work, *Timber: or, Discoveries* (1641), has been found to be virtually a commonplace book of ideas culled mainly from classical writers, and thus the view expressed in his alleged remark to Drummond of Hawthornden that 'he thought not Bartas a Poet but a Verser, because he wrote not Fiction'[3] is not unexpected. A poet, he claimed:

. . . is a Maker, or a Fainer: his Art, an Art of imitation or faining, expressing the life of man in fit measure, numbers and harmony . . . Hence he is called a *Poet*, not he which writeth in measure only, but that fayneth and formeth a fable, and writes things like the truth. For

[1] *Arte of English Poesie*, op. cit., p. 19.
[2] Bacon, *De augmentis scientiarum*, op. cit., iv, 336.
[3] Ben Jonson, 'Conversations with William Drummond'; ed. C. H. Herford and E. Simpson, *Ben Jonson* (8 vols., Oxford, 1947), i, 133.

the Fable and Fiction is, as it were, the form and Soul of any Poeticall worke or Poeme.[1]

Other writers such as Sir William Alexander, whose *Anacrisis* (1634?) was mentioned earlier in this chapter, continued to argue the Aristotelian thesis of imitation, but the interest aroused seems to have been infinitely less than that arising later in the century from such questions as the rivalry of rhyme and blank verse, and other stylistic controversies. Edward Benlowes, in the Preface to his *Theophilia, or Loves Sacrifice. A Divine Poem* (1652) provides a mid-century statement of Sidney's idealism, associated with the Platonic idea of the divine inspiration of the poet. The Preface is no more than a pastiche of traditional ideas—on the subject of 'judgement' and 'fancy' Benlowes will be found later to have been equally conventional. Notice, however, that in this passage he is like Bacon in seeing satisfaction of the soul rather than knowledge as the achievement of poetry:

. . . *Divine Poesie* is the internal Triumph of the Mind, rapt with *S. Paul* into the third Heaven, where She contemplates Ineffables: 'tis the sacred Oracles of Faith put into Melodious Anthems that make Musick ravishing, no earthly Jubilation being comparable to It. It discovers the *Causes, Beginnings*, Progresse, and *End* of Things, It instructeth Youth, comforteth Age, graceth Prosperity, solaceth Adversity, pleaseth at Home, delighteth abroad, shortneth the Night and refresheth the Day; No Star in the Sphear of *Wisdom* outshines It: Natural Philosophy hath not anything in it which may satisfie the Soul, because that is created to something more excellent than all Nature: but this *Divine Rapture* chains the Minde with harmonious Precepts from a Divine Influence.[2]

For Dryden the concept of imitation seems one to be taken for granted rather than discussed. In his 'Defence of an Essay of

---

[1] Jonson, *Timber; or Discoveries* (London, 1641), Sec. 128; ed. Herford and Simpson, op. cit., viii, 635. On the other hand, Drummond also reported (op. cit., i, 143) Jonson as saying: 'That verse stood by sense without either Colours or accent, which yett other tymes he denied.'

[2] Edward Benlowes, Preface to *Theophilia, or Loves Sacrifice. A Divine Poem* (London, 1652).

Dramatic Poesy' (1668) he makes a typical mention of it—in passing:

I never heard of any other foundation of Dramatic Poesy than the imitation of Nature . . . But 'tis very plain, that he has mistaken the foundation for that which is built upon it, though not immediately: for the direct and immediate consequence is this; if Nature be to be imitated, then there is a rule for imitating Nature rightly; otherwise there may be an end and no means conducing to it.[1]

Imitation of nature may be the foundation of poetry, but like most of his contemporaries Dryden is less interested in this foundation than he is in the 'means conducing to it'—an attitude to be summed up later by Pope in *An Essay on Criticism* (1711):

> Learn hence for ancient rules a just esteem;
> To copy nature is to copy them.[2]

Of all the issues raised by Dryden's *An Essay of Dramatic Poesy* the controversy as to the relative merits of rhyme and blank verse seems to have caused the greatest excitement; and it is clear that behind this controversy there was a much less dynamic concept of the identification of poetic form or technique and the imitation than there had been, for example, in Lionardi's or Fracastoro's treatment of poetic ornament. The ornament and the imitation are seen as quite separate things, in keeping with the prevalent idea of poetic ornament as something added to make the subject more attractive and the treatment consequently more persuasive. This relationship between ornament and imitation is put quite clearly by Dryden:

'Tis true, that to imitate well is a poet's work; but to affect the soul, and excite the passions, and above all, to move admiration (which is the delight of serious plays) a bare imitation will not serve. The converse, therefore, which a poet is to imitate, must be heightened with all the arts and ornaments of poesy . . .[3]

At its most advanced level the Renaissance theory of poetic ornament has seen the ornaments as giving life and truth beyond the

---

[1] Dryden, 'Defence of an Essay of Dramatic Poesy', op. cit., i, 123.
[2] *An Essay on Criticism*, ll. 139–40.
[3] Dryden, 'Defence of an Essay of Dramatic Poesy', op. cit., i, 113.

merely accidental to the subject-matter of poetry, thereby themselves creating the imitation; for Dryden the ornament serves
simply 'to move admiration'.

All the evidence from the seventeenth century is of a simple
acceptance of the traditional ideas rather than of any revitalizing of
the concept of imitation; there is no suggestion that the influence of
the scientific attitude, which had led Bacon to neglect poetry's
claim to knowledge beyond that offered by philosophy or history,
caused Dryden, or anyone else, to search for a new, or different concept of poetic reality, or a deeper view of utility than that held by
the scientists. Rather the reverse, in fact, since the purely rhetorical
concept of imitation—the imitation of classical models—gained
strength with neo-classicism. In 1711 Pope could still write:

> Thus RULES of old, discover'd, not deviz'd,
> Are Nature still, but nature methodiz'd; &c.[1]

But it is hard to see how his words could be anything more than an
empty formula, a transfer to the old tradition of the new emphasis
on method. How, it might be asked, could Aristotle have 'method-
ized' nature satisfactorily, when the true order of nature was only
then being revealed by the work of the scientists—by Galileo,
Descartes, or Newton.

Dissatisfaction with the concept of imitation is expressed in one
of the strangest essays of the neo-classic period. Leonard Welsted's
Dissertation concerning the State of Poetry (1724). Eighty per cent
rubbish that thoroughly deserved the scorn it drew from John
Dennis, this work none the less contains some ideas which, had
Welsted been capable of developing them, could have placed him
well in the forefront of his time. These ideas, however, belong
mainly to the next chapter, since they refer to the nature of the
imagination: but as part of his primary purpose of attacking neo-

---

[1] *An Essay on Criticism*, ll. 88–89. The emphasis on rules was, of course, an
aspect of neo-classicism, but the use of the term 'imitation' to cover the
imitation of classic models was already common in antiquity and had remained
so. Only perhaps the identification of imitation of nature and imitation of
models was a neo-classic extravagance.

classic rules Welsted also included an attack on imitation: 'What I contend against is this, the common traditionary Rules; such as, for Example, *"Poetry is an imitation; it has Nature for its object . . ."* '[1] Elsewhere in the *Dissertation*, however, it becomes apparent that for Welsted imitation is likely to mean only the imitation of other writers. In this passage, for example, which puts forward what was becoming a common feature of eighteenth-century criticism, a plea for originality:

Imitation is the Bane of Writing, nor ever was a good Author, that entirely form'd himself on the Model of another; for Poetry, in this respect, resembles Painting; no other Performance in it can be valuable, which is not an Original, and the Reason is, that to imitate is purely mechanical, whereas to write is a work of Nature . . .[2]

Whether this is the same rule as he had rejected earlier, or another, is uncertain. Indeed, it may be, as Dennis rather testily puts it, 'this Author neither understands what poetry is, nor what Imitation is, nor what a Poeticall work of nature, but without understanding what he says throws out his words at Random, and as a man does his arms who gropes his way in the Dark'.[3] In rejecting the idea of poetry as imitation which 'has Nature for its Object', and at the same time saying that 'to write is a Work of Nature', Welsted may have had in mind some positive substitute for the traditional concept of poetry as an imitation of nature. More likely, however, apart from his emphasis on originality, his attitude to imitation was no more than part of a general rejection of 'rules' with no immediate significance for the history of the concept itself.

John Dennis was in no doubt on the subject of imitation: 'Now if to imitate is purely mechanical', he wrote in criticism of Welsted, 'why then all poetry is mechanical because all poetry is an Imitation of nature. Whoever writes poetically imitates, and every work of

---

[1] Leonard Welsted, *A Dissertation concerning the Perfection of the English Language, the State of Poetry, &c.* (London, 1724); ed. W. H. Durham, *Critical Essays of the Eighteenth Century 1700–1725* (London, 1915), p. 370.

[2] Ibid., p. 377.

[3] John Dennis, *The Causes of the Decay and Defects of Dramatic Poetry, and of the Degeneracy of the Publick Tast* (London, 1725); ed. Hooker, op. cit., ii, 285.

T.H.–K

nature that is poeticall, is a Downright imitation.'[1] The basic idea of imitation accepted by Dennis is completely within the neo-classic tradition. There is, however, a significant emphasis given to it by his stress on the 'passions'. The essential mark of poetry is passion, and because passions exist only in the human mind the proper subject for imitation is humanity. Here Dennis is only following Aristotle; but in helping to bring poetry back to a study of mental experience, even though within the concept of imitation, he was helping to open the way to new developments. This subject belongs, however, to the next chapter, since the advance lay in the emphasis given to the passions as the subject-matter of poetry, and not as part of the poetic ornament or colouring by which the imitation was given verisimility; and as such it is connected with the development of the concept of the creative imagination. Indeed the development in which Dennis played a part was to lead ultimately to the final denial of imitation as the basis of poetry.

The conclusion to be drawn from the treatment of imitation in the seventeenth and earlier eighteenth centuries is that, although the concept itself survived actively well into the eighteenth century, it was unable to provide poetry with any new directions in the face of the rise of science. The neo-classic period could see poetry as utilitarian in the sense of providing delight or moral instruction, but it was difficult for it to be convincing beyond this level.[2] Not until

---

[1] John Dennis, *The Causes of the Decay and Defects of Dramatic Poetry, and of the Degeneracy of the Publick Tast* (London, 1725); ed. Hooker, op. cit., ii, 285.

[2] The neo-classic critics continued to pay lip-service to the Platonic concepts on which Sidney's view of the transcendent utility of poetry was based. Thus for Dennis, in imitating nature the poet should aim 'not to draw after particular Men, who are but Copies and imperfect Copies of the great universal Pattern; but to consult that Innate Original, and that universal Idea, which the Creator has fix'd in the minds of ev'ry reasonable Creature, and so make a true and a just Draught'. (*Reflections Critical and Satyrical upon a Late Rhapsody, call'd an Essay upon Criticism*, London, 1711; op. cit., i, 418). As a general rule, however, Dennis reveals the lack of strength of these concepts by accepting the empiricists' denial of the existence of innate ideas. For a detailed treatment of Platonic phraseology in neo-classic criticism see L. Bredvold, 'The Tendency toward Platonism in Neo-Classical Esthetics', *ELH*, i, (1934), 91–119.

new concepts of the nature and function of poetry had led towards the complete overthrow of imitation was poetry able to achieve, though in a new direction, a position at all comparable in status to that which it could be seen as occupying in the Renaissance world. The development of these concepts, associated as they are with new ideas of the nature of the imagination, go beyond considerations of utility, and will therefore be the subject of another chapter.

CHAPTER FOUR

Poetry and the Imagination

True wit is Nature to advantage dress'd
What oft was thought, but ne'er so well express'd.[1]

WHEN Alexander Pope wrote these lines in his *Essay on Criticism* he almost certainly meant no more than that the art of poetry consists in saying things supremely well—in putting them in the most apt and appropriate form. That is, he was expressing a view that would have been understood and accepted since the time of Chaucer and before. It is what might be described as the rhetorical view of poetry, and arises at least in part from the association of poetry and rhetoric discussed in a previous chapter.

But if these lines are taken from their context they may be understood as expressing a paradox: 'What oft was thought but ne'er so well expressed'—if the thought had never before been expressed in quite the way the poet expressed it, then until the moment of its expression by the poet the thought had never really existed; it would, in fact, be something unique, created in the process of its expression. This would be the view, for example, of the school of aestheticians of whom Croce is the prophet and Professor R. G. Collingwood perhaps the leading apostle. For them the language of poetry is to be distinguished from intellectualized or 'symbolic' language, and is an imaginative process by which the poet becomes aware of his own emotions.[2] Language in this sense is regarded as synonymous with poetry (or art,) and consequently poetry has a unique function which can be performed in no other

[1] *An Essay on Criticism*, ll. 297–8.
[2] 'Art as such contains nothing that is due to the intellect. Its essence is that of an activity by which we become aware of our emotions.' (R. G. Collingwood, *The Principles of Art*, Oxford, 1938, p. 292).

way.[1] It is not simply the most effective, or persuasive, or even the most artistically perfect way of saying something; it is the only way of saying it, because the saying of it is itself the final realization of the experience, and until it has been said the experience cannot be claimed to exist. It is probably something like this that A. E. Housman meant, rather than simply a repetition of Pope's cliche, when he declared that poetry is not a thing said but a way of saying it.

Poetry has at many times in its history tended to be seen as opening the way to knowledge or experience not otherwise to be reached; or at least as providing means for the communication of knowledge or experience beyond the powers of other forms of discourse. It has apparently seemed necessary that poetry should have some unique justification for its existence; mere entertainment, or persuasiveness, or artistic perfection, have not satisfied. Professor Frank Kermode, writing in a recent issue of the *Observer*, has said:

In the case of hysterical paralysis the part of the body affected is often one where an organic paralysis would be impossible: the patient has a primitive, not a doctor's idea of anatomy. Yet his choice has its own accuracy, and meets a desperate need. The accuracy of poetry, though as Wallace Stevens says it is 'an accuracy with respect to the structure of reality' is of this kind. 'Dr. Zhivago' is the great poem of our time because it weighs this kind of accuracy against others which omit humanity and decides for the fiction, for the accuracy of the human error.
. . . poetry is literally expert beyond experience; its peculiar pleasures and its special information are not obtainable elsewhere, and are necessary to anybody who likes being human.[2]

Ideas as to the kind of experience or knowledge that poetry is uniquely able to reach or to communicate have varied from age to age; the Aristotelian concept of the imitation by the poet of the universal element in nature, discussed in the last part of the

[1] 'In its original or native state, language is imaginative or expressive; to call it imaginative is to describe what it is, to call it expressive is to describe what it does.' (Collingwood, op. cit., p. 225.)

[2] Frank Kermode, 'The Defence of Poetry', in the *Observer*, March 12th, 1961, p. 31.

previous chapter, by which poetry is seen as freeing man's search for knowledge from concern with the immediate and accidental events of everyday life, is only one—albeit one of the most pervasive—of such views that men have held.

It has already been suggested that the Aristotelian concept of the unique function of poetry received no more than a token acceptance from the later seventeenth century, in the face of the experimental approach to knowledge. Indeed, this period is one that it is difficult not to see as an era when any such ideas of the unique function of poetry, in any form, were less widely held and less sincerely believed, than at most times before or since; as an era, that is, when the rhetorical function of poetry dominated most completely any uniquely poetic function, and when at most poetry was seen as a specially effective or persuasive way of saying things. Yet such a relative lack of emphasis on the special functions of poetry would be surprising if, as has been alleged, this period was also one in which there was a growing consciousness of the distinction between poetry and prose.[1]

Without entering into any detailed discussion of modern aesthetic theory, it would be safe to say that the unique functions of poetry have, during the past century and a half, been seen as associated in some way with its essentially imaginative nature; either, that is, with the poet's special powers of imaginative expression or with the imaginative relationship between the language of poetry and man's inner life. It is also true that the seventeenth century has been suggested as a time when the distinction between poetry and prose on the basis of the former's imaginative qualities began to be thought of more clearly than ever before.

However, the emphasis of the nineteenth and twentieth centuries has been on the autonomy of the poet's imaginative activity, on its ability to present or to express immediately and intuitively the mental experience of the poet or of man; it is something like this that in the post-Romantic era has been seen as distinguishing poetry

[1] See for example R. F. Jones ('The Attack on Pulpit Eloquence in the Restoration', op. cit., 205): 'In general, poetry was related more closely to the imagination and emotions, prose to the rational mind.'

from other 'intellectualized' forms of discourse, which have meaning or value only with reference to systems of thought or ideas outside the discourse itself. Poetry has not been thought of simply as a more imaginative form of expression. The mere fact, therefore, that the seventeenth century associated poetry with the imagination would not necessarily mean that it was beginning to evolve new concepts of the unique function of poetry; for this association had always been made, either implicitly or directly. Any more fundamental distinction of poetry from prose on the basis of its imaginative qualities would only be possible as a result of new concepts of the nature and role of the imagination. The main purpose of this chapter will be to review the evidence for the emergence of any such concepts.

Francis Bacon has already been mentioned as having written of poetry at the beginning of the seventeenth century in terms which might seem to place him in the line of development leading to the concept of the creative imagination. He seeks from two points of view to define the special nature and functions of poetry, or at least to distinguish it from the other parts of 'human learning'—history and philosophy. Firstly, in terms of the 'three intellectual faculties' —Memory, Imagination, and Reason—poetry is essentially associated with the Imagination:

I now come to Poesy, which is a part of learning in measure of words for the most part restrained, but in all other points extremely free and licensed; and therefore (as I said at first) it is referred to the Imagination, which may at pleasure make unlawful matches and divorces of things . . .[1]

And secondly, at least in its highest forms, poetry is able either to reveal truths otherwise difficult to convey, or to conceal them where necessary from the irreverent or uninitiated:

But Parabolical Poesy is of a higher character than the others, and appears to be something sacred and venerable; especially as religion itself commonly uses its aid as a means of communication between

[1] Bacon, *De augmentis scientiarum*, op. cit., iv, 314–15.

divinity and humanity . . . It is of double use and serves for contrary purposes; for it serves for an infoldment; and it likewise serves for illustration. In the latter case the object is a certain method of teaching, in the former an artifice for concealment. Now this method of teaching, used for illustration, was very much in use in ancient times. For the inventions and conclusions of human reason (even those that are now common and trite) being then new and strange, the minds of men were hardly subtle enough to conceive them, unless they were brought nearer to the sense by this kind of resemblance and examples . . . And even now, and at all times, the force of parables is and has been excellent; because arguments cannot be made so perspicuous nor true examples so apt.

But there remains yet another use of Poesy Parabolical, opposite to the former; wherein it serves (as I said) for an infoldment; for such things, I mean, the dignity whereof requires that they should be seen as it were through a veil; that is when the secrets and mysteries of religion, policy, and philosophy are involved in fables or parables. [1]

Bacon may thus be seen as distinguishing poetry from other forms of discourse in terms both of its psychological basis in the mind of the poet and of the manner in which it deals with its subject-matter. In both respects, nevertheless, he is being as thoroughly traditional as he has already been found in his treatment of imitation.

It is particularly significant that while Bacon acknowledged that imagination may work on its own authority, and that 'in matters of faith and religion our imagination raises itself above our reason', he is careful in the same passage to make it clear that even so reason is the seat of divine illumination, which makes use of imagination only as an instrument:

. . . not that divine illumination resides in the imagination; its seat being rather in the very citadel of the mind and understanding; but that the divine grace uses the motions of the imagination as an instrument of illumination, just as it uses the motions of the will as an instrument of virtue; which is the reason why religion ever sought access to the mind by similitudes, types, parables, visions, dreams.[2]

[1] Bacon, *De augmentis scientiarum*, op. cit., iv, 316–17.
[2] Ibid., iv, 406.

And he reiterates his conviction that neither imagination, nor poetry, can lead to knowledge: 'Nevertheless, I see no cause to alter the former division; for imagination hardly produces sciences; poesy (which in the beginning was referred to the imagination) being to be accounted rather a pleasure or play of wit than a science.'[1]

Bacon's treatment of imagination is based on medieval faculty psychology, and stems originally from Aristotle's De Anima. For Aristotle the imagination was an image-making faculty by which pictures previously presented to the mind by the senses were able to be recalled at will;[2] it stood on the border line between sense and intellect, and without it intellect could not operate because of lack of matter.[3] The two aspects of this concept of the imagination that are most important for the present purpose remained unchanged into the seventeenth century; these are its lack of any truly 'creative' element, and the manner of its association with the intellect. Combined with the view of man as essentially a 'rational' being, these elements in the traditional psychology of the imagination placed severe limits on the development of any concept of poetry as an imaginative activity.[4]

[1] Ibid.
[2] Aristotle, De anima, III, iii, 17–20.
[3] Ibid., 5–16.
[4] Bacon's treatment of the imagination in relation to rhetoric is in some ways more interesting and revealing than his treatment of it in relation to poetry, and perhaps shows even more clearly the traditional nature of his ideas regarding it. Rhetoric he sees as the 'illustration of tradition'—'illustration' here being itself used in the rhetorical sense of a figure of speech 'by which the form of things is so set foorth in words, that it seemeth rather to be seen with the eies, then heard with the ears' (John Marbecke, A Booke of Notes and Commonplaces, London, 1581; quoted from OED, s.v. 'illustration'). The task of rhetoric is 'to apply Reason to Imagination for the better moving of the Will', which in the system that Bacon adapts from Plato means combining the forces of the imagination and reason in order to defeat the passions in the struggle for the control of the will. The will is superior to either the imagination or the passions, but a coalition of the latter could possibly defeat it; and it is the task of rhetoric or eloquence to circumvent the formation of such an alliance. For a fuller discussion of this particular aspect of Bacon's treatment of imagination and reason see W. S. Howell, Logic and Rhetoric in England 1500–1700, op. cit., pp. 371–2.

The emphasis with Bacon is on the 'inventive' power of the imagination. His 'invention', however, is essentially a joining together of objects in the external world; there is no suggestion of the dynamic power of the imagination in creating entirely new mental experiences, such as was the basis, for example, of Coleridge's theory of the imagination. For Bacon, the emphasis is outward from the mind, on what the imagination can do with objects in the external world, rather than inward to the life of the imagination itself:

Poesy, in the sense in which I have defined the word, is also concerned with individuals; that is, with individuals invented in imitation of those which are the subject of true history; yet with this difference, that it commonly exceeds the measure of nature, joining at pleasure things which in nature would never have come together, and introducing things which in nature would never have come to pass; just as Painting likewise does. This is the work of Imagination.[1]

The Aristotelian theory of imitation, which is repeated here, by its stress on the fictional nature of poetry, had implied the necessity for some such function of the imagination in order to provide poetry with its materials. But Aristotle was himself more interested in the relationship between poetry and external reality than in the psychological process by which this relationship was achieved. The role he gave to imagination in poetic imitation can only be inferred from his treatment of the subject in his *De Anima*.

Medieval interest in faculty psychology was strong, but it was perhaps not until the sixteenth century that this interest became closely associated with poetry. In the sixteenth century, as M. W. Bundy has pointed out,[2] the 'invention' of rhetoric began to be explicitly connected with the imagination of the poets, by such writers as Ronsard, Puttenham, and Sidney. Gascoigne, too, shows this identification clearly:

The first and most necessarie poynt that euer I founde meete to be considered in making of a delectable poeme is this, to grounde it vpon

[1] Bacon, *De augmentis scientiarum*, op. cit., iv, 292.
[2] M. W. Bundy, ' "Invention" and "Imagination" in the Renaissance', *JEGP*, xxix (1930), 535–45.

some fine inuention . . . If I should vndertake to wryte in prayse of a gentlewoman, I would neither praise hir christal eye, nor hir cherrie lippe, etc. For these things are *trita et obuia*. But I would either finde some supernaturall cause whereby my penne might walke in the superlatiue degree, or els I would vndertake to aunswere for any imperfection that shee hath, and therevpon rayse the prayse of hir commendacion. Likewise, if I should disclose my pretence in loue, I would eyther make a strange discourse of some intollerable passion, or finde occasion to pleade by the example of some historie, or discouer my disquiet in shadowes *per Allegoriam* . . .[1]

Stephen Hawes, it will be remembered, in *The Pastime of Pleasure* (1509), made imagination one of the elements of invention in a treatment of rhetoric which virtually appropriates the terminology of classical rhetoric to the use of the poets. During the sixteenth century, also, the great Italian controversy concerning Dante used 'imagination' to denote the fictional character of Dante's vision, as part of the process of accommodating the allegory of the *Divina Commedia* to fit into Aristotle's theory of imitation.[2]

The inventive power of the imagination as its functions were understood by the sixteenth century can be regarded as 'creative' only in the sense that it was able to make new combinations out of the materials furnished to it by experience. Even by Sidney the imagination was not seen as a truly idealizing activity, but rather as an 'invention' of such as will transcend the individual species in nature. And although the interest in the imagination was based on a psychological theory, the real centre of this interest was not the mental life of the poet, or of man, but simply what the imagination could do with the objects presented to it by the senses; the interest was in matters almost wholly external to the poet, and there was no suggestion of the poet's imaginative activity as primarily the expression or revelation of his own mental life. It is, in fact, the same

---

[1] Gascoigne, *Certayne Notes of Instruction*, op. cit., i, 47–48.

[2] The central work in this controversy, perhaps one of the greatest in literary history, was the *Della difesa della Comedia di Dante* (1587) of Jacopi Mazzoni. Many other writers of the time were also involved. A detailed account of the quarrel is provided by Bernard Weinberg, *A History of Literary Criticism in the Italian Renaissance*, op. cit., ii, 819–911.

kind of emphasis as Bacon was to give to his treatment of poetry as a function of the imagination.

This lack of creative power is reflected, too, in the second survival from Aristotle, the role given to the imagination in relation to the reason or intellect. The imagination does no more than provide the intellect with its materials: and so, for Hawes, 'estimacyon' (judgement) follows invention in order to provide the necessary check of the rational mind upon the activities of the imagination:

> And fourtely by good estymacyon
> He must nombre all the hole cyrcumstaunce
> Of this mater with breuyacyon
> That he walke not by longe contynuaunce
> The perambulat wayc full of all varyaunce
> By estymacyon is made annuncyate
> Whether the mater be longe or breuyate
>
> For to inuencyon it is equypolent
> The mater founde ryght well to comprehende
> In suche a space as it is conuenyent
> For properly it doth euer pretende
> Of all the purpose the length to extende
> So estymacyon maye ryght well conclude
> The parfyte nombre of euery symylytude.[1]

And Puttenham at times treats even invention itself as apparently a 'post imaginative' process:

. . . For as the euill and vicious disposition of the braine hinders the sounde iudgement and discourse of man with busie and disordered phantasies, for which cause the Greekes call him φαντάστικος, so is that part being well affected, not onely nothing disorderly or confused with any monstrous imaginations or conceits, but very formall, and in his much multiforities *vniform*, that is well proportioned, and so passing cleare, that by it as by a glasse or mirrour, are represented vnto the soule all maner of bewtifull visions, whereby the inuentive parte of the mynde is so much holpen, as without it no man could deuise any new or rare thing . . .[2]

---

[1] Hawes, *The Pastime of Pleasure*, ll. 736–49; op. cit., pp. 34–35.
[2] Puttenham, *The Arte of English Poesie*, op. cit., pp. 18–19.

The concept of the imagination inherited by the seventeenth century is consequently a very indifferent and insecure basis for conceiving of poetry as a unique form of discourse, performing a unique function. Imagination thought of as 'invention' tends to be what Miss Tuve has called part of the 'pre-poem' process;[1] that is, a necessary but nevertheless preparatory stage of the poet's work: an attitude reflected in the Ramist removal of invention from rhetoric to dialectic. It follows from this that there could be no real concept of poetry as itself an imaginative process—no true identification of poetic and imaginative activity. When Bacon says that poetry is 'referred to the Imagination' he can mean no more than that poetry deals with materials provided for it by the imagination; but in actually dealing with these materials its methods are not part of the imaginative process, nor is poetry unique in thus making use of the imagination. Puttenham, for instance, sees imagination as essential to poetry, but it also is the possession of all such persons who, being:

. . . illuminated with the brightest irradiations of knowledge and of the veritie and due proportion of things . . . are called by the learned men not *phantastici* but *euphantasiote*, and of this sort of phantasie are all good Poets, notable Captaines stratagematique, all cunning artificers and enginers, all Legislators Polititiens & Counsellours of estate, in whose exercises the inuentive part is most employed and is to the sound and true iudgement of man most needful.[2]

Again, as in its relation to the external world, imagination is seen as having no autonomous life or function of its own, and as existing only to present material to the intellect: and poetry, in so far as it is thought of as imaginative must be similarly lacking in autonomy. Within the concept of faculty psychology this position would indeed seem to be inevitable.

The other main aspect of Bacon's treatment of poetry, his

---

[1] Tuve, *Elizabethan and Metaphysical Imagery*, op. cit., p. 388.
[2] Puttenham, op. cit., pp. 19–20. This is a most interesting passage in view of the present-day emphasis on the role of the imagination in science, particularly in the formation of scientific hypotheses on a high level. The same idea is repeated by the Spaniard Huarte (see below, p. 157 n. 2).

reference to *Allusive* or *Parabolicall* poetry, is even more deeply rooted in medieval poetics than his ideas of the imagination, the particular connexion being, of course, with the tradition of poetic allegory. Allegory is a form of metaphor and as such is as old as language itself; but as something explicit in the structure of whole poems it has its beginnings in the later classical period. The great age of allegory is the medieval period, but perhaps more than any other aspect of medieval literature it carries over into the Renaissance. From Chaucer's *Parlement of Foules* to Spenser's *Faerie Queen*, allegory is a constantly recurring form in English poetry.

For Bacon allegory is obviously a substitute for rational discourse, but only when the subject is too difficult to be grasped directly, or is such as should be revealed only obscurely, 'as it were through a veil'. There is no suggestion that through allegory poetry can reveal truth directly without the intervention of reason; it simply aids the reason in providing conveniently apt examples or illustrations.[1] It is a means of communication rather than of thought.[2]

---

[1] George Chapman has already been mentioned as standing out from his contemporaries in stressing that 'plainness' was out of place in poetry, and his emphasis on the function of obscurity is more subtle than Bacon's, and has a more 'modern' ring about it. None the less it remains within the concept of poetry as an art of ornamentation. The 'darkness' at which he aims is included in the rhetorical figure 'enargia' and is seen as the proper clothing of the inventions of the poet, the means by which he gives his imitation 'motion, spirit and life'; 'That *Enargia*, or *cleerness of representation*, requird in absolute Poems is *not* the perspicuous delivery of lowe invention; but high and harty invention exprest in most *significant* and unaffected phrase; it serves not a skilfull Painters turne to drawe the figure of the face onely to make knowne who it represents; but hee must lymn, give luster, shaddow, and heightening; which though ignorants will esteeme spic'd, and too curious, yet such as have the iudiciall perspective, will see it hath, *motion spirit and life* . . .' (Preface to *Ovids Banquet of Sence*, op. cit.,) *Enargia* (often confused during the Renaissance period with *energia*) is, of course, a part of classical rhetoric, treated particularly by Quintilian.

[2] C. S. Lewis (*The Allegory of Love*, Cambridge, 1960, pp. 44–48) provides a clear basis for distinguishing between allegory, in the sense that Bacon refers to as parabolic poetry, and symbolism. His statement concludes: 'There is nothing "mystical" or mysterious about medieval allegory; the poets know quite clearly what they are about and are well aware that the figures they present to us are fictions. Symbolism is a mode of thought, but allegory is a mode of expression. It belongs to the form of poetry, more than to its con-

Bacon's exposition of the myths of Pan, Perseus, and Dionysius,[1] which form the most extended part of his treatment of poetry, are simply rationalizations; he is interested in images not as something transcending rational processes, but as the visible symbol of the rational idea. Again, as with his treatment of the imagination, Bacon's concept of the allegorical function of poetry makes it at best a convenient means of assisting or enforcing the dictates of reason.

Bacon is essentially a man of prose and of the reason, and what he says of poetry and of the imagination is likely to be coloured by his prime interests. Consequently, while his views on these matters may yet be safely taken as reflecting the traditional views as they were popularly accepted at the beginning of the seventeenth century, it would be desirable to inquire whether his simple allegorical concept of poetry holds the sum total of the medieval and Renaissance heritage of ideas as to the ability of poetry to aid or to transcend the powers of reason.[2]

The writings of Dante stand at the centre of interest and controversy regarding the nature and function of medieval allegory. His own statements on the subject are, at times, clear and unequivocal, but they are not always consistent, and their relationship to his practice, particularly to the *Commedia Divina*, leaves room for considerable argument. In *La Vita Nuova* (*c.* 1293) he writes:

Wherefore, inasmuch as greater license in speech is conceded to poets than to composers in prose and as they who compose in rhyme are no other than poets in the vernacular, it is seemly and reasonable that greater license be vouchsafed to them than to other writers in the vulgar tongue; wherefore if any figure or rhetorical colour is conceded to the poets it is also conceded to the rhymers. Therefore if we see

tent.' Leaving aside the question of its justice for medieval poetry, this distinction is particularly useful, and will be followed in the present study.

[1] Bacon, *De augmentis scientiarum*, op. cit., iv, 318–35.

[2] The meaning of the term 'allegory' in the English Renaissance has been studied by J. McClennen, 'On the Meaning and Function of Allegory in the English Renaissance', *Uni. of Mich. contrib. in Mod. Phil.*, iv (1947). His conclusions point clearly to the traditional nature of Bacon's treatment, and also to the lack of any Renaissance concept of symbolism.

that the poets have spoken to inanimate things as if they had sense
and reason and have made them speak together, and not only real
things but unreal things (that is they have said of things which do
not exist that they speak and have said that many qualities of things
speak as if they were beings and men), the composer in rhyme has a
right to do the like; not indeed without some reason, but *with a reason
which it were possible afterwards to make clear in prose* [my italics.][1]

And again, to place the point beyond doubt:

And in order that no witless person may take any license therefrom I
say that neither did the poets speak thus without reason, nor should
they who rhyme speak thus, without having some interpretation in
their own minds of what they should say; for deep shame were it to
him who should rhyme under cover of a figure or of a rhetorical colour
and, afterwards, being asked, knew not how to strip such vesture from
his words, in such wise that they should have a real meaning.[2]

Here the reference seems to be to allegory pure and simple; the
poets must have 'some interpretation in their own minds of what
they say'; and there can be no question of allegory forming the
experience in the process of expression or of it enabling poetry to
express the otherwise inexpressible.

However, in *Il Convivio* (1308?), Dante recognizes two kinds of
allegory: 'an allegory of the poets', and 'an allegory of the theologians':

I say that, as was told in the first chapter, this exposition must be
both literal and allegorical; and that this may be understood it should
be known that writings may be taken and should be expounded
chiefly in four senses. The first is called literal, and it is that one that
extends no further than the letter as it stands; the second is called the
allegorical, and is the one that hides itself under the mantle of these
tales, and is a truth hidden under beauteous fiction . . . And why
this way of hiding was devised by the sages will be shown in the last
treatise but one. It is true that the theologians take this sense otherwise than the poets do, but since it is my purpose here to follow the

[1] Dante Alighieri, *La Vita Nuova*, xxv; (Dent, London, 1906), p. 99.
[2] Ibid., xxv; p. 101.

method of the poets I shall take the allegorical sense after the use of the poets . . .

. . . The fourth sense is called the anagogical, that is to say 'above the sense'; and this is when a scripture is spiritually expounded which even in the literal sense, by the very things it signifies, signifies again some portion of the supernal things of eternal glory . . . which although it be manifestly true according to the letter is none the less true in its spiritual intention . . .[1]

Il Convivio itself, in so far as it was completed, was obviously as Dante himself said intended as an 'allegory of the poets'; that is, as an allegory like the *Faerie Queen* in which the first and literal sense is a fiction devised only for the sake of expounding the second and allegorical sense which is true. The 'allegory of the theologians', which despite some confusion appears in the above passage to be identified with the fourth method of interpretation (or rather perhaps with all four methods, but with the fourth being especially peculiar to it), is much closer to symbolism; for here the first and literal meaning itself is true, and therefore cannot be devised simply or arbitrarily for the sake of the second meaning. In such allegory the words have an immediate meaning in pointing to a real event or thing; and this event or thing in its turn has a meaning, because the things wrought by God themselves yield a higher spiritual meaning.

Whether the *Commedia Divina* is an 'allegory of the poets' or an 'allegory of the theologians' remains a problem for argument beyond the scope of this study. The continued presence of the problem, even up to the present day, nevertheless, is an indication that the medieval allegorical tradition was not a simple one. And it is complicated by its association with Scriptural interpretation, for whether or not the *Commedia Divina* is to be interpreted in terms of the fourfold meaning of the Scriptures, Dante shows clearly from his comments in the *Convivio*, and also in the letter to Can Grande, that as poet the exegetical tradition was very much in his mind. In this letter to Can Grande—if, in fact, Dante did write it and it is not a later invention to justify a commentator's zeal in interpreting the

[1] Dante, *Il Convivio* (*c.* 1308), II, i, 2–4; (Dent, London, 1903), pp. 63–64.

allegory of the *Commedia*[1]—he appears to mention allegory in the Scriptural or 'theological' sense in the immediate context of a discussion of the allegory of the *Commedia*:

> To elucidate, then, what we have to say, be it known that the sense of this work is not simple but on the contrary it may be called polysemous, that is to say, 'of more senses than one; for it is one sense we get through the letter, and another which we get through the thing the letter signifies; and the first is called literal, but the second allegorical or mystic. And this mode of treatment, for its better manifestation, may be considered in this verse: 'When Israel came out of Egypt, and the house of Jacob from the people of strange speech, Judea became his sanctification, Israel his power.' For if we inspect the letter alone the departure of the children of Israel from Egypt in the time of Moses is presented to us; if the allegory, our redemption wrought by Christ; if the moral sense, the conversion of the soul from the grief and misery of sin to the state of grace is presented to us: if the anagogical, the departure of the holy soul from the slavery of this corruption to the liberty of eternal glory is presented to us. And although these mystic senses have each their special denominations, they may all in general be called allegorical, since they differ from the literal and historical.[2]

There seems to be here a clear acceptance of a connexion between poetic allegory and the symbolic revelation of truth.

Symbolic thought in the Christian tradition is based on the *Epistles* of Saint Paul; and in the writings of the Church Fathers on Scriptural interpretation, particularly those of Origen, Tertullian, and Philo, there is a mixture of both symbolism and allegory. Saint

[1] The authenticity of the letter to Can Grande, as part of opposing views on the whole matter of the symbolic interpretation of the *Commedia*, is discussed by C. S. Singleton, 'Dante's Allegory', *Speculum*, xxv (1950), 78–86, and M. W. Bloomfield, 'Symbolism in Medieval Literature', *MP*, lvi (1958–9), 73–81. C. S. Lewis (*The Allegory of Love*, p. 48n) believes that 'the exegetical tradition is less important for an understanding of secular allegory than is sometimes supposed. Certainly it will be difficult to prove that multiple senses played any part in the original intention of any erotic allegory. Dante himself while parading four senses . . . makes singularly little use of them to explain his own work.'

[2] Dante, *Epistola*, x, 7; (Dent, London, 1904), pp. 347–8.

Augustine combines this tradition with the forms of classical logic and rhetoric, and with neo-Platonism, to form a new concept of divine wisdom and eloquence, in which the modes of logic, the topics and tropes of rhetoric, are seen as springing directly from the mind's spontaneous and unconscious activity upon the elements of experience. Such eloquence is not simply the best way of saying a thing, it is the only way of saying it:

Here someone may enquire whether our authors, whose divinely inspired writings have formed the canon with a most wholesome authority for us, are merely wise or may also be called eloquent. This question is most easily solved for me and for those who think like me. For where I understand these authors, not only can nothing seem to to me more wise than they are, but also nothing can seem more eloquent. And I venture to say that all who understand rightly what they say, understand at the same time that it should not have been said in any other way . . . there is a kind of eloquence fitting for men most worthy of the highest authority and clearly inspired by God.[1]

This kind of eloquence—what Augustine calls the 'high' style—comes very close to Professor Collingwood's 'natural' language; it is a mode of thought rather than of expression (or as Collingwood would put it, a mode of expression rather than of communication). Language at this level is the immediate embodiment of thought, the internal voice speaking within us that teaches us the truth without the intervention of reason.

Saint Augustine, however, is concerned with prose, primarily the prose of the sermon, and with the reading and understanding of the prose of the Scriptures. Despite the closeness of his ideas to modern concepts of symbolic expression, there is no sign except perhaps in the work of Dante of their having influenced medieval poetic theory or practice. Followers of Saint Augustine, such as Peter Abelard, attacked poetry; and Platonism, which alone of classical influences worked in the direction of symbolism, was basically hostile to poetry in the Middle Ages. The rediscovery of Aristotle's *Poetics*, together with the strengthening of the bonds between poetry and

[1] Saint Augustine, *De doctrina Christiana*, IV, vi, 9; see also Ibid., xvii, 34—xx, 43; and *De magistro*, ii, 38.

rhetoric during the Renaissance, led thinking about poetry in other directions.

One further contribution to medieval ideas on poetry should be mentioned, which is interesting, however, rather as an isolated phenomenon than as part of any general development of ideas. Saint Thomas Aquinas, in a discussion aimed at justifying the use of metaphor in the Scriptures, links this use of metaphor with the metaphors of poetry in a manner that is not altogether complimentary to poetry. Metaphor, he says, seems to be a device distinctive of poetry, and it may therefore be asked whether metaphor can also be properly used in theology, which he is seeking to establish as a strict science. He answers his own question in this way:

> The science of poetry is about things which because of their deficiency of truth cannot be laid hold of by the reason. Hence the reason has to be drawn off to the side by means of certain comparisons. But then, theology is about things which lie beyond reason. Thus the symbolic method is common to both sciences, since neither is of itself accommodated to [human reason].[1]

Poetry, like the mysteries of religion, demands a direct, intuitive, rather than a rational response. As Saint Thomas goes on to explain, its 'truths' are unlike those of ordinary knowledge, in that they cannot be reached by a process of abstraction. However, unlike St. Augustine, Thomas does not seem to posit an immediate connexion between thought and expression, at least for poetry. The passage quoted above comes in a discussion of metaphor, and it is as metaphor rather than as symbol in the strict sense of the word that Saint Thomas's concept of the concretions of poetry is apparently to be understood. Metaphor for him is still a mediate form of expression; it allows some understanding of the subject to be reached without going through the usual reasoning process, but there seems to be no idea of the metaphor as the direct embodiment of the subject, as the figures of the Bible were the embodiments of divine reason for Augustine.

[1] Saint Thomas Aquinas, *In sententia Petri Lombardi commentaria*, prolog., q. 1. a. 5. ad. 3; trans. Ong, 'Wit and Mystery: a revaluation in Medieval Latin Hymnody', *Speculum*, xxii (1947), 324.

Despite its incidental nature, Saint Thomas's insight into the intuitive nature of poetry's method of operation has a distinctly modern flavour. In its own time it seems to have been virtually unique, and its influence to have been slight. W. J. Ong sees a connexion with the paradoxical wit of Thomas's own Latin hymns and with those of Adam of Victor, and traces its influence to the metaphysical wit of the earlier seventeenth century.[1] A similar strain of wit may be found perhaps in the ironies and paradoxes exploited by George Herbert in *The Sacrifice*, whose origins are in the liturgy of the medieval church and in the medieval religious lyric. Indeed, whenever medieval poetic theory or practice moves towards a transcendence of the rational processes of thought it seems to be as a result of the transference of habits of thinking associated with the mysteries of religion. Something akin to this, in fact, has already been noticed in the earlier discussion of the defence of Biblical rhetoric in the seventeenth century.

To sum up, then, it is apparent that symbolic modes of thought were not unknown, but with the possible exception of Dante their connexion with poetry was only incidental and well below the surface. The main stream of the seventeenth-century inheritance contained little that would provide the basis for a theory of poetic creation independent of reason and performing a unique function. Imagination was still tied to the reason by the system of faculty psychology, and served only as a preliminary in the poetic process.[2]

---

[1] Ibid.

[2] The Spaniard Juan de Dios Huarte was one who apparently saw poetry (and eloquence in general) as the product of imagination and independent of reason. His work is discussed by C. DeW. Thorpe, *The Aesthetic Theory of Thomas Hobbes* (Ann Arbor, 1940), who claims that he may have influenced both Bacon and Hobbes. Huarte's *Examen de ingenios para las sciencas* (1578?) was translated by Richard Carew in 1594 and four editions appeared by 1616. However, Huarte's concept of the imagination is still within that of faculty psychology, and his influence did not, for either Bacon or Hobbes, serve to free the poetic imagination from the control of the reason. Also the limitations of his theory as a basis for a uniquely poetic theory is shown by the fact that, like Puttenham, he sees imagination as the basis of all the 'Arts and Sciences', including not only 'Poetrie, Eloquence, Musicke and the skill of preaching', but also 'Physicke, the Mathematicals, Astrologie, the gouerning of the Commonwealth: the art of Warfare . . .'

It now remains to be seen how far, if at all, this position was changed during the seventeenth century.[1]

'The most receiv'd Opinion', according to Pierre Charron, in a work translated into English in 1707,

. . . is that deriv'd from Aristotle importing, That the Mind understands and is instructed by the Senses: That it is naturally and of itself, a perfect Blank, a clean white Paper; and that whatever is written afterwards in it, must be dictated by the Senses, and cannot be convey'd thither any other way.[2]

This statement of the empiricist position indicates the role of the imagination to be virtually the same as that given it by Aristotle. 'The Fancy, or Imaginative Faculty', Charron declares,

. . . first collects the several Images receiv'd by the Senses, forms Ideas out of them, and lays them up for use. This is done in so accurate and faithful a manner, that the Objects themselves be far distant, nay, though the Man be asleep, and all his Senses lock'd up, yet this Faculty represents them to the Mind and Thoughts, in Images so strong, so lively, that the Imagination does the very same to the Understanding now, which the Object it self did, by the first and freshest Impression heretofore.[3]

This basically Aristotelian concept of the imagination as standing on the border line between sense and intellect can be found stated repeatedly throughout the seventeenth century. Robert Burton, in his *Anatomy of Melancholy* (1621), speaks of sense impressions as first conveyed by the 'animal spirits' to the 'common sense', 'by whom we discern all differences of objects; for by mine eye I do not know what I see, or by mine ear that I hear, but by my common

---

[1] A most useful detailed treatment of seventeenth-century views of the imagination, and one to which the following section is considerably indebted, is to be found in two articles by D. F. Bond—' "Distrust" of Imagination in English Neo-Classicism', *PQ*, xiv (1935), 54–69; and 'Neo-Classical Psychology of the Imagination', *ELH*, iv (1937), 245–64.

[2] Pierre Charron, *Of wisdom*, I, xiii; trans. G. Stanhope (2 vols., London, 1707), i, 123–4.

[3] Ibid., I, xii; i, 109.

sense . . .': from thence the impressions go to the 'Phantasie', or Imagination, conceived by Burton as:

. . . an inner sense, which doth more fully examine the Species perceaved by common sense, of things present or absent, and keeps them longer, recalling them to minde again, or making new of his owne. In time of sleep this facultie is free, & many times conceaves strange, stupend, absurd, shapes, as in sicke men we commonly obserue. His *Organ* is the middle cell of the braine; his *Obiects* all the Species communicated to him by the *Common sense*, by comparison of which hee fains infinite other vnto himself. In *Melancholy* men this facultie is most powerful and strong . . . In Poets and Painters *Imagination* forcibly workes, as appears by their several fictions, Anticks, Images . . .[1]

Joseph Glanvill (1665) puts it more simply: 'Now our *simple* apprehension of corporal objects, if *present*, we call *Sense*, if absent, we properly name it *Imagination*.'[2] And Hobbes, with supreme simplicity, calls imagination 'decaying sense'.[3]

At best, then—that is when it is treated by those accepting the empiricist position, as against the rationalists and neo-Platonists, who, it will be seen, gave to the imagination a much lowlier position —the imagination remains, as it had been for Bacon and the medieval psychologists from whom he derived his ideas, the servant of the intellect, a necessary but preparatory stage in the process of understanding. The imagination, declared one defender of empiricism against the claims of the rationalists, 'hath been bestow'd on man for the service of the Understanding'. And: 'So often and whensoever the understanding is busied about any thing the imagination also acts its part by presenting it with the image of the same thing or some other.'[4] The imagination, he says, using an image

---

[1] Robert Burton, *The Anatomy of Melancholy, What it is. With all the Kindes, Causes, Symptomes, Prognostickes, and Severall Cures of it* . . . (London, 1621), I, I, ii, 7; quoted from 2nd ed. (London, 1624), p. 22.

[2] Joseph Glanvill, *Scepsis scientifica* (London, 1665), p. 71.

[3] Thomas Hobbes, *Leviathan* (London, 1651), II; (Everyman, London, 1914), p. 5.

[4] J(ohn) D(avies), trans., *Reflections upon Monsieur Des Carte's Discourse of a Method* . . . (London, 1655), p. 71.

later echoed by Dryden, 'always accompanies the Understanding, as a Dog follows his master every where . . .'

This role of the imagination is accepted explicitly by seventeenth-century poetic theory. Poetry is a function of the imagination, but because imagination is itself subservient to the judgement its use in poetry must be similarly under control. Thomas Rymer, in *The Tragedies of the Last Age* (1678), makes what seems like a significant analogy between poetry and the mysteries of religion, but then qualifies it out of existence:

. . . *Fancy*, I think, in Poetry, is like *Faith* in Religion: it makes far discoveries, and soars above reason, but never clashes or runs against it. *Fancy* leaps and frisks, and away she's gone, whilst *reason* rattles the chains and follows after. *Reason* must consent and ratify what-ever by *fancy* is attempted in its absence, or else 'tis all *null* and void in law. However, in the contrivance and economy of a Play, reason is always principally to be consulted. Those who object against reason are the *Fanaticks* in Poetry, and are never to be sav'd by their good works.[1]

Sixty-five years later a writer is quoted in the *Gentleman's Magazine* as having expressed similar ideas concerning the fancy:

When the Imagination and Invention are so busy, Reason and Judgement are seldom allowed time enough to examine the Justness of a Sentiment, and the Conclusiveness of an Argument. Many of our Poets, the most celebrated for their Ingenuity, have been very incorrect and injudicious, as well as irreligious and immoral, in their Sentiments. They seem to have studied rather to say *fine* things than *just* ones, and have often shewn their Fancy at the Expense of their Understanding, which is buying reputation at a very extravagant Price.[2]

Here there is the association of imagination with poetic invention, as well as the necessity for both to be under the control of reason.

[1] Thomas Rymer, *The Tragedies of the Last Age* (London, 1687); ed. Spingarn, op. cit., ii, 185.
[2] *Weekly Miscellany* (Sept. 28, 1734), referring to the *Gentleman's Magazine* (Sept. 1734), p. 499.

The same elements were present, seventy years previous, in one of Dryden's earliest critical pronouncements, the Epistle Dedicatory to *The Rival Ladies* (1664):

This worthless present was designed you, long before it was a play; when it was only a confused mass of thoughts, tumbling over one another in the dark; when the fancy was yet in its first work, moving the sleeping images of things towards the light, there to be distinguished, and then either chosen or rejected by the judgement; it was yours, my Lord, before I could call it mine.[1]

And again in the same essay Dryden gives as his strongest reason for tying himself to rhyme that: '. . . imagination in a poet is a faculty so wild and lawless, that like a high-ranging spaniel, it must have clogs tied to it, lest it outrun the judgement.'[2] Only once in his discussions of such matters as wit, fancy, or imagination does Dryden treat them as being relatively free from the judgement. This is in the Preface to his *Annus Mirabilis* (1667):

The composition of all poems is, or ought to be, of wit; and wit in the poet, or *Wit writing* (if you will give me leave to use a school-distinction) is no other than the faculty of imagination in the writer, which, like a nimble spaniel, beats over and ranges through the field of memory, till it springs the quarry it hunted after; or, without metaphor, which searches over all the memory for the species or ideas of those things which it designs to represent. *Wit written* is that which is well defined, the happy result of thought, or product of imagination . . . So then the first happiness of the poet's imagination is properly invention, or finding of the thought; the second is fancy, or the variation, deriving, or moulding of that thought, as the judgement represents it proper to the subject; the third is elocution, or the art of clothing and adorning that thought, so found and varied, in apt significant, and sounding words: the quickness of imagination is seen in the invention, the fertility in the fancy, and the accuracy in the expression.[3]

[1] Dryden, Epistle Dedicatory to *The Rival Ladies*, op. cit., i, 1.
[2] Ibid., i, 8.
[3] Dryden, Preface to *Annus Mirabilis*, op. cit., i, 14–15.

Bringing all the parts of the poetic process under the single head of imagination, with only 'fancy' associated in a secondary way with the judgement, may seem to be a significant advance. But in the full context of Dryden's theories, and of their Renaissance background, the passage becomes no more than a rearrangement of conventional terms: imagination is virtually a synonym for poetic rhetoric, and its parts thinly disguised versions of the parts of classical rhetoric. It is therefore not surprising to find him writing in the following year:

> Imagination in a man, or reasonable creature, is supposed to partici-pate of Reason, and when that governs, as it does in the belief of fiction, Reason is not destroyed, but misled or blinded . . . Reason suffers itself to be so hoodwinked, that it may better enjoy the pleasures of the fiction; but it is never so wholly made captive, as to be drawn headlong into a persuasion of those things which are most remote from probability . . . Fancy and Reason go hand in hand; the first cannot leave the last behind: and though Fancy, when it sees the wide gulf, would venture over, as the nimbler, yet it is withheld by Reason . . .[1]

Certainly if Dryden's statement in the *Annus Mirabilis* Preface is to be taken at its face value, as a relatively unqualified statement of the primacy of the imagination in the process of poetic creation, it is no more than the exception that proves the rule. For while it would be very difficult to parallel if taken in that sense, statements of the interdependence of imagination and judgement may be quoted almost *ad infinitum* from all manner of writers of the period. The emphasis may differ from writer to writer, mainly according to whether he is concerned to defend or to attack poetry, but the general tenor is that of this passage from Sir Thomas Blount's com-pendium of critical commonplaces, *De re poetica* (1694):

> Rapin observes, That nothing can more contribute to the perfection of *Poetry*, than a *Judgement* proportioned to the *Wit;* for the greater that the *Wit* is, and the more Strength and Vigour that the Imagina-tion has to form those *Ideas* that enrich *Poesie;* the more Wisdom and

---

[1] Dryden, 'Defence of an Essay of Dramatic Poesy', op. cit., i, 127–8.

Discretion is requisite to moderate that heat, and govern its natural *Fury*. For *Reason* ought to be much stronger than the *Fancy*, to discern how far the Transports may be carried.[1]

Two further examples of the prevailing attitude will suffice. One is from Nahum Tate's remarks 'To the Reader', prefixed to Cowley's *Six Books of Plants* (1689):

Yet in all this liberty, you find him nowhere diverted from his Point, Judgement . . . being never carried too remote by the heat of his Imagination and quickness of his Apprehension. His Invention exerts its utmost Faculties, but so constantly over-rul'd by the Dictates of Sense, that even those Conceits which are so unexpectedly started, and had lain undiscover'd by a less piercing Wit, are no sooner brought to light, but they appear the result of a genuine Thought, and naturally arising from this Matter.[2]

And finally, Sir William Temple, in his *Of Poetry* (1690):

There must be a spritely Imagination or Fancy, fertile in a thousand Productions, ranging over infinite Ground, piercing into every Corner, and by the Light of that true Poeticall Fire discovering a thousand little Bodies or Images in the World, and Similitudes among them, unseen to common Eyes, and which could not be discovered without the Rays of that Sun.

Besides the heat of Invention and liveliness of Wit, there must be the coldness of good Sense and Soundness of Judgement, to distinguish between things and conceptions which at first sight or upon short glances seem alike . . . Without the Forces of Wit all Poetry is flat and languishing; without the Succours of Judgement 'tis wild and extravagant.[3]

Most discussions of imagination introduce at some point the term 'wit', and the use of this latter term during the later seventeenth century provides some additional insight into the prevailing

---

[1] Sir Thomas Blount, *De re poetica: or, Remarks upon Poetry* (London, 1694), p. 17.

[2] Nahum Tate, 'To the Reader', prefixed to Abraham Cowley's *Six Books of Plants* (London, 1689); *The Works of Abraham Cowley* (8th ed., London, 1693).

[3] Sir William Temple, *Of Poetry* (London, 1690); ed. Spingarn, op. cit., iii, 81.

attitude. Wit is accepted as perhaps above all things the essence of poetry. Donne is acclaimed by Thomas Carew as 'a king that rul'd as he thought fit the universal monarchy of wit',[1] and to Abraham Cowley wit is a thing of 'a thousand different shapes', the very essence of poetic genius, an intangible mystery of which we can only ask:

> What is it then, which like the Power Divine,
> We only can by Negatives define?[2]

Wit is frequently identified with the imaginative element in poetry, as it is by Temple in the passage quoted above, and even more explicitly by Dryden in the Preface to *Annus Mirabilis*—'. . . wit in the poet . . . is no other than the faculty of imagination in the writer . . .' On the other hand, however, Dryden can say that 'if we are not so great wits as Donne, yet certainly we are better Poets'.[3]

On the subject of seventeenth-century 'wit', C. S. Lewis has recently written:

The difficulty here is to find, for our own purpose, a word to express what *ingenium* and *wit* both clearly mean. One cannot call it either 'talent' or 'genius' without foisting upon the Roman or English writers a far later and Romantic, distinction . . . But what is hard to express is easy to understand. What is being talked about is the thing which, in its highest exaltation, may border on madness; the productive, seminal (modern cant would say 'creative') thing, as distinct from the critical faculty of *judicium;* the thing supplied by nature, not acquired by skill (ars); the thing which he who has it may love too well and follow intemperately. It is what distinguishes the great writer and especially the great poet.[4]

This is very true, yet it is also inadequate because it sees wit as something separate and distinct from judgement, which the seventeenth century also did, without at the same time seeing it in relation to judgement, which the seventeenth century almost never failed to do, either explicitly or by implication. Within the context

[1] Thomas Carew, *An Elegie upon the death of the Deane of Pauls, Dr John Donne* (London, 1633), ll. 95–96.
[2] Cowley, *Ode; of Wit* (1656), ll. 55–56.
[3] Dryden, *Original and Progress of Satire*, op. cit., ii, 102.
[4] C. S. Lewis, *Studies in Words* (Cambridge, 1960), p. 92.

of faculty psychology, wit, like the imagination with which it was frequently identified, could be seen as deriving partly from judgement, or it could be contrasted with judgement while still at the same time being seen as perverted if not under the control of the judgement. Edward Benlowes, for example, writing in 1652, makes wit the joint outcome of 'invention' and judgement:

. . . Now 'tis *Judgement* begets the Strength, *Invention* the Ornaments of a Poem; both These joyn'd form Wit, which is the Agility of Spirits: Vivacity of *Fancie* in a florid Style disposeth Light and Life to a Poem, wherein the Masculine and refined Pleasures of the *Understanding* transcend the feminine and Sensual of the Eye . . .[1]

And John Dennis was expressing an attitude which would have been found equally acceptable, not only at the time when he wrote (1711) but throughout the sixteenth and seventeenth centuries, when he connected wit with imagination, and demanded that both be curbed by the judgement:

Tho perhaps no one is more truly pleas'd by the Charms of a beautiful Imagination than my self, yet I have always been of opinion, that there is no one Quality of a human Mind, that makes a Man a more impertinent extravagant Blockhead, than that which they call Wit, when 'tis not corrected by good Sense, and restrain'd by Judgement; as a Dose of Mercury uncorrected and unfix'd naturally causes Driveling. And that which they call Wit in Conversation, without good Sense, and without Judgement, is generally without Good-Nature likewise, and vents itself in Slander.[2]

Joseph Glanvill, on the other hand, in 1678 saw true wit as the perfection of all the faculties, of the understanding as well as of the imagination:

I do not . . . reprehend all Wit whatsoever in Preaching, nor any thing that is truly such: For True Wit is a perfection in our Faculties, chiefly in the Understanding, and Imagination; Wit in the Understanding is a Sagacity to find out the Nature, Relations and Consequences of things; Wit in the Imagination is a quickness in the

[1] Edward Benlowes, Preface to *Theophilia,* op. cit.
[2] Dennis, *An Essay upon Publick Spirit,* op. cit., ii, 397.

phancy to give things proper Images; now the more of these is in Sermons, the more of Judgement and Spirit, and Life: and without Wit
of these kinds Preaching is dull, and unedifying. The Preacher should
endeavour to speak sharp, and quick thoughts, and to set them out in
lively colours.[1]

The seventeenth century could, without incongruity, either
connect wit and imagination with judgement or separate them,
because there was always the understanding that any mental
activity worthy of man as a rational being would be under the
control of the reason, whether or not this connexion was actually
made explicit.[2]

Thomas Hobbes identified 'wit' and 'fancy' and opposed these to
judgement when he said that those who are readily able to discern
similitudes and likenesses of images 'are sayd to have a *Good Wit*; by
which, in this occasion, is meant a *Good Fancy*'. Those who are able
to observe difference 'are sayd to have a good Judgement'.[3] But
none the less he makes it quite clear that if judgement is absent
from a work then true wit will also be wanting:

. . . in any Discourse whatsoever, if the defect of Discretion be
apparent, how extravagant soever the Fancy be, the whole discourse
will be taken for a signe of want of wit; and so will it never when the
Discretion is manifest, though the Fancy be never so ordinary.[4]

And it is also significant that the poetic wit which the later seventeenth century came to prefer to that of the 'metaphysicals' was the
kind which Hobbes here relates to a good judgement rather than a
good fancy; that is, wit based on nice balances or oppositions, rather

---

[1] Glanvill, *An Essay concerning Preaching*, op. cit., pp. 71–72.
[2] The meaning of 'wit' in the neo-classical period is discussed by G. E.
Williamson, 'The Restoration Revolt against Enthusiasm', *SP*, xxx (1933),
571–603; W. Lee Ustick and Hoyt Hudson, 'Wit, "Mixt Wit", and the Bee in
Amber', *HLB*, viii (1935), 103–30; R. M. Krapp, 'Class Analysis of a Literary
Controversy: Wit and Sense in Seventeenth Century English Literature',
Science and Society, x (1946), 80–92; and E. N. Hooker, 'Pope on Wit: *The Essay
on Criticism*', in *The Seventeenth Century* (Stanford, 1951), pp. 225–46.
[3] Hobbes, *Leviathan*, I, viii; op. cit., p. 33.
[4] Ibid.; p. 34.

than on the 'heterogeneous ideas yoked with violence together' that Dr. Johnson objected to in the poetry of the earlier part of the century.[1]

In so far as Hobbes would completely rule out the imagination in discourse of a scientific nature—'In Demonstration, in Councell, and all rigourous search of Truth, Judgement does all'[2]—and also in sermons, he may be seen as presenting a new distinction between poetry and prose. Yet the distinction is primarily made from the point of view of prose. His emphasis on the non-imaginative nature of scientific prose may be new, or at least what amounts to an identification of figurative and imaginative language may be so; but for poetry he introduces no new concepts, although he does perhaps emphasize the imagination more and make more explicit what had been implicit in Renaissance attitudes regarding the role of the imagination in poetic imitations. Yet, if anything, his manner of doing this serves rather to emphasize more strongly the relationship between imagination and reason, and consequently to tie poetry, as imaginative discourse, more closely to the purely rational discourse of science. And in all these respects Hobbes is typical of his age.

Mark van Doren, in his study of the poetry of Dryden, is led by Hobbes's identification of a good wit and a good fancy to see him as having made poetry purely a product of the imagination, with no relation to the judgement. He believes this to have seriously harmed the cause of imaginative writing in the later seventeenth century:

When Hobbes and Davenant separated Fancy from Judgement and sent it off to play alone, they condemned it to dull company. Their aesthetics, in setting reason over against imagination, did reason no great service and did imagination real harm. Dryden belonged on the side of so-called reason. He was not a child of fancy; he never lived what is sometimes too glibly termed the life of the imagination. His true home was the house of the Judgement, and his true game was the adult game of common sense.[3]

---

[1] Samuel Johnson, 'Life of Cowley', in *Lives of the English Poets* (London, 1779); Worlds Classics (2 vols., Oxford, 1906), i, 14.

[2] Hobbes, *Leviathan*, I, viii; op. cit., p. 34.

[3] Mark Van Doren, *John Dryden: A Study of his Poetry* (New York, 1946), p. 31.

This view is difficult to accept in the full context of Hobbes's writing; like Lewis's treatment of wit, it loses sight of the fact that when Hobbes separates imagination from judgement he does so against the background of their essential relatedness. Yet supposing it were true, to say that the separation, at that particular time in literary history, of imagination and judgement would necessarily have been harmful to the development of imaginative writing is itself questionable: as, indeed, is the opposite view of C. D. Thorpe, who sees one of Hobbes's achievements as his having found a place in poetry for both imagination and judgement, and who for this reason gives him an important place in the line of aesthetic development leading to Coleridge and Kant.[1] The relationship of imagination and judgement described by Hobbes was well known before him, and in his own time was on the level of a commonplace. And perhaps more important, the line of development of the creative imagination, when it did begin to be apparent in the eighteenth century, did not depend on imagination and reason learning to live together more closely; rather it depended on imagination finding a new, independent, and creative life of its own. The movement stressing the role of the intellect in imaginative creation, though in a manner very different from that associated with faculty psychology, belongs to the twentieth, rather than to the eighteenth or nineteenth centuries.

However, before going on to discuss briefly the beginnings of these new developments in poetic theory, one further aspect of the seventeenth-century attitude to the imagination needs to be considered. This relates to the effect on concepts of the imagination of Cartesian rationalism, and movements associated with it, which though relatively less important in England than in France, never-

---

[1] C. DeW. Thorpe, *The Aesthetic Theory of Thomas Hobbes*, op. cit. I am not denying that certain aspects of Hobbes's theory of the imagination, notably his ideas on 'association' may have been influential in the development of later concepts of literary creativeness. I am only concerned here to say that his treatment of the imagination in relation to poetry was predominantly traditional, and retained most of the characteristics which would have to be got rid of before views based on the creative power of the imagination could be developed.

theless did provide considerable opposition to views based on the prevailing empiricism such as have been so far discussed in this chapter.

Imagination, it has been suggested in the previous discussion, was for the seventeenth century 'at best' the necessary servant of the judgement or reason in the work of the poet. The other side of the picture is associated with seventeenth-century rationalism, and may be illustrated from the words of Cambridge Platonist Ralph Cudworth, for whom there is a higher type of knowledge in which the imagination can play no part:

Phantasms are nothing else but Sensible Ideas, Images or Pictures of Outward Objects, such as are caused in the Soul by Sense; whence it follows that nothing is the *Object of Fancy*, but what is also the *Object of Sense*, nothing can be fancied by the Soul but what is perceptible by Sense. But there are many Objects of our Mind, which we can neither See, Hear, Feel, Smell nor Taste, and which did never enter into it by any Sense; and therefore we can have no Sensible Pictures or Ideas of them, drawn by the Pencil of that Inward Limner or Painter which borrows all his Colours from Sense, which we call Fancy; and if we reflect on our own Cogitations of these things, we shall sensibly perceive that they are not Phantastical, but Noematical. As for Example, Justice, Equity, Duty and Obligation, Cogitation, Opinion, Intellection, Volition, Memory, Verity, Falsity, Cause, Effect, Genus, Species, Nullity, Contingency, Possibility, Impossibility, and innumerable more such there are that will occur to any one that shall turn over the Vocabularies of any Language, none of which can have any Sensible Picture drawn by the Pencil of the Fancy.[1]

This view, which limits the role of the imagination to aiding in the visualization of material things, was shared by the Cartesian rationalists. For Descartes, by way of illustration, the difference between a chiliogene and other polygons may be understood but not imagined; which he takes as evidence of a difference between the

---

[1] Ralph Cudworth (d. 1685), *A treatise concerning eternal and immutable morality;* quoted from 1731 edition, pp. 140–1.

products of imagination and those of pure intellection that are in no way dependent on the imagination.[1]

The direct influence of Cartesian rationalism in England before the last years of the seventeenth century was probably limited,[2] and it was in the writings of the rational theologians like Cudworth[3] that statements of the inadequacy of the imagination were most likely to have been found.[4] As might have been expected, the theory of innate ideas by which these rationalists, or Cambridge Platonists as they are commonly known, sought to explain the presence in the mind of ideas which were thought of as unimaginable (i.e. as not able to be derived through the senses), tended to echo the Platonism of St. Augustine.[5] The latter, for example, speaks of the manner in which we have knowledge of universals: 'Concerning universals of which we can have knowledge, we do not listen to anyone speaking and making sounds outside ourselves. We listen to Truth which presides over our minds within us, though of course we may be bidden to listen to someone using words.'[6]

The rationalist side of seventeenth-century thought, therefore, tended to bring together on the one side a theory of innate or intuitive ideas which are known directly and immediately and from which imagination is wholly excluded because of its dependence on the senses: and, on the other, the strongest classical and medieval influence towards symbolic modes of thought, that associated with the philosophy of Plato. This state of affairs has two important

---

[1] Descartes, *Six Metaphysical Meditations* (Paris, 1641); ed. C. Adam and P. Tannery, *Oeuvres de Descartes* (11 vols., Paris, 1904), ix, 57.

[2] See, however, M. Nicholson, 'The Early Stage of Cartesianism in England', *SP*, xxvi (1929), 356–74, which argues for a more widespread diffusion of the influence of Descartes than is generally accepted.

[3] The main link between the Cambridge Platonists and Descartes was, of course, the writings and teachings of Henry More (1614–87).

[4] Such statements should perhaps be distinguished from the kind of attacks made on imaginative style that were discussed in the previous section of this chapter. However, the line is often very difficult to draw, particularly in those statements coming from the pens of members of the Royal Society.

[5] E. Gilson, *Études de philosophie medievale* (Strasbourg), 1921, pp. 172–89, discusses the manner in which contemporaries of Descartes such as Silhon and Mersenne sought to adapt Augustinian Platonism to a theory of innate ideas.

[6] Saint Augustine, *De magistro*, ii, 38.

implications for poetic theory, which become more pronounced the more closely poetry is identified with the activities of the imagination.

The first and general effect is, of course, to lower the status of poetry. As a product of the imagination poetry could have no connexion with the higher or spiritual kinds of knowledge, which are known without the intervention of the senses—witness Boilean's remark that Descartes had 'cut the throat of poetry'. This is indeed the usual charge levelled against rationalism—by, for example, Basil Willey when he declares that the development of rationalist ideas 'could not fail to result in a lowering of the status of poetry, as an activity which by its very nature foreswore the only methods by which, it was now felt, truth could be reached'.[1] Seventeenth-century poetic theory and practice did not, however, as a general rule 'foreswear' the use of the intellect—quite the reverse in fact. Also it is difficult to make the connexion between the imagination and the feelings which Willey implies when he says:

The Cartesian spirit made for the sharper separation of the spheres of prose and poetry, and thereby hastened that 'dissociation of sensibility' which Mr. Eliot has remarked as having set in after the time of the Metaphysical poets. The cleavage then began to appear, which has become so troublesomely familiar to us since, between 'values' and 'facts'; between what you *felt* as a human being or as a poet, and what you *thought* as a man of sense, judgement and enlightenment. Instead of being able, like Donne or Browne, to think and feel simultaneously either in verse or prose, you were now expected to think prosaically and to feel poetically.[1]

This seems to be quite wrong, if only from the fact that the connexion habitually made by the seventeenth century was between the senses and the imagination, not the feelings or emotions and the imagination.

In any event there is little direct evidence of the influence of rationalism on English poetry, most criticism of, and theorizing about poetry being in terms of those views of the imagination

[1] Basil Willey, *The Seventeenth Century Background,* op. cit., p. 88.

associated with the prevalent empiricism, although the rationalist climate of ideas no doubt influenced to some extent the attitude to imaginative language expressed particularly by the members of the Royal Society. More important for its effect on poetic theory is the rationalist view of the relationship (or rather complete lack of relationship) between imagination and innate or intuitive knowledge. Platonism, in its origins and throughout its history, had been traditionally hostile to poetry. It is true that the tradition of Biblical exegesis, culminating in the divine wisdom and eloquence of Augustine, could be seen as opening the way, as indeed it may have done for Dante, to a view of poetic metaphor as a direct or intuitive mode of thought: that is, as symbolism in the fullest sense of the term. Nevertheless, the form taken by seventeenth-century rationalism, with its opposition of imaginative and intellectual activity, and its identification of intuitive knowledge wholly with the latter, was not a milieu in which this concept of poetry could be expected to flourish.

Ruth Wallerstein has argued cogently for the influence, on Donne in particular, of St. Augustine and other writers of the Christian symbolic tradition. 'Their symbolic explication of faith', she declares 'is the core of Donne's method, both in verse and prose.'[1] This general question lies outside the scope of the present study, but whether or not this symbolic tradition did, in fact, influence the poetry of the earlier seventeenth century, the point at issue here remains the manner in which seventeenth-century ways of thinking acted against the development of symbolic modes of expression. One part of the medieval tradition that Wallerstein sees as having vitally affected Donne is also relevant to the present discussion: this is the use of 'strong lines', a mode of statement originating apparently with Tertullian.[2] The essence of these 'strong lines' was their rejection of all amplification, their brevity, their concentration of a

[1] Wallerstein, *Studies in Seventeenth Century Poetic*, op. cit., p. 73.

[2] For discussions of 'strong lines' see Wallerstein, *Studies in Seventeenth Century Poetic*, op. cit., pp. 73–81 *passim*.; G. E. Williamson, 'Strong Lines', *Eng. Studies*, xviii (1936), pp. 152–9; also W. F. Mitchell, *English Pulpit Oratory from Andrewes to Tillotson* (London, 1932), *passim*.

thought or idea within a single metaphor or paradox.[1] Their aim seems to be to make language a mode of thought, to make it reflect thought directly.

The same general aim seems also to have helped form another stylistic movement of the earlier seventeenth century. This was the 'Senecan' movement in prose that was described by Professor Croll in a passage quoted in an earlier chapter and seen by him as having passed from prose into poetry. As with 'strong lines' the aim of Senecan style, according to Croll, was to express the idea as it comes to the mind—to express it at 'the moment in which truth is still imagined'. Here the symbolic intention is perhaps less clearly apparent than it is in the idea of 'strong lines', but each carries the same implication that language is to act directly as the embodiment of thought, without the intervention of elaborate artifice.

This impulse to treat language as the immediate expression of thought is, of course, to be seen also in the demands of the Royal Society for a 'close, naked, natural way of speaking'. According to Sprat, writing in 1667, the Society was:

. . . most rigorous in putting in execution, the only Remedy, that can be found for this *extravagance*; and that has been, a constant Resolution, to reject all the amplifications, digressions, and swellings of style: to return back to the primitive purity, and shortness, when men deliver'd so many *things*, almost in an equal number of *words*.[2]

Here there is the same rejection of unnecessary amplification and formality, yet the gulf between the Royal Society's idea of the relationship between words and things and any poetic development based on the symbolic use of language is apparent from such a passage as this, written in 1666 by Samuel Parker, who was also a member of the Royal Society:

Now to Discourse of the Natures of Things in Metaphors and Allegories is nothing else but to sport and trifle with empty words, because these Schems do not express the Natures of Things, but only their

[1] Cf. Longinus's contrast between 'intensity', with which sublimity is more often associated, and amplification. (See above, p. 50.)

[2] Sprat, *History of the Royal Society*, op. cit., p. 113.

Similitudes and Resemblances, for Metaphors are only words, which properly signifying one thing are apply'd to signifie another by reason of some Resemblance between them. When therefore any thing is express'd by Metaphor or Allegory, the thing it self is not express'd, but only some Similitude observ'd or made by Fancy . . . All those theories in Philosophie which are express'd only in metaphorical Termes, are not real Truths, but the meer Products of Imagination, dress'd up (like Childrens babies) in a few spangled empty words . . . Thus their wanton and luxuriant fancies climbing up into the Bed of Reason, do not only defile it by unchast and Illegitimate Embraces, but instead of real conceptions and notices of Things, impregnate the mind with nothing but Ayerie and Subventaneous Phantasmes.[1]

The target of Parker's wrath is, strangely enough, the Platonic philosophy that had placed imagination and intellect in opposition to each other, but this does not prevent him from directing his attack against the metaphorical use of language—using language, incidentally, which is itself hardly free of metaphor. The main point, however, is that if there was any connexion between the 'plain' styles of the earlier and later seventeenth century, then once again, this time at the hands of the Royal Society, a concept which might have led poetry away from its traditionally rhetorical and didactic functions towards a more unique form of expression was developed in a manner directly opposed to any such poetic movement. The whole treatment of language by the Royal Society was as a problem in the accurate communication of thought, and not in the formation of thought itself; and, if a renewed interest in 'strong lines', or some of the characteristics of metaphysical poetry and Senecan prose style, did in fact indicate an earlier seventeenth-century tendency toward the symbolic or directly imaginative expression of thought, the impulse seems to have been side-tracked into what was clearly a 'prose' rather than a poetic direction—in the direction, for instance, of Wilkins's *Real Character, and a Philosophical Language*. Indeed, as

[1] Samuel Parker, *A free and impartial censure of the Platonick philosophie* (London, 1666), pp. 75–76. Parker will be remembered for his suggestion of a law banning the use of metaphors.

early as 1621 'strong lines' could be included in a general condemnation of the 'affected' use of language. *The Anatomie of Melancholy*, its author claims, was written: '. . . with as small deliberation as I doe ordinarily speake, without all affectation of big words, fustian phrases, jingling terms, strong lines, strains of wit, elegies, exornations, etc. which so many affect.'[1]

Seventeenth-century rationalism, because of its denigration of the imagination, and by banishing it from what might seem to be its legitimate field, that of immediate, intuitive knowledge, could undoubtedly have had an actively repressive effect on poetry as a distinctively imaginative form of discourse; although the extent to which this effect did actually operate is uncertain. On the other hand, the view of poetry, and of the imagination generally, associated with empiricism did little more, good or bad, for poetry than to cause it to stand still in a situation which perhaps called for movement in order to enable poetry to maintain its relative importance in the scheme of discourse.

Indeed, the whole significance of the seventeenth-century treatment of the imagination is not that it resulted in its belittlement. Obviously, apart from the rationalists, seventeenth-century writers did not seek to belittle the imagination, although like their predecessors of the Renaissance they were generally careful of it; there are far too many references to the power of the imagination and its function in poetry for there to be any real doubt on this point. The exaltation of the reason is not made at the expense of the imagination; or at least in so far as it is, this is not anything new, but simply a continuation of the traditional pattern of faculty psychology and of the view of man as a rational being.

This view of man as a 'rational animal', sharing with the animal world the bodily senses which supply the imagination with its materials, and with the spiritual world his rational soul, which the seventeenth century inherited from the past, was a stronger influence in forming its concepts of imagination and judgement than

[1] Burton, *The Anatomy of Melancholy*, op. cit., 'Democritus to the Reader'. p. 9.

was that of the new scientific attitude. And it was the paradox of faculty psychology that, while it sharply distinguished the powers of the mind from each other, it was less able than later, more integrated concepts of mind, to conceive of imagination as an independent, autonomous function; for, at the same time as distinguishing between the powers of the mind, faculty psychology also set up reason as the characteristic which lifted man above the level of the beasts, and consequently as the only one of the mind's powers strong enough to stand alone:

> Mean while the Mind, from pleasure less
> Withdraws into its happiness:
> The Mind, that Ocean where each kind
> Does streight its own resemblance find;
> Yet it creates transcending these,
> Far other Worlds, and other Seas;
> Annihilating all that's made
> To a green Thought in a green Shade.[1]

To men like Marvell who, at least as poets, still held to the traditional view of man's state, the transcendence of the immediate events of the mortal world was to be achieved, not through the imagination but through the intellect, through the pure activity of the rational soul.

It is this faculty psychology, inherited from the past, rather than any new exaltation of the reason associated with the scientific attitude, which governs most directly the attitude of the seventeenth century towards imaginative literature. It is for this reason unnecessary to think of neo-classic poetry as essentially unimaginative only because of the homage it pays to the reason; nor is this homage wholly to be associated with the neo-classic period as an age of reason. At the same time, however, the relationship of imagination and reason within the context of faculty psychology meant that there was not likely to be the wide gulf between imaginative poetry and other forms of discourse based wholly on reason that would become possible when imagination could be thought of as being

[1] Marvell, *The Garden*, ll. 41–49.

able to stand alone, and this relationship consequently provided a fertile ground for the influence on poetry of the scientific attitude.

The position in which poetry was placed in the later seventeenth century was due in part to a fundamental change in the centre of philosophic interest. Medieval philosophy had concentrated on metaphysics; and, in this concern with the nature of truth, poetry had played its part, as one of the great arts of communication, in the task of achieving a valid or effective statement of reality. At its highest level poetry could be seen as a means to the revelation of the universal element in nature; at its lowest, perhaps, to use St. Thomas's phrase, it served to deal with matters so far removed from absolute certainty that the decision could incline to one of the parts of a contradiction only because of the manner of its presentation in poetry. But in either case poetry had a role to fill, a justification for its existence over and above its mere ability to give delight.

During the seventeenth century the centre of philosophical interest shifted from metaphysics to epistemology; from a concern with the nature and verbalization of truth to a primary interest in the way in which truth can become known. And it has already been claimed in the previous sections of this chapter that neither of the prevalent epistemological systems of the seventeenth century— neither, that is, the empiricism of Hobbes or Locke, nor the rationalism of Descartes—provided poetry with a satisfactory role. Neither gave to poetry the opportunity to claim powers of 'knowing' truth tantamount to those it had formerly enjoyed as an art of statement. In the epistemological world of the Royal Society, poetry as imitation could have little real meaning, for poetry was given no special access to knowledge as a basis for its imitations; and in consequence poetry became limited, even more completely than it had been previously, to a delightful form of rhetoric, or simply a means of entertainment.

Philosophically, this position had to await the arrival of Kant before a satisfactory solution was provided. However, well before this happened the dissatisfaction of poets and literary theorists began to be expressed in new concepts of the nature of poetry.

Nowhere is this dissatisfaction more forcibly declared, or more clear-cut answers provided, than in the *Scienza Nuova* (1725) of Giambattista Vico,[1] and some extracts from this work will serve as illustrations of the changes beginning to take form in the early eighteenth century:

> Throughout this book it will be shown that only so much as the poets had first sensed of vulgar wisdom did the philosophers later understand of esoteric wisdom; so that the former may be said to have been the sense and the latter the intellect of the human race. What Aristotle said of the individual man is therefore true of the race in general: *Nihil est in intellectu quin prius fuerit in sensu.* That is, the human mind does not understand anything of which it has no previous impression . . . from the senses. Now the mind uses the intellect when, from something it senses, it gathers something which does not fall under the senses . . .[2]

Here the old commonplace of the historical primacy of the poets is combined with Aristotelian faculty psychology to give a new concept of the relationship between the senses and the intellect in which imagination, as the product of the senses, is no longer seen as under the domination of the reasoning judgement.

Thus: 'Imagination is more robust in proportion as reasoning power is weak.'[3] And:

> Men at first feel without observing, then they observe with a troubled and agitated spirit, finally they reflect with a clear mind.
>
> This axiom is the principle of the poetic sentences, which are formed with the senses of passions and affections, in contrast with philosophic sentences, which are formed by reflection and reasoning. The more the latter rise towards universals, the closer they approach to truth; the more the former take hold of particulars, the more certain they become.[4]

---

[1] The first version of the *Scienza Nuova* (1725) developed ideas on the nature of poetry outlined four years earlier in Vico's *De constantia iurisprudentis.* The second *Scienza Nuova* (1731) added two new books.

[2] Giambattista Vico, *Scienza Nuova seconda* (1731), bk. ii, intro.; ed. T. G. Bergin and M. H. Fisch. *The New Science of Giambattista Vico translated from the third edition (1744)* (New York, 1948), p. 98.

[3] Ibid., elem. xxxvi; p. 63.

[4] Ibid., elem. liii; pp. 67–68.

Argument and reflection may be put into verse, but they do not thereby become poetry: '. . . abstract sentences are the work of philosophers, because they contain universals, and reflections on the passions are the work of false and frigid poets.'[1]

The divisions made by Vico between poetry and philosophy, between imagination and intellect, and between poetry and prose, are drawn with a distinctiveness quite untypical of the seventeenth century and leaving no room for confusion. The distinction between poetry and philosophy in relation to the imagination is made especially clear in this passage:

The studies of Metaphysics and Poetry are in natural opposition one to the other; for the former purges the mind of childish prejudice and the latter immerses and drowns it in the same; the former offers resistance to the judgement of the senses, while the latter makes this its chief rule: the former debilitates, the latter strengthens, imagination.[2]

Benedetto Croce in his study of Vico's philosophy admirably sums up the latter's attitude and shows clearly its relevance to the theme of the present study:

Vico adopted a theory of poetry which was then and was still for a time to be a bold and revolutionary innovation . . . He criticised at once the three doctrines of poetry as a means of adorning and communicating intellectual truth, as merely subservient to pleasure, and as a harmless mental exercise for those who can do it. Poetry is not esoteric wisdom: it does not presuppose the logic of the intellect: it does not contain philosophic judgements . . . it is the primary activity of the human mind. Man, before he has arrived at the stage of forming universals, forms imaginary ideas. Before he reflects with a clear mind he apprehends with faculties confused and disturbed; before he can articulate he sings: before speaking in prose he speaks in verse: before using technical terms he uses metaphors . . . So far from being a fashion of expounding metaphysics poetry is distinct from and opposed to metaphysics . . . the judgements of poetry are composed

[1] Ibid., bk. ii, ch. iii; p. 237.
[2] Vico, *Scienza nuova prima* (1715), bk. iii, ch. 26; quoted from Croce, *Aesthetic*, trans. D. Ainslie, New York, 1909, pp. 221–2.

of sense and emotion, those of philosophy are composed of reflection . . .[1]

The remainder of this chapter will be concerned to see the manner in which this break with tradition was also being accomplished in England, so that by the mid-eighteenth century Bishop Lowth, in a passage quoted in an earlier chapter, could declare that 'the language of the passions is totally different . . . reason speaks literally, the passions poetically'.

One of the most significant facts of seventeenth-century literary history was undoubtedly the 'rediscovery' of the treatise *On the Sublime* of 'Longinus'; for in this work lay the clue to a solution of the dilemma in which poetic theory found itself, deprived of much of its traditional function and unprovided with any alternative by the new epistemologies. The treatise had, in fact, never really been lost for it to be rediscovered;[2] it had been published by Robortello in 1554, but it was not translated into English until almost a hundred years later, and not until the appearance of a French translation by Boileau in 1674 was it well known or widely quoted in England.

Whether as a cause or a symptom, the significance of the later seventeenth-century renewal of interest in 'Longinus' comes from the fact that of all the classical literary theorists he is the most clearly concerned with a psychological approach to discourse; he is

[1] Croce, *The Philosophy of Giambattista Vico* (1910); trans. R. G. Collingwood (London, 1913), pp. 47–48.

[2] The first modern edition of *On the Sublime* was that of Robortello (Basle, 1554), and the first English translation that of John Hall (London, 1652). The influence of 'Longinus' in England has been studied by, among others, S. H. Monk, *The Sublime: A Study of Critical Theories in XVIII-Century England* (New York, 1935), and also, more incidentally, by G. McKenzie, *Critical Responsiveness: A Study of the Psychological Current in Later Eighteenth Century Criticism* (Berkeley, 1949); the subject, along with much else relevant and valuable to the present study is also treated by N. Maclean, 'From Action to Image: Theories of the Lyric in the Eighteenth Century', in R. S. Crane (ed.), *Critics and Criticism*, op. cit., pp. 408–60. The post classical to Renaissance career of *On the Sublime* is traced by B. Weinberg, 'Translations and Commentaries of Longinus *On the Sublime* to 1660: A Bibliography', *MP*, xlvii (1950), 145–51, and the logical basis of the treatise is analysed by Elder Olson, 'The Argument of Longinus *On the Sublime*', *MP*, xxxix (1942), 225–58.

interested above all in the unique experience to be gained from a particular use of words and the manner in which this experience is to be induced. He makes no clearer distinctions between poetry and oratory than did many other writers, but for him the 'sublime' arouses not persuasion but 'transport',[1] and ultimately he is interested in the nature and source of sublimity rather than in its effect. Also, as regards his eighteenth-century influence, the qualities of discourse emphasized by him are so far removed from those sought for contemporary prose that discussions of sublimity at that time are almost always confined to poetry. For these reasons, the influence of *On the Sublime* on modern literary theory, despite its original connexion with oratory, lies largely outside the rhetorical tradition.

'Sublimity', says 'Longinus', 'is the echo of a great soul.'[2] Almost without exception, other critics from Plato to Dryden who thought at all of the poet as 'inspired' saw the inspiration as coming from outside both poet and poem—the 'divine frenzy' of Plato's *Ion*.[3] For 'Longinus', however, the inspiration is seen as the combination, in the act of creation, of on the one hand the concepts and passions of the poet or orator, and on the other the resources of language. Of the five sources of sublimity two are constituents of the soul, while the other three are the verbal means of expressing these first two:

There are, it may be said, five principal sources of elevated language. Beneath these five varieties there lies, as though it were the common foundation, the gift of discourse, which is indispensable. First and most important is the power of forming great conceptions, as we have elsewhere explained in our remarks on Xenophon. Secondly there is

---

[1] 'Longinus', *On the Sublime* I; op. cit., p. 43. See also above, p. 53.
[2] Ibid., IX; p. 61.
[3] 'For all the epic poets, the good ones, utter all their beautiful poems not through art but because they are divinely inspired and possessed, and the same is true of the good lyric poets. For just as the Corybantes are not in their right minds, so the lyric poets are not in their right minds . . .' Fracastoro, it will be remembered, was one of the few who saw the inspiration as coming from within the poem. For a seventeenth-century statement of the poet's divine inspiration see the passage from Benlowes Preface to his *Theophilia* quoted above, p. 134.

vehement and inspired passion. These two components of the sublime are for the most part innate. Those which remain are partly the product of art. The due formation of figures deals with two sorts of figures, the first those of thought and the second those of expression. Next there is noble diction, which in turn comprises choice of words, and use of metaphors, and elaboration of language. The fifth cause of elevation—one which is the fitting conclusion of all that have preceded it—is dignified and elevated composition.[1]

In this view poetry exists to provide a suitable medium which the spirit of the poet transcends and illuminates. Sublimity is to be understood in neither a wholly moral nor a wholly stylistic sense; it is the expression of the elevated soul, made possible by the perfection both of the soul and of art. As such it links together the resources of poetic language and the sensitivity of the poet in a manner which has no parallel in the rhetorical treatment of poetry.

Whether *On the Sublime* gave the poets of the seventeenth century the lead they were looking for, or whether the renewed interest in 'Longinus' was simply one aspect of a general movement in poetic ideas, the end of the century did see the clear growth of a tendency to regard the mental life of the poet as an important subject for poetry. And it is this which is the beginning of the end of the rhetorical domination of poetry, the beginning of the shift from an emphasis on the audience to an emphasis on the poet himself, from seeing poetry as a means of moving the reader to one of allowing the poet to express his emotions.[2]

The first important statement in this new direction came from John Dennis, whose *Impartial Critic* (1693) has already been noted for its insistence on prose 'correctness' in poetic statement. Only three years later, in his *Remarks on Blackmore's Prince Arthur*, he declared that a poet is obliged always to speak to the heart:

---

[1] 'Longinus', op. cit., VIII; pp. 57–59.

[2] This study is concerned with the seventeenth century and when it ventures into the eighteenth century does so only in order to throw light, chiefly by contrast, on seventeenth-century ideas and attitudes. When it does so venture, particularly in the present section, it owes a considerable debt to what I consider to be one of the most valuable studies of this period—Norman Maclean's *From Action to Image*, op. cit.

As no Pleasure can be very great, if it is not surprizing, so no Surprize can be very great if it is not pathetick; from whence it follows by manifest Consequence, that if *Mr. Blackmore's* Narration is not pathetick, it cannot be very delightful. Indeed, a Poet ought always to speak to the Heart. And the greatest Wit in the World, when he ceases to do that, is a Rhimer and not a Poet. For a Poet, that he may be sure to instruct, is oblig'd to give all the Delight that he can, as we have prov'd above. Now nothing that is not pathetick in Poetry can give very much delight; For he who is very much pleas'd, is at the same time very much mov'd: and Poetical Genius, as we shall prove in another Place, is it self a Passion. A Poet then is oblig'd always to speak to the Heart. And it is for this reason, that Point and Conceit, and all that they call Wit, is to be forever banish'd from true Poetry. Because he who uses it, speaks to the Head alone . . .[1]

In his *Advancement and Reformation of Poetry* (1701) Dennis attempts what he believes to be the first definition of poetry: 'Poetry then is an Imitation of Nature, by a pathetick and numerous Speech'.[2] Here he repeats the link made by 'Longinus' between the poet's soul and the verbal qualities of poetry; and of the two elements of poetry, passion and harmony, the latter is of less importance, passion being the 'characteristical mark of poetry':

That the Speech, by which Poetry makes its Imitation, must be pathetick, is evident; for Passion is still more necessary to it than Harmony. For Harmony only distinguishes its Instrument from that of Prose, but Passion distinguishes its very Nature and Character. For, therefore, Poetry is Poetry, because it is more Passionate and Sensual than Prose. A discourse that is writ in very good Numbers, if it wants Passion, can be but measured Prose. But a Discourse that is every where extremeley pathetick, and consequently, every where bold and figurative, is certainly Poetry without Numbers.

Passion then, is the Characteristical Mark of Poetry, and, consequently must be every where: For where-ever a Discourse is not

---

[1] Dennis, *Remarks on a Book entituled Prince Arthur, an Heroick Poem, with some general Critical Observations and Several New Remarks upon Virgil* (London, 1696); op. cit., i, 127.

[2] Dennis, *The Advancement and Reformation of Modern Poetry* (London, 1701); op. cit., i, 215.

Pathetick, there it is Prosaick. As Passion in a Poem must be every where, so Harmony is usually diffus'd throughout it. But Passions answers the Two Ends of Poetry better than Harmony can do . . .[1]

The concept of imitation is retained in this passage, but instead of imitation it is the passion that is the essence of poetry, separating it from prose more definitely than any stylistic elements.

Among the passions, Dennis distinguishes between the 'Vulgar' and the 'Enthusiastick' passions as sources of poetry:

First, Vulgar Passion, or that which we commonly call Passion, is that which is moved by the Objects themselves, or by the Ideas in the Ordinary Course of Life . . .

Secondly, Enthusiastick Passion, or Enthusiasm, is a Passion which is moved by the Ideas in Con-Templation or the Meditation of things that belong not to common Life . . .[2]

The 'vulgar' passions have a wider but lower common appeal, whereas the 'enthusiastick' passions, which arise from man's highest ideas, his religious contemplations, are more subtle and lofty. These 'enthusiastick' passions, Dennis finds, are most purely expressed in those parts of epic poetry 'where the Poet speaks himself', and in the 'greater Ode'.[3]

Many of Dennis's ideas are traditionally based, and his ostensible point of reference for judging poetry remains its effect on an audience; none the less his analysis is centred less on the power of poetry to move men than on the source of this power, which in the highest poetry he finds in the spiritual life of the poet: '. . . Poetical Genius, in a Poem, is the true Expression of Ordinary or Enthusiastick Passions proceeding from Ideas to which it naturally belongs; and Poetical Genius, in a Poet, is the Power of expressing such

---

[1] Dennis, *The Advancement and Reformation of Modern Poetry* (London, 1701) op. cit., i, 215. Milton had, of course, already remarked that poetry was 'more simple, sensuous and passionate' than rhetoric (*Treatise of Education, to Master Samuel Hartlib*, 1644; ed. Spingarn, op. cit., i, 206).

[2] Dennis, *The Grounds of Criticism in Poetry* (London, 1704); op. cit., i, 338-9.

[3] Ibid., i, 339.

Passion worthily . . .'[1] He accepts from 'Longinus' that great thoughts lead inevitably to passion; and poetic language he believes to be the natural consequence of passion. The 'divine inspiration' has, in fact, been replaced by the personal emotions of the poet, as in part it had been for 'Longinus':

. . . first, Greatness of Thought supposes Elevation, they being Synonymous Terms: and, secondly, the Enthusiasm or the Pathetique, as *Longinus* calls it, follows of course; for if a Man is not strongly mov'd by great Thoughts, he does not sufficiently and effectually conceive them. And, thirdly, the figurative Language is but a Consequence of the Enthusiasm, that being the Natural Language of the Passions. And so is, fourthly, the Nobleness of the Expression, supposing a Man to be Master of the Language in which he writes. For as the Thoughts produce the Spirit or the Passion, the Spirit produces and makes the Expression, which is known by Experience to all who are Poets . . .[2]

Whether this passage goes so far in the direction of modern concepts of poetic expression as to justify E. N. Hooker's claim that from it may be inferred that 'in the moment of Poetic inspiration the passion and the expression of it were inseparably linked in the poet's mind—that there was a kind of organic unity between the idea and the words and figures which clothed it',[3] is perhaps doubtful, attractive as it may be to make such an inference. But how far Dennis is from the conventional seventeenth-century concept of the poetic expression of passion may be judged by a comparison with this passage from Blount's *De re poetica* (1694):

The Passions, says Rapin, give no less Grace to *Poetry*, than the *Manners;* when the Poet has found the Art to make them move by their *natural Springs.* Quintilian tells us, without the Passions all is cold

---

[1] Dennis, *The Advancement and Reformation of Modern Poetry*, op. cit., i, 222.

[2] Dennis, *The Grounds of Criticism in Poetry*, op. cit., i, 359.

[3] E. N. Hooker, *The Critical Works of John Dennis*, op. cit., ii, xcvi; Hooker's interpretation may perhaps be confirmed from a more succinct statement of a similar concept from Dennis (*The Advancement and Reformation of Modern Poetry*, op. cit., i, 222): 'Poetical Genius, in a Poem, is the true Expression of Ordinary or Enthusiastick Passions proceeding from Ideas to which it naturally belongs: and Poetical Genius, in a Poet, is the Power of expressing such Passion worthily.'

T.H.–N

and flat in the *Discourse*; for they (says Rapin) are, as it were, the *Soul* and *Life* of it; but the Secret is to express them according to the several Estates, and different degrees of their Birth: and in this distinction consists all the Delicacy, wherewith the Passions are to be handled, to give them their *Character*, which renders them *admirable* by the Secret *Motions* they impress on the *Soul* . . . To conclude, 'tis this exact Distinction of the different Degrees of *Passion* that is of the most effect in Poetry.[1]

Here 'passion' is still only an 'ornament' of poetry, something which lends verisimilitude to the discourse.

Before leaving Dennis, the difficulty in which he found himself regarding religion as a subject for poetry might be mentioned for the light it throws on the transitional nature of his views. In his *Remarks on Prince Arthur* (1696) Dennis had quoted with approval Boileau's attack on the Christian epic, contained in the latter's *Art Poetique*:

Boileau tells us with a great deal of reason in the Third Canto of his *Art of Poetry*, though it is spoken in rhyme:

> 'That the terrible mysteries of the Christian faith are not capable of delightful ornaments, that the Gospel offers nothing to us but repentance on the one side or eternal torments on the other, and that the criminal mixture of poetical fictions gives a fabulous air even to its most sacred truths'.

Now if this be reasonable in the Roman church, I cannot but think it must have as much force in a much purer religion.[2]

Poetry as an art of ornamentation, therefore, is seen as having nothing to offer religion. Despite this, however, and in keeping with the changing view of the nature of poetry, Dennis's writing as a whole, and particularly his *The Grounds of Criticism in Poetry* (1704) shows clearly that religion is accepted as the basis of all great poetry. '. . . religious ideas', he declares, 'are the most proper to give greatness and sublimity to a discourse.'[3] It is a measure of

---

[1] Sir Thomas Blount, *De re poetica*, op. cit., pp. 24–25.
[2] Dennis, *Remarks on Prince Arthur*, op. cit., p. i, 53.
[3] Dennis, *The Grounds of Criticism in Poetry*, i, 357.

the growing 'inwardness' of poetry that though poetry cannot adorn religious ideas, those ideas are the inspiration of the finest poetry.

A man whom Dennis frankly despised, Leonard Welsted, was responsible for perhaps an even more significant contribution than those of Dennis himself to the store of evidence that the seventeenth-century concepts of poetry were changing. In his *Dissertation concerning the State of Poetry* (1724), which was noted in the previous chapter for its rejection of imitation, Welsted gave what was possibly the first clear indication of a breakdown in the system of faculty psychology on which ideas of the poetic imagination had been based since the time of Aristotle. Welsted declared that reason as it is used in mathematics is different from that used in poetry, and that poetic reason includes imagination:

. . . Reason operates differently, when it has different Things for its Object; poetical Reason is not the same as mathematical Reason; there is in good Poetry as rigid Truth, and as essential to the Nature of it, as there is in a Question of *Algebra*, but that Truth is not to be prov'd by the same Process or way of Working; Poetry depends much more on Imagination, than other Arts, but is not on that Account less reasonable than they; for Imagination is as much a Part of Reason, as is Memory or Judgement, or rather a more bright Emanation from it, as to paint or throw Light upon Ideas, is a finer Act of the Understanding, than simply to separate or compare them: the Plays, indeed, and the Flights of Fancy, do not submit to that sort of Discussion, which moral or physical Propositions are capable of, but must nevertheless, to please, have Justness and natural Truth: The Care to be had, in judging of things of this Nature, is to try them by those Tests that are proper to themselves, and not by such as are proper to other Knowledges. Thus Poetry is not an irrational Act, but as closely link'd with Reason, exerted in a right Way, as any other Knowledge; what it differs in, as a Science of Reason, from other Sciences, is, that it does not equally with them, lie level to all Capacities, that a Man, rightly to perceive the Reason and Truth of it, must be born with *Taste* or a Faculty of Judging, and that it cannot be reduc'd to a formal Science, or taught by any set Precepts.[1]

[1] Welsted, *A Dissertation concerning the State of Poetry*, op. cit., pp. 367-8.

T.H.–N*

It is doubtful whether Welsted's ideas had any direct influence. His importance is rather as an indicator of the way the current of ideas was running towards a position which would free the poetic imagination from domination by a faculty of reason, seen as something separate from imagination itself and superior to it. Welsted does not deny that poetry is rational; he is, indeed, surprisingly 'modern' in the manner of his insistence on the rational quality of poetry's 'flights of fancy'. He does, however, deny the absolute distinction which faculty psychology had made between the various powers of the mind; and when these distinctions were demolished the domination of the imagination by the reason could be demolished also.

A more definitive statement of the end of the sole reign of faculty psychology was, in fact, provided, only seven years after Welsted had written, by William Law:

We say . . . that our passions paint things in false colours, and present to our minds vain appearances of happiness.

But this is no more strictly true, than when we say, our *imagination* forms castles in the air. For the imagination signifies no distinct faculty from our reason, but only reason acting upon our own ideas.[1]

These so-called faculties, he says, are really linguistic rather than psychological distinctions:

For the distinction of our Reason from our Passions, is only a distinction in language, made at pleasure; and is no more real in the things themselves, than the *desire* and *inclination* are really different from the *will*. All therefore that is weak and foolish in our passions, is the weakness and folly of our reason; all the inconstancy and caprice of our humours and tempers, is the caprice and inconstancy of our reason.[2]

In the mid-eighteenth century, in a work which Joseph Warton thought to be 'the richest augmentation literature has lately received', Bishop Robert Lowth made a distinction between 'in-

---

[1] William Law, *The Case of Reason, or Natural Religion, Fairly and Fully Stated* (London, 1731), p. 157.
[2] Ibid., p. 152.

ternal' and 'external' poetry. He followed the traditional concept of poetry as imitation, but included among the objects of imitation 'whatever the human mind is able to conceive'.[1] These objects of imitation he divided into 'internal' and 'external', external poetry being that 'which exhibits great objects', whereas internal poetry arises from 'Longinus's' two sources of innate sublimity, the concepts and passions of the poet.[2] Poetry thus internally derived is superior because:

. . . that sublimity which arises from the vehement agitation of the passions, and the imitation of them, possesses a superior influence over the human mind; whatever is exhibited to it from without, may well be supposed to move and agitate it less than what it internally perceives, of the magnitude and force of which it is previously conscious.[3]

Much of Lowth's particular significance for literary history arises from his interest in linguistic problems. As was noticed in the earlier discussion of style, he differentiates between the 'normal' use of language in prose—grammatically regular, uniform and non-rhythmic, avoiding the unusual in meaning and application—and the 'totally different' language of poetry. This normal mode of expression he sees as a reflection of a mind concerned with the matter-of-fact, and similarly the language of poetry becomes a reflection of the passionate mental experience of the poet. Even more explicitly than with Dennis, Lowth re-establishes the link made by 'Longinus' between the experience of the poet and the unique language of poetry. 'Poetry is said to consist in imitation', he agrees, but his whole attitude leans towards the view of poetry as the actual, personal expression of emotion rather than its imitation. The language of poetry, he says, is 'the effect of mental emotion. Poetry itself is indebted for its origin, character, complexion, emphasis, and application, to the effects which are produced upon the mind and

[1] Lowth, *Lectures on the Sacred Poetry of the Hebrews*, Lect. XVII, 'Of the Sublime of Passion'; op. cit., p. 178.

[2] Lowth, 'Of the Sublime in General and Sublimity of Expression in Particular'; op. cit., p. 149.

[3] Lowth, 'Of the Sublime of Passion', op. cit., pp. 178-9.

body, upon the imagination, the senses, the voice, and respiration, by the agitation of passion.'[1] And again: 'As poetry . . . derives its very existence from the more vehement emotions of the mind, so its greatest energy is displayed in the expression of them . . .'[2]

Of particular interest, too, is Lowth's treatment of allegory, which is the direct result of his attitude to poetry and to language. His ideas here are very much a repetition of the distinction which Dante had made between the 'allegory of the poets' and the 'allegory of the theologians'. Lowth distinguishes three types of allegory—continued metaphor, and parable, which correspond to the usual kind of medieval allegory, and what he terms 'mystical' allegory. The latter type of allegory is similar to Dante's 'allegory of the theologians', in that there is nothing fictional or arbitrary in its first, or literal, meaning:

. . . in those other forms of allegory (metaphor and parable) the exterior or ostensible imagery is fiction only; the truth lies altogether in the interior or remote sense, which is veiled as it were under this thin and pellucid covering. But in the allegory of which we are now treating, each idea is equally agreeable to truth. The exterior or ostensible image is not a shadowy colouring of the interior sense, but is in itself a reality; and although it sustains another character, it does not wholly lay aside its own.[3]

Lowth's interest in this mystical allegory is related directly to his study of the sacred Hebrew poetry; nevertheless the appearance at this time of what seems to have been the first clear statement at least since the Middle Ages, of the symbolic use of poetic allegory is one more sign of the direction in which thinking about poetry was tending. In the context of Lowth's concept of the unique nature of poetic language as the expression of personal emotion, this awareness of symbolism becomes particularly interesting and significant.

Both Dennis and Lowth accepted the traditional concept of poetry as an art of imitation. Welsted, on the other hand, has already been mentioned as having attacked the emphasis on imita-

[1] Lowth, 'Of the Sublime of Passion,' op. cit., p. 177.
[2] Ibid., p. 178.
[3] Lowth, Lect. XI, 'The Mystical Allegory'; op. cit., p. 116.

tion, and this became an increasingly popular attitude during the eighteenth century, particularly in so far as imitation was taken to mean the imitation of classic models. Perhaps the best-known expression of this attitude is that of Edward Young, in his *Conjectures on Original Composition* (1759). 'What comes from the writer's hearts reaches ours',[1] he says. And again: '. . . there is something in poetry beyond prose reason; there are mysteries in it not to be explained . . .'[2]

A more complete and explicit break with the tradition is accomplished by the philologist Sir William Jones, who in 1772 made what was apparently the first clear distinction between imitative and expressive poetry:

. . . almost all the philosophers and criticks, who have written on the subject of *poetry*, *musick*, and *painting*, how little soever they may agree in some points, seem of one mind in considering them as arts merely *imitative*: yet it must be clear to anyone, who examines what passes in his own mind, that he is affected by the finest *poems*, pieces of *musick*, and *pictures*, upon a principle, which whatever it be, is entirely distinct from imitation . . . It shall be my endeavour in this paper to prove that, though *poetry* and *musick* have, certainly, a power of *imitating* the manners of men, and several objects in nature, yet, that their greatest effect is not produced by *imitation*, but by a very different principle; which must be sought for in the deepest recesses of the human mind.[3]

The conclusion he reaches is that: '. . . the finest parts of poetry, musick and painting, are expressive of the *passions*, and operate on our minds by *sympathy* . . .' The inferior parts are based on another principle, that of imitation, or as he now calls it, 'substitution': '. . . the inferior parts of them are *descriptive* of natural *objects*, and affect us chiefly by *substitution*.'[4]

[1] Edward Young, *Conjectures on Original Composition, in a letter to the author of 'Sir Charles Grandison'* (1759); ed. E. D. Jones, *English Critical Essays (Sixteenth, Seventeenth and Eighteenth Centuries)* (Oxford, 1922), p. 351.
[2] Ibid., p. 326.
[3] Sir William Jones, 'On the Arts, Commonly called Imitative', in *Poems Consisting Chiefly of Translations from the Asiatick Languages* (Oxford, 1772); ed. Lady Jones, *The Works of Sir William Jones* (6 vols., London, 1799), v, 549–50.
[4] Ibid., v, 561.

Once 'expression' is directly opposed in this way to 'imitation' (or substitution), the step towards making expression synonymous with 'creation' is neither a long nor a difficult one; however, more immediately important, perhaps, is Jones's argument that poetry 'expressive of the emotions', which he identifies with lyric poetry, is the basis of all types of poetry, including even epic and drama, which are poetry only in so far as they contain lyrical elements.[1]

Writing in the *Rambler* of September 21st, 1751, Samuel Johnson had endeavoured to maintain the neo-classic position that poetry was bound by the same laws of logic as other forms of discourse. He criticized the lack of logical development in the eighteenth-century ode: they were modelled, he said, upon a primitive form of poetry, written when the imagination was 'vehement' and rapid, and before science had been sufficiently developed to accustom the mind to close inspection and control. 'From this accidental peculiarity of the ancient writers', he declared,

. . . the critics deduce the rules of lyrick poetry, which they have set free from all the laws by which other compositions are confined, and allow to neglect the niceties of transition, to start into remote digressions, and to wander without restraint from one scene of imagery to another.[2]

Johnson was answered in due time by one Robert Potter, in a manner typical of the changes taking place: the lyricists, said Potter, 'knew that rapture, not argumentation, was the constituent part of that species of poetry they cultivated'.[3]

---

[1] Sir William Jones, 'On the Arts, Commonly called Imitative', in *Poems Consisting Chiefly of Translations from the Asiatick Languages* (Oxford, 1772); ed. Lady Jones, *The Works of Sir William Jones* (6 vols., London, 1799), v, 550–1. Cf. Bacon, who had denied that lyric poetry was poetry at all, on the grounds that it contained no imitation.

[2] Samuel Johnson, *Rambler*, 21st September 1751; ed. L. T. Bergeur, *The British Essayists* (45 vols., London, 1823), xxi, 275–6. Cf. the comments of Cowley on the lack of logical connexions in the Pindaric Ode (see above, p. 21).

[3] Potter, *An Inquiry into Some Passages in Dr. Johnson's 'Lives of the English Poets'; Particularly his Observations on Lyric Poetry, and the Odes of Gray* (London, 1783), p. 13.

This exaltation of the lyric as the expression of personal passion, already seen in the writings of Lowth, Jones, and Potter, is the main theme of later eighteenth-century criticism. Joseph Warton, for example, in an Essay written in 1756 primarily to bestow praise on Pope, nevertheless divides poetry into four kinds and will allow Pope only a superiority over all others in the second of these kinds— moral, ethical, and panegyrical poetry,[1] in which there is seen 'true poetical genius in a more moderate degree',[2] as compared with the first kind which is distinguished by the sublime and the pathetic, 'the two chief nerves of all genuine poetry'.[3] This first kind of poetry Warton refers to as 'pure' poetry,[4] perhaps the first use of the term in this sense, reflecting the desire to purify poetry by separating it from other, non-poetic influences.

By the end of the century 'imagination', 'lyric', and 'poetry' could be virtually synonymous terms. For Mrs. Barbauld, writing in 1797, only lyric poetry is 'pure'; all other poetry—epic, dramatic, descriptive, didactic, &c.—makes use of the 'charms of verse', but only to illustrate subjects 'which in their own nature are affecting or interesting', and thus is dismissed the whole medieval and Renaissance tradition of poetry as an art of ornamentation. Quite apart from this use of poetry is:

. . . what may be called pure Poetry, or Poetry in the abstract. It is conversant with an imaginary world, peopled with beings of its own creation. It deals in splendid imagery, bold fiction and allegorical personages. It is necessarily obscure to a certain degree; because, having to do chiefly with ideas generated within the mind, it cannot be at all comprehended by any whose intellect has not been exercised in similar contemplations; while the conceptions of the Poet (often highly metaphysical) are rendered still more remote from common apprehension by the figurative phrase in which they are clothed. All that is properly *Lyric Poetry* is of this kind.[5]

---

[1] Joseph Warton, *An Essay on the Genius and Writings of Pope* (London, 1756); ed. Scott Elledge, *Eighteenth-Century Critical Essays* (2 vols., New York, 1961), ii, 717.

[2] Ibid., ii, 720.   [3] Ibid., ii, 719.   [4] Ibid., ii, 717.

[5] Mrs. A. L. Barbauld, Preface to *The Poetical Works of Mr. William Collins* (London, 1797), pp. iii–iv.

As part of this exaltation of the lyric there is everywhere an impulse to see it as the most spiritual kind of poetry, as more completely than any other poetic form the expression of the imagination, and therefore as the form of poetry furthest removed from the prose which in the later seventeenth century had been appropriated to science and the intellect. Joseph Trapp (1711), in a passage quoted in an earlier chapter, says of the lyric that 'it is of all Kinds of Poetry the most poetical'; and Edward Young, in his *On lyrick Poetry* (1728), thinks of it as 'more spirituous and more remote from Prose than any other, in Sense, Sound, Expression and Conduct'.[1]

This interest in the lyric provides the first undeniable evidence of a conscious, deep-rooted desire to distinguish poetry from prose —evidence such as it has not been possible to find from the seventeenth century. Poetry is moving towards the point where it will become thought of as emanating wholly from the soul of the poet, of whose emotions it is seen as the natural and unique means of expression. This may have been the inevitable reaction against the later seventeenth-century domination of the arts of discourse by attitudes that were essentially associated with prose, or at least alien to poetry; indeed, the forms of eighteenth-century literary theory which have been surveyed above strongly suggest that this may have been the case. But this reaction was something which, except in so far as its 'cause' may have lain there, belonged hardly at all to the seventeenth century. And only with the completion of this movement in the nineteenth century can the process of separation of poetry and prose, as distinct forms of discourse, be said to have reached its culmination. At least part of the efforts of the twentieth century has been towards a blurring of this distinction.

[1] Young, 'On lyrick Poetry'; preface to *Ocean: an Ode* (London, 1728), p. 18.

CHAPTER FIVE

Conclusion

G REAT movements in the history of ideas do not necessarily affect all areas of human endeavour simultaneously: changes in one field may eventually cause changes elsewhere, but the process of change may take considerable time to complete itself, or even to begin. In the foregoing chapters it has been suggested that the ideas manifesting the arrival of the 'modern' world in the seventeenth century were primarily concerned with physical science, and that their immediate effect on discourse was largely confined to one type of discourse, namely 'utilitarian' prose, which was most closely associated with the needs and attitudes of the scientists. The world of Letters, though not unaffected, remained largely under the control of the older influences; and literary discourse, particularly poetry, remained basically unchanged until the eighteenth century, the process of change even then being slow. In so far as the growth of the new scientific attitude affected literature it did so at first only as an influence from the outside, and consequently without causing any fundamental changes in the structure of literary discourse, or in the concepts of its nature and function on which literary effort was based.

For this reason the usual practice of regarding the predominantly literary movement known as the Renaissance as having ended somewhere about the end of the sixteenth century, in time for the beginnings of the modern world in the seventeenth, can be misleading. It has led, for example, to the widespread acceptance of earlier seventeenth-century poetry as a first burgeoning of the 'modern', 'romantic' spirit in poetry under the influence of the new ideas, which is not only wrong in itself but also accentuates the position of the poetry of the later part of the century as an arid desert of regression before the final arrival of Romanticism. Changes of taste there certainly were between the beginning and end of the seventeenth century, but these were relatively minor and superficial compared with the fundamental concepts of the nature and function of poetry that remained unchanged. Donne and Dryden alike wrote their poetry according to ideas formulated in the Renaissance rhetorical poetics—ideas which in many respects were closer to the medieval than to the modern concept of poetry.

It was stated in the opening chapter of this study that it was not intended to *prove* anything, nor to provide any complete explanation of developments in poetic theory or practice during the seventeenth and eighteenth centuries. None the less some sort of thesis, or hypothesis at least, has emerged in the foregoing chapters, and it would seem desirable at this stage to attempt a formulation of this thesis; and in doing so to endeavour to state as briefly and clearly as possible its basic tenets and its implications for the history of poetic theory and practice.

The thesis itself may be stated as follows: the prevailing concept of verbal utility, or of the useful function of words, underwent a far-reaching change as part of the final emergence in the seventeenth century of the 'modern' scientific attitude, with its emphasis on 'things' rather than words and on reasoning based on spatial rather than verbal analogies: and the nature of the change was such that the position of poetry, in what had previously been a relatively homogeneous pattern of discourse, became no longer tenable. As a result the eighteenth century was led to search for concepts of the nature and function of poetry that would be independent of the new kind of emphasis given to verbal utility by experimental science, thus separating poetry from other forms of discourse more completely than it had hitherto been.

The basic assumption made by this thesis is that poetry, and indeed all 'creative' writing, will always insist on being a mode of thought as well as a mode of communication: that is, it assumes that such a statement as A. E. Housman's that 'poetry is not the thing said but a way of saying it' has no real validity, because for the poet the two cannot be separated. Poetry will not long continue to be satisfied with retailing, no matter how well or attractively, goods of someone else's manufacture. When the normal usage of words is such that they are seen primarily as a means of communication poetry will be likely to emphasize its own special interest in words as a mode of thought or 'expression'. This is the situation at the present day.

On the other hand, in a verbally centred world such as that of the Renaissance, a world in which words stand at the very centre of thought and learning—in which words are seen as supplying thought with the very forms or modes in which to operate—poetry (and literary or creative writing in general) will not feel this need to stress its unique powers of expression in quite the same way. For in such a world, though communication may be emphasized, there will always be the underlying assumption that words are also the primary means of formulating thought, in all its various forms.

In the sixteenth century particularly, as a result of the humanist emphasis on rhetorical and literary learning, the whole weight of the intellectual tradition was towards the coherence of the arts of discourse. There was no consistent or fundamental pressure towards a distinction between literary and non-literary discourse, or between poetry and other forms of writing. Such distinctions as there were tended to be formal, or vague and close to the surface. This is in spite of the philosophical distinctions made by such writers as Sidney between poetry, as an imaginative art—as an art of imitation —and other forms of discourse such as history and philosophy. For the rhetorical tradition, with its emphasis on the role of the audience, gave to poetry a predominantly moral and didactic colour-ing and ensured that most weight was given to its function as an art of communication, which it shared most obviously with other forms of discourse, while at the same time its creative power of 'knowing' or ordering the matter it communicated was not denied.

In the seventeenth century, however, the position was changed. For the scientists, thought came to be organized on the basis of mechanically or spatially rather than linguistically framed analogies, and words were seen as performing a secondary, utilitarian role, subsequent to thought rather than as an integral part of it. Instead of supplying the forms which enabled thought to be organized, the position was reversed: the form of words was seen as determined by thought and the ideal style that which followed most faithfully the order of thought. Verbal utility was envisaged wholly and specifically in terms of communication, even to the extent of the scientist supplying the poet or literary artist with 'many new things to be nam'd, adorn'd, and describ'd' in their discourse'. In consequence, the cohesive force that had previously caused poetry to remain closely associated with other forms of discourse—the central position of words in the world of thought—lost its power.

This study has suggested that in its initial stages this seventeenth-century movement led to an emphasis on the utilitarian value of words as a convenient means of communication (that is, to an emphasis on 'plain' prose), without immediately having any fundamental effect on the traditional attitudes to poetry. There was found to be much evidence from the later seventeenth century to suggest that the prevalent concepts of poetry were basically those which had been developed during the previous century, their ties with other forms of discourse being if anything made stronger by whatever influence they did feel from the new movements in prose. There was, in fact, found to be less of a tendency for poets to see themselves as separated from writers in other forms than for the new prose writers to see poetry as something distinct and separate from prose.

But despite this it was inevitable that the new movements would have their effect eventually. Words, in themselves, could no longer be assumed to be anything more than a convenient means of communication, and at the same time whole areas of knowledge, particularly nature itself, had become the preserve for investigation of the new non-verbal modes of thought from which poetry was by its nature cut off, except as a means of communication. In these circumstances, if it was to maintain its position as a mode of thought or expression as well as of communication, poetry had no option but to seek for fields in which these non-verbal modes of thought would be ineffective, and to make these its own; or alternatively it could

seek to become a way of manipulating words independent of anything outside itself, as patterns of sound or verbal imagery existing
wholly for their own sake. The attempt to achieve one or both of
these things has occupied much of the attention of poets and critics
of poetry from the eighteenth century onwards, beginning with
the eighteenth-century emphasis on the passions or emotions of the
poet as the unique subject of poetry.

Because experimental science and utilitarian prose were associated primarily with the rational and the logical, it seems natural that
poetry, in its search for a new or independent function, should turn
first as it did to the emotional life of the poet, and see itself as
expressing this in poetical rather than logical terms. 'Reason',
declared Robert Lowth, 'speaks literally, the passions poetically.'
Similarly, the breakdown of faculty psychology, whether as part of
the movement taking place or as a convenient coincidence, made
possible the development of new concepts of poetry as itself an
imaginative activity independent of reason—concepts very different
from those of the Renaissance, for whom poetry was 'imaginative'
only in so far as it dealt with materials presented to it by the imagination or 'invention' of the poet. The decline of the classical theory
of imitation, too, meant that poetry need no longer claim to reveal
the true order of nature—an order that in the new scientific world
was the preserve of Galileo, Descartes, and Newton.

There were without doubt other important factors which influenced the development of poetic theory and practice after the
middle of the seventeenth century; nevertheless it is claimed here
that the particular direction taken by these developments is
inextricably related to the changes manifested in seventeenth-
century England by the founding of the Royal Society of London.

Certainly it must be admitted that in seeking to investigate what
the seventeenth century thought about poetry by looking at the
kind of distinctions it habitually made between poetry and prose,
there has been an inevitable concentration on conscious intention—
on what men *thought* they were doing when they chose to write in
poetry rather than prose, or vice versa, rather than what they
actually were doing. These things may not always be the same, for

much in the poetry of any age is likely to be independent of conscious intention. Nevertheless, this study has been undertaken in the belief that a knowledge of consciously held attitudes to poetry is at least necessary for a proper understanding of the poetry written in the light of those attitudes.

Those ideas and attitudes which for the time being men may have held are a less constant thing than is human nature itself; and therefore those aspects of poetry that have their origins in man's psychological make-up would be the most likely to remain constant, in spite of conscious changes in ideas or changes of taste. For this reason, changes in the nature of poetry that are believed to have taken place during the seventeenth century may perhaps be approached more realistically through a study of consciously held ideas than through any psychologically based theory of change such as T. S. Eliot's doctrine of the 'dissociation of sensibility'. To say that at a certain time in history men ceased to think and feel simultaneously is a psychological generalization that would be very difficult to sustain, even if its exact meaning could be made clear in psychological rather than poetic terms: it would be very much more difficult to maintain than a belief that at that time men ceased to see the emotional expression of thought as the unique or primary function of poetry—not that I believe either of these things, or anything very like them, actually to have happened during the seventeenth century.

Concerning the poetry of the seventeenth century, a distinguished scholar of the period, Ruth Wallerstein, has said that:

. . . lack of sure and ready sympathy and judgement prevents our entering fully into the humanistic value of what we read. For it is only in logic that our experience of the beauty and of the moral or intellectual intention of a poem or of the substance of life in it can really be separated. Much of the present uncertainty and disagreement as to Donne's significance arises from lack of precise insight into poetic method and intention, no less than from our own divergencies in values and aesthetic approach. Dryden even more than Donne illustrates our condition.[1]

[1] Ruth Wallerstein, *Studies in Seventeenth Century Poetic*, op. cit., p. 3.

This study has been directed towards some further alleviation of
this condition, particularly as it affects the age of Dryden. As for
Donne and the earlier part of the century, thanks to such scholars as
Rosamund Tuve, Helen Gardner, and Louis Martz, we are perhaps
now less in need of enlightenment.[1]

Finally, then, what is the basic meaning of all this for poetry,
particularly for the poetry of the later seventeenth century? Dryden,
it is claimed, belongs as a poet to the older tradition. His poetry is to
be understood and appreciated fully only in terms of concepts which,
though they recognized the special qualities of poetry, were based
ultimately on an acceptance of the homogeneity of all discourse as
the means by which man, as a rational being, could know and
control the universe he lived in. Dryden is difficult for the twentieth
century to appreciate fully, because his own judgements and those
of his age recognized no final distinction between the literary and
non-literary, or between the poetic and non-poetic uses of language.
In writing poetry, Dryden would seek to give it qualities, in addition to those thought of as specifically poetic, which it would share
with other forms of discourse. Ultimately for him poetry must succeed not merely as poetry but as discourse: it cannot be judged
wholly by poetic criteria, because it is never envisaged as having a
sufficiently autonomous existence as poetry for this to be done.

Poetry, for Dryden, is something which may adorn discourse,
make it delightful, convincing, verisimilar. But it cannot make the
discourse itself, which is seen as controlled originally not by any
particular form of words, such as poetry, logic, or rhetoric, but by
the forms of thought, which all discourse serves as a means to order.
Poetry itself may be imaginative, but by the nature of man thought
—and therefore discourse—is essentially rational. Consequently

[1] Some of the works that have contributed particularly to this end are
Tuve's *Elizabethan and Metaphysical Imagery*, op. cit., and her *Reading of George
Herbert* (London, 1952); also Helen Gardner's *John Donne: The Divine Poems*
(Oxford,1952), and Louis Martz's *Poetry of Meditation*, op. cit. Articles such as
J. V. Cunningham, 'Logic and Lyric', *MP*, li (1953), 33–41; A. J. Smith, 'The
Metaphysic of Love', *RES*, ix (1958), 362–75; and the same author's 'On
Metaphysical Poetry', in *Determinations*, ed. F. R. Leavis (London, 1934), pp.
10–45 also provide valuable orientation to the poetry of the period.

poetry, thought of as discourse, must also be rational, and its imaginative character can do no more than give an imaginative colouring to it. Poetry cannot claim to transform discourse into something wholly imaginative, because in that case it would cease to be discourse and would become no longer worthy of man as a rational creature.

The later seventeenth century may have been an age of prose and reason, but this can account for no more than the surface characteristics of Dryden's poetry. The new scientific attitudes may have had a sobering effect on his poetry; they may have tied it down, more than poetry had hitherto been restricted, to the achievement of persuasive and delightful statement, instead of allowing it to soar into the new realms of discovery that had become the preserve of the scientists. But science did not prescribe this role for poetry, nor was it responsible for poetry's underlying rationality. Both these characteristics of seventeenth-century poetry—the rhetorical and the rational—which tend to divide it off from that of the nineteenth century, were part of its inheritance from the medieval and Renaissance past, and they had been as effective for Donne as they were for Dryden, though in Donne's poetry their manifestations were different.

Far from imposing a rational basis on poetry, the new science, by its divorce of words and reason, made inevitable the eventual destruction of the concepts which had given poetry its rational character. But this was something that came too late to affect Dryden.[1]

---

[1] I hope shortly to publish a study of Dryden's 'poetry of statement' in which some of the definitions arrived at in this work will be applied to reach an appreciation of Dryden's achievement, in terms of concepts of the nature and function of poetry that he himself would have understood and accepted.

Bibliography

This bibliography lists all works referred to in the text and notes. It is in two sections:— I. PRIMARY SOURCES (which covers works published for the first time prior to 1800) with references to such modern editions as have been used; and II. SECONDARY SOURCES (covering works published for the first time after 1800).

ABBREVIATIONS: In addition to the usual abbreviations of journal titles, the following abbreviations have been used:

Hooker: E. N. Hooker (ed.), *The Critical Works of John Dennis* (2 vols., Baltimore, 1939).

Ker: W. P. Ker (ed.), *Essays of John Dryden* (2 vols., Oxford, 1900).

Smith: Gregory Smith (ed.), *Elizabethan Critical Essays* (2 vols., Oxford, 1904).

Spingarn: J. E. Spingarn (ed.), *Critical Essays of the Seventeenth Century* (3 vols., Oxford, 1909).

I. PRIMARY SOURCES

AENEAS, SYLVIUS, *De liberorum educatione* (1450); trans. W. H. Woodward, *Vittorino da Feltre and other Educators* (Cambridge, 1897).

ALEXANDER, SIR WILLIAM, Earl of Stirling, *Anacrisis: or, a censure of some poets ancient and modern* (London, 1634); ed. Spingarn, i, 180–9.

AQUINAS, SAINT THOMAS, *In libros posteriorum analyticorum expositio; Opera omnia iussi impensaque Leonis XIII. P.M. edita* (12 vols., Rome, 1882–1906), i, 137–271.

——, *In sententia Petri Lombardi Commentaria.*

ARDERNE, JAMES, *Directions concerning the matter and style of sermons* (London, 1671); ed. J. Mackay (Oxford, 1952).

ARISTOTLE, *De anima.*

——, *Poetics;* ed. S. H. Butcher, *Aristotle's Theory of Poetry and Fine Art* (London, 1898).

——, *Rhetoric.*

ASCHAM, ROGER, *The Scholemaster: or, plaine and perfite way of teaching children to understand, write and speake the Latin tong . . .* (London, 1570); ed. A. M. Wright, *Roger Ascham, English Works* (Cambridge, 1904), pp. 170–302.

——, *Toxophilus: or, The schole of shooting conteyned in two books* (London, 1545); ed. A. M. Wright, *Roger Ascham, English Works* (Cambridge, 1904), pp. 1–119.

AUGUSTINE, AURELIUS, Saint, Bishop of Hippo, *Confessions.*

——, *De doctrina christiana.*

——, *De magistro.*

BACON, FRANCIS, Baron Verulam, Viscount St. Albans, *De dignitate et augmentis scientiarum libros ix* (London, 1623); ed. J. Spedding and R. H. Ellis, *The Philosophical Works of Francis Bacon* (5 vols., London, 1861), iv, 275–497 (trans. of Bks. I–VI).

——, *The twoo bookes of Francis Bacon, of the proficiencie and advancement of learning, divine and humane* (London, 1605); ed. J. Spedding and R. H. Ellis, *The Philosophical Works of Francis Bacon* (5 vols., London, 1861), iii, 253–492.

BARBAULD, (Mrs.) A. L., (ed.), *The Poetical Works of Mr. William Collins* (London, 1797).

BENLOWES, EDWARD, *Theophilia; or, Loves Sacrifice: A Divine Poem* (London, 1652).

BILSTEN, JOHANN, *Syntagma Philippo-Ramaeum* (1596).

BLACKMORE, SIR RICHARD, *Prince Arthur. An Heroick Poem in ten books* (London, 1695); 2nd ed. (London, 1695).

BLOUNT, SIR THOMAS POPE, *De re poetica: or, Remarks upon poetry* (London, 1694).

BLOUNT, THOMAS, *The Academie of Eloquence* (London, 1654).

BRINSLEY, JOHN, *Ludus literarius: or, The Grammar School* (London, 1612); ed. E. T. Campagnac, *Brinsley's Ludus Literarius, reproduced from the 1627 edition* (Liverpool, 1917).

BRUNI, L., *De studiis et literis* (*c.* 1405); trans. W. H. Woodward, *Vittorina da Feltre and other Educators* (Cambridge, 1897).

BURNET, GILBERT, (trans.), *More's Utopia* (London, 1684).

BURTON, ROBERT, *The Anatomy of Melancholy, what it is, with all Kindes, Causes, Symtomes, Prognostickes, and Severall Cures* (London, 1621).

BUTLER, CHARLES, *Oratoriae libri duo* (London, 1629).

——, *Rhetoricae libri duo . . .* (London, 1598).

BUTLER, SAMUEL, *Characters and Passages from Note-Books*, ed. A. R. Waller (Cambridge, 1908).

BYSSHE, EDWARD, *Art of English Poetry* (London, 1702).

CARPENTER, NATHANIEL, 'Logica pugno, Rhetorica palmae, non recte a Zenone comparatur', in *Philosophia libera* (Oxford, 1622), pp. 158–61; trans. W. S. Howell, 'Nathaniel Carpenter's Place in the Controversy between Dialectic and Rhetoric', *Speech Monographs*, i (1934), 20–41.

CASTELVETRO, LODOVICO, *Poetica d'Aristotele vulgarizzata et sposta* (Vienna, 1570).

CHAPMAN, GEORGE, *Ovid's Banquet of Sence: A Coronet for his Mistresse Philosophie and his amorous Zodiacke* (London, 1595).

——, Preface to the Reader, prefixed to the translation of Homer (London, 1610–16?); ed. Spingarn, i, 67–74.

CHARRON, PIERRE, *Of Widsom*; trans. G. Stanhope (2 vols., London, 1707).

CICERO, *De inventione.*

——, *De optimo genere oratorum.*

——, *De oratore.*

——, *Orator.*

COOPER, ANTHONY ASHLEY, 3rd Earl of Shaftesbury, *Characteristicks of Men, Manners, Opinions, Times* (3 vols., London, 1711).

COOPER, T., *Thesaurus amphistre* (c. 1565–75).

COWLEY, ABRAHAM, *Works* (London, 1668).

COX, LEONARD, *The Arte or Crafte of Rhetoryke* (London, c. 1530).

CUDWORTH, RALPH (d. 1685), *A treatise concerning the eternal and immutable morality*; quoted from edit. of 1731.

DANIEL, SAMUEL, *A Defence of Ryme, against a pamphlet entituled: Observations in the Art of English Poesie* (London, 1603?); ed. Smith, ii, 356–84.

DANTE ALIGHIERI, Letter to Can Grande della Scala, in *Epistolae* (Dent, London, 1904), pp. 343–62.

——, *La Vita Nuova* (Dent, London, 1906).

——, *Il Convivio* (Dent, London, 1903).

D(AVIES), J(OHN) (trans.), *Reflections upon Monsieur Des Cartes Discourse of a Method* (London, 1655).

DENNIS, JOHN, *The Advancement and Reformation of Modern Poetry* (London, 1701); ed. Hooker, i, 197–278.

——, *The Causes of the Decay and Defects of Dramatick Poetry, and of the Degeneracy of the Publick Tast* (London, 1725?); ed. Hooker, ii, 275–99.

——, *The Grounds of Criticism in Poetry* (London, 1704); ed. Hooker, i, 325–73.

——, *The Impartial Critic: or, some observations upon a late book entituled a short view of tragedy written by Mr. Rymer* (London, 1693); ed. Hooker, i, 11–14.

——, *Reflections Critical and Satyrical, upon a late rhapsody, called an Essay upon Criticism* (London, 1711); ed. Hooker, i, 396–419.

——, *Remarks on a book entituled Prince Arthur, an Heroick Poem, with some general critical observations and several remarks upon Virgil* (London, 1696); ed. Hooker i, 46–144.

——, *Remarks upon Mr. Pope's Translation of Homer . . .*; ed. Hooker, ii, 115–58.

DESCARTES, RENE, 'Meditations touchant La Premiere Philosophie', in *Les Meditationes Metaphysiques de Rene Descartes* (Paris, 1641); ed. C. Adam and P. Tannery, *Oeuvres de Descartes* (11 vols., Paris, 1904), ix, 13–72.

DIGBY, SIR KENELM, *The Second Treatise: declaring the Nature and Operations of Mans Soul . . .* (London, 1657); in *Two Treatises in the one of which the Nature of Bodies, in the other the Nature of Mans Soul is looked into . . .* (London, 1658).

DIONYSIUS of Halicarnassus, *De compositione verborum*.

DRYDEN, JOHN, 'The Author's Apology for Heroic Poetry and Poetic Licence', prefixed to *The State of Innocence and Fall of Man, an Opera* (London, 1677); ed. Ker, i, 178–90.

——, 'A Defence of an Essay of Dramatic Poesy', prefixed to the second edition of *The Indian Emperour* (London, 1668); ed. Ker, i, 110–33.

——, *A Discourse concerning the Original and Progress of Satire* (London, 1693); ed. Ker, ii, 15–114.

——, 'Epistle Dedicatory to the Duke of York', prefixed to *Almanzor and Almahide: or, The Conquest of Granada* (London, 1672); ed. Sir Walter Scott and George Saintsbury, *The Works of John Dryden* (18 vols., London, 1882–92), iv, 11–17.

——, The Epistle Dedicatory to *The Rival Ladies* (London, 1664); ed. Ker, i, 1–9.

——, *An Essay of Dramatic Poesy* (London, 1668); ed. Ker, i, 28–108.

——, Preface to *Annus Mirabilis: The Year of Wonders MCDLXVI* (London, 1667); ed. Ker, i, 10–20.

——, Preface to *Fables, Ancient and Modern* (London, 1700); ed. Ker, ii, 246–73.

——, Preface to *Religio Laici: A Poem* (London, 1682); ed. G. R. Noyes, *The Poetical Works of Dryden* (Cambridge, Mass., 1909), pp. 157–62.

EACHARD, JOHN, *The grounds & occasions of the contempt of the clergy and religion enquired into in a letter written to R.L.* (London, 1670); ed. E. Arber, *An English Garner* (8 vols., London, 1895), vii, 245–316.

ELYOT, SIR THOMAS, *The Boke named the Governour* (London, 1531).

ERASMUS, Desiderius, *Ciceronianus, sive de optimo genere dicendi* (Paris, 1528).

——, *De conscribendis epistolis* (Paris, 1521).

——, *De copia verborum* (Paris, 1511); trans. W. H. Woodward, *Erasmus concerning Education* (Cambridge, 1904).

——, *Moriae encomium* (Paris, 1509).

——, *De ratione studii, et instituendi pueros commentari totidem . . .* (Paris, 1510?).

FAGE, ROBERT, *Peter Ramus of Vermandois, The Kings Professor, his Dialectica in two bookes . . .* (London, 1632).

FÉNELON, *Dialogus sur l'Eloquence* (written *c.* 1679, pub. 1717, trans. into English, London, 1722); ed. W. S. Howell, *Fénelon's Dialogues on Eloquence: A Translation with an Introduction and Notes* (Princeton, 1951).

FENNER, DUDLEY, *The Artes of Logicke and Rhetorike* (London, 1584).

FOCLIN, ANTOINE, *La Rhetorique Francoise d'Antoine Foclin de Chauncy en Vermandois* (Paris, 1555).

FRACASTORO, GIROLAMO, *Girolamo Fracastoro Navgerius sive de poetica dialogvs* (1555); trans. R. Kelso, *Uni. of Ill. St. in Lang. and Lit.,* ix (1924), no. 3, pp. 49–88.

FRAUNCE, ABRAHAM, *The Arcadian Rhetoricke: or, the precepts of rhetoricke made plaine . . .* (London, 1588); ed. E. Seaton (Luttrell Soc., Oxford, 1950).

——, *The Lawyiers Logike: exemplifying the precepts of logike by the practice of the common law* (London, 1588).

FREIGIUS, JOHN THOMAS, *Paedogogus* (1582).

GASCOIGNE, GEORGE, *Certayne Notes of Instruction concerning the making of verse or rhyme in English, written at the request of Master Eduardo Donati* (London, 1575); ed. Smith, i, 46–57.

GIL, ANDREW (the elder), *Logonomia Anglica* (London, 1619).

GLANVILL, JOSEPH, *An Essay concerning Preaching: written for the direction of a young divine* (London, 1678).

——, *Scepsis scientifica: or, Confest Ignorance, the way to Science* (London, 1665).

——, *The Vanity of Dogmatizing: or, Confidence in Opinions* (London, 1661); (The Facsimile Text Soc., New York, 1931).

GRANT, EDWARD, *Graecae linguae spicilegum . . .* (London, 1595).

GRAHAM, SIR RICHARD, *Angliae speculum morale* (London, 1670).

GRAY, THOMAS, *Correspondence;* ed. P. Toynbee and L. Whibley (3 vols., Oxford, 1935).

GUARINI, BATTISTA, *De ordine docendi et studendi* (1459).

HALL, JOHN, Περὶ ὕψους: or, *Dionysius Longinus of the Height of Eloquence rendered out of the original . . .* (London, 1652).

HARINGTON, SIR JOHN, 'A Preface, or rather a Briefe Apologie of Poetrie, and of the Author and Translator', prefixed to his translation of *Orlando Furioso* (London, 1591); ed. Smith, ii, 194–222.

HAWES, STEPHEN, *The Pastime of Pleasure* (London, 1509); ed. W. E. Mead, *EETS*, 173 (1928).

HOBBES, THOMAS, *Leviathan* (London, 1651); (Everyman, London, 1914).

HOOLE, CHARLES, *A new discovery of the old art of teaching schoole, in four small treatises* (London, 1660—probably written *c.* 1637); ed. E. T. Campagnac (Liverpool, 1913).

HORACE, *Ars Poetica.*

HUARTE, JUAN DE DIOS, *Examen de ingenios para las sciencias* . . . (Pamplono, 1578); trans. R. Carew, *The Examination of Mens Wits* . . . (London, 1594).

JEWEL, JOHN, *Oratio contra rhetoricum* (London, 1548); ed. H. H. Hudson, 'Jewel's Oration against Rhetoric: a Translation', *QJS*, xiv (1928), 374–92.

JOHN OF GARLAND, *Poetria magistri Johannis anglici de arte prosayca metrica et rithmica*; ed. G. Mari, *RF*, xiii (1902), 881–965.

JOHNSON, SAMUEL, *Lives of the English Poets* (London, 1779); (Worlds Classics, 2 vols., Oxford, 1906).

——, *Rambler*; ed. L. T. Berguer, *The British Essayists* (45 vols., London, 1823), vols. 20–24.

JONES, SIR WILLIAM, 'On the Arts, commonly called Imitative', in *Poems consisting chiefly of translations from the Asiatick Languages* (Oxford, 1772); ed. Lady Jones, *The Works of Sir William Jones* (6 vols., London, 1799), iv, 549–61.

JONSON, BEN, 'Conversations with Drummond of Hawthornden'; ed. C. Herford and E. Simpson, *Ben Jonson* (12 vols., Oxford, 1947), i, 89–142.

——, *Timber: or, Discoveries: Made upon Men and Matter; As they have flow'd out of his daily Readings; or had their Refluxe in his Peculiar Notions of the Times* (London, 1640); ed. C. H. Herford and E. Simpson (12 vols., Oxford, 1947), viii, 561–649.

LAW, WILLIAM, *The Case of Reason, or Natural Religion, Fairly and Fully Stated* (London, 1731).

LESSING, GOTTFRIED EPHRAIM, *Laokoon* (Berlin, 1766).

LIONARDI, ALESSANDRO, *Dialogi di Messer Alessandro Lionardi, della inventione poetica* (Venice, 1554).

LOCKE, JOHN, *Some Thoughts concerning Education* (London, 1693); *The Works* (10 vols., London, 1812), ix.

——, *An Essay concerning Human Understanding* (London, 1690); ed. A. C. Fraser (2 vols., Oxford, 1894).

'LONGINUS', *On the Sublime*; ed. W. R. Roberts, *Longinus on the Sublime* (Cambridge, 1899).

LOWTH, ROBERT, *De sacra poesi Hebraeorum praelectiones academicae* (London, 1753); trans. G. Gregory, *Lectures on the Sacred Poetry of the Hebrews* (London, 1835).

LUCIAN, *Quomodo historia conscribenda.*

MACILMAINE, ROLAND, *The Logike of the Moste Excellent Philosopher P. Ramus, Martyr* (London, 1574).

MARBECKE, JOHN, *A Booke of Notes and Commonplaces* (London, 1581).

MAZZONI, JACOPO, *Della difesa della comedia di Dante* (Cesena, 1587).

MILTON, JOHN, *A fuller institution of the Art of Logic, arranged after the method of Peter Ramus* (London, 1672), ed. F. A. Patterson *et al.* *The Works of John Milton* (18 vols., New York, 1931–8).

——, *Treatise of Education, to Master Samuel Hartlib* (London, 1644); ed. Spingarn, i, 206.

MORE, SIR THOMAS, *Utopia* (London, 1516).

NASHE, THOMAS, *The Anatomie of Absurditie* (London, 1589); ed. Smith, i, 321–37.

——, 'To the Gentlemen Students of both Universities', prefixed to Robert Greene's *Menaphon* (London, 1589); ed. Smith, i, 307–20.

PARKER, SAMUEL, *A Discourse of Ecclesiastical Politie* (London, 1671).

——, *A free and impartial censure of Platonick philosophie* (London, 1666).

PATRICK, SIMON, *A friendly debate between a conformist . . .* (London, 1666).

PEACHAM, HENRY (the elder), *The Garden of Eloquence, conteyning figures of grammar and rhetorick* (London, 1577).

PHILLIPS, EDWARD, *Theatrum Poetarum; or, a compleat Collection of the Poets; with some Observations and Reflections upon many of them, particularly those of our own Nation* (London, 1675); ed. Spingarn, ii, 256–72.

PLATO, *Ion*.

——, *Phaedrus*.

——, *Republic*.

PLUTARCH, *De audendis poetis*.

POLITIAN, *Politiani Opera*; ed. Gryphius (Lyon, 1537–39).

POOLE, JOSHUA, *The English Parnassus: or, a help to English poesie*, with a Preface by J. D. (London, 1657).

POTTER, ROBERT, *An inquiry into some passages in Dr. Johnson's 'Lives of the Poets': Particularly his observations on lyric poetry and the Odes of Gray* (London, 1783).

PUTTENHAM, GEORGE, *The Arte of English Poesie* (London, 1589); ed. G. D. Willcock and A. Walker (Camb., 1936).

QUINTILIAN, *De institutione oratoria*.

RAINOLDE, RICHARD, *A Booke called the Foundacion of Rhetorike, because all other partes of rhetorike are grounded thereupon . . .* (London, 1563).

RAMUS, PETER (Pierre de la Ramée), *Scholae in liberales artes* (Basle, 1569).

RAMUS, PETER, and TALAEUS, AUDOMARIS (Omar Talon), *Petri Rami Professoris Regii & Audomari Talaei Collectionae Praefationes, Epistolae, Orationes* (Marburg, 1599, Preface dated Paris, 1544).

RAVENSCROFT, EDWARD, *Mammamouchi: or, The Citizen turn'd Gentleman: A Comedy* (London, 1675).

ROBORTELLO, FRANCESCO, *Francisi Robortelli Vtinensis in librum Aristotelis de arte poetica explicationes* (Florence, 1548).

——, Διονισίον Λογγίνου ῥήτορς περὶ ὑψους βιβλίον *Dionysii Longini rhetoris* (Basle, 1554).

ROSS, ALEXANDER, *Medicus Medicatus* (London, 1645).

RYMER, THOMAS, *The Tragedies of the Last Age* (London, 1678); ed. Spingarn, ii, 181–208.

SCALIGER, JULIUS CAESAR, *Ivlii Caesaris Scaligeri, Uiri Clarissimi, Poetices libri septem* (1561).

SHERLOCK, WILLIAM, *A defence and continuation of the discourse concerning the knowledge . . .* (London, 1675).

SIDNEY, SIR PHILIP, *An Apologie for Poetrie* (London, c. 1583); ed. Smith, i, 148–207.

SOUTH, ROBERT, *Sermons preached on several occasions;* (7 vols., Oxford, 1823).

——, *Dr. South's Sermons* (2 vols., Oxford, 1855).

SMITH, JOHN, *The Mysterie of Rhetorique Unvail'd wherein above 130 of the tropes and figures are severally divided from the Greek into English together with lively definitions . . .* (London, 1657).

SPENCER, THOMAS, *The Art of Logick, delivered in the precepts of Aristotle and Ramus* (London, 1657).

SPRAT, THOMAS, *The History of the Royal Society of London for the improving of Natural Knowledge* (London, 1667).

TATE, NAHUM, 'To the Reader', prefixed to Abraham Cowley's *Six Books of Plants* (London, 1689); *The Works of Abraham Cowley* (8th edit., London, 1693).

TEMPLE, SIR WILLIAM, *Of Poetry* (London, 1690); ed. Spingarn, iii, 73–109.

TRAPP, JOSEPH, *Praelectiones poeticae* (London, 1711); trans. as *Lectures on Poetry* (London, 1742).

VALLA, LORENZO, *Elegantiae linguae latinae* (c. 1435).

VERGERIUS, *De ingenuis moribus* (c. 1404); trans. W. H. Woodward, *Vittorina da Feltre and other Educators* (Cambridge, 1897).

VICO, GIAMBATTISTA, *Scienza nuova prima* (Naples, 1725).

——, *Scienza nuova seconda* (Naples, 1731); trans. T. G. Bergin and M. H. Fisch, *The New Science of Giambattista Vico, translated from the third edition (1744)* (New York, 1948).

VIVES, JUAN LUIS, *De causis corruptarum artium* (1531).

——, *De ratione dicendi, libri tres* (1533).

——, *De ratione studii* (1523).

——, *De tradendis disciplinis* (1531); trans. F. Watson, *Vives on Education* (Cambridge, 1913).

WARTON, JOSEPH, *An Essay on the Genius and Writings of Pope* (London, 1756); ed. Scott Elledge, *Eighteenth Century Critical Essays* (2 vols., New York, 1961), ii, 717–63.

WEBSTER, JOHN, *Academiarum examen* (London, 1653).

WELSTED, LEONARD, *A dissertation concerning the perfection of the English tongue, and the State of Poetry &c.* (London, 1724); ed. W. H. Durham, *Critical Essays of the Eighteenth Century 1700–1725* (New Haven, 1915), pp. 355–95.

WESLEY, SAMUEL, *An Epistle to a friend concerning Poetry* (London, 1700).

WILKINS, JOHN, *An Essay towards a Real Character and a Philosophical Language* (London, 1668).

WILSON, THOMAS, *The Arte of Rhetorique, for the use of all suche as are studious of eloquence* . . . (London, 1553); ed. G. H. Mair, *Wilson's Arte of Rhetorique 1560* (Oxford, 1909).

——, *The Rule of Reason, conteyning the Arte of Logique, set forth in Englishe* (London, 1551).

WOTTON, SAMUEL, *The Art of Logick, gathered out of Aristotle, and set forth in due forms, according to his instructions* (London, 1626).

YOUNG, EDWARD, *Conjectures on original composition* (London, 1759); ed. E. D. Jones, *English Critical Essays (Sixteenth, Seventeenth and Eighteenth Centuries)* (Oxford, 1922), pp. 315–64.

——, 'On lyric poetry', preface to *Ocean, an Ode* (London, 1728).

II. SECONDARY SOURCES

ARNOLD, MATTHEW, 'The Study of Poetry', in *Essays in Criticism (Second Series)*, ed. S. R. Littlewood (London, 1938).

ATKINS, J. W. H., *English Literary Criticism: The Medieval Phase* (London, 1952).

——, *English Literary Criticism: The Renascence* (London, 1947).

——, *English Literary Criticism: 17th & 18th Centuries* (London, 1951).

——, *Literary Criticism in Antiquity* (2 vols., London, 1952).

BAKER, H., *The Wars of Truth* (London, 1952).

BALDWIN, C. S., *Ancient Rhetoric and Poetic* (New York, 1924).

——, *Medieval Rhetoric and Poetic* (New York, 1928).

BALDWIN, C. S., and CLARK, D. L., *Renaissance Literary Theory and Practice* (New York, 1939).

BALDWIN, T. W., *William Shakspere's Small Latin & Lesse Greeke* (2 vols., Urbana, Ill., 1944).

BARKER, G. F. R., *Memoir of Richard Busby D.D. (1606-1695)* (London, 1895).

BETHELL, S. L., *The Cultural Revolution of the Seventeenth Century* (London, 1951).

BLOOMFIELD, M. W., 'Symbolism in Medieval Literature', *MP*, lvi (1958–9), 73–81.

BOEHNER, P., *Medieval Logic* (Manchester, 1952).

BOND, D. F., ' "Distrust" of Imagination in English Neo-Classicism', *PQ*, xiv (1935), 54–69.

——, 'Neo-Classical Psychology of the Imagination', *ELH*, iv (1937), 245–64.

BREDVOLD, L., 'Dryden, Hobbes, and the Royal Society', *MP*, xxv (1928), 417–38.

——, *The Milieu of John Dryden* (Ann Arbor, 1934).

——, 'The Tendency toward Platonism in Neo-Classical Esthetics', *ELH*, i (1934), 91–119.

BROWN, W. C., *The Triumph of Form: A Study of the Later Masters of the Heroic Couplet* (Chapel Hill, 1948).

BUNDY, M. W., 'Bacon's True Opinion of Poetry', *SP*, xxvii (1930), 244–64.

——, ' "Invention" and "Imagination" in the Renaissance', *JEGP*, xxix (1930), 535–45.

CHAGNARD, B., *Rhetoric and Poetry in the Renaissance* (New York, 1922).

CLARK, D. L., *Milton at St. Paul's School* (New York, 1948).
——, *Rhetoric and Poetry in the Renaissance* (New York, 1922).
COLLINGWOOD, R. G., *The Principles of Art* (Oxford, 1938).
CRAIG, HARDIN, *The Enchanted Glass* (New York, 1936).
CRANE, W., *Wit and Rhetoric in the Renaissance* (New York, 1946).
CROCE, BENEDETTO, *Aesthetic* (1901); trans. D. Ainslie (New York, 1909).
——, *The Philosophy of Giambattista Vico* (1910); trans. R. G. Collingwood (London, 1913).
CROLL, M. W., 'Attic Prose in the Seventeenth Century', *SP*, xviii (1921), 79–128.
——, 'The Baroque Style in Prose', in *Studies in English Philology*, ed. K. Malone and M. B. Ruud (Minneapolis, 1929), pp. 427–56.
——, 'The Cadence of English Oratorical Prose', *SP*, xvi (1919), 1–55.
CRUTTWELL, P., *The Shakespearean Moment* (London, 1954).
CULLER, A. D., 'Edward Bysshe and the Poet's Handbook', *PMLA*, lxiii (1948), 858–85.
CUNNINGHAM, J. V., 'Logic and Lyric', *MP*, li (1953), 33–41.
CURTIUS, E. R., *Europäische Literatur und Lateinisches Mittelalter* (Berne, 1948); trans. W. R. Trask, *European Literature and the Latin Middle Ages* (London, 1953).
DAVIE, DONALD, *Articulate Energy* (London, 1955).
DEANE, C. V., *Dramatic Theory and the Rhymed Heroic Play* (Oxford, 1931).
DUHAMEL, P. A., 'The Logic and Rhetoric of Peter Ramus', *MP*, xlvi (1949), 163–71.
——, 'Sidney's "Arcadia" and Elizabethan Rhetoric', *SP*, xlv (1948), 134–50.
FEDER, LILIAN, 'John Dryden's use of Classical Rhetoric', *PMLA*, lxix (1954), 1258–78.
FISCH, H., 'The Puritans and the Reform of Prose Style', *ELH*, xix (1952), 229–48.
GARDNER, HELEN, *John Donne: The Divine Poems* (Oxford, 1952).
GILSON, ETIENNE, *Études de philosophie medievale* (Strasbourg, 1921).
GRIERSON, H. J. C., *Cross Currents of Literature of the XVIIth Century* (London, 1929).
HALE, E. E. (Jr.), 'Ideas on Rhetoric in the Sixteenth Century', *PMLA*, xviii (1903), 424–44.
HOOKER, E. N. (ed.), *The Critical Works of John Dennis* (2 vols., Baltimore, 1939).
——, 'Pope on Wit: the Essay on Criticism', in *The Seventeenth Century, from Bacon to Pope* (Stanford, 1951), pp. 225–46.
HOWARD, L., 'The "Invention" of Milton's "Great Argument": A Study of the Logic of "God's Ways to Men",' *HLQ*, lx (1946), 149–61.
HOWELL, W. S., *Logic and Rhetoric in England, 1500–1700* (Princeton, 1956).
——, 'Nathaniel Carpenter's Place in the Controversy between Dialectic and Rhetoric', *Speech Monographs*, i (1934), 20–41.
——, 'Oratory and Poetry in Fénelon's Literary Theory', *QJS*, xxxvii (1951), 1–10.
——, 'Ramus and English Rhetoric', *QJS*, xxxvii (1951), 299–310.

HUDSON, H. H., 'Jewel's Oration against Rhetoric: A Translation', *QJS*, xiv (1928), 374–92.

JEBB, R. C., *The Attic Orators* (2 vols., London, 1893).

JOHNSON, F. R., 'Two Renaissance Textbooks of Rhetoric', *HLQ*, vi (1942–3), 427–44.

JONES, R. F., 'The Attack on Pulpit Eloquence in the Restoration', *JEGP*, xxx (1931), 188–217.

——, 'Science and Criticism in the Neo-Classical Age of English Literature', *JHI*, i (1940), 381–412.

——, 'Science and English Prose Style in the Third Quarter of the Seventeenth Century', *PMLA*, xlv (1930), 977–1009.

——, 'Science and Language in England of the mid-Seventeenth Century', *JEGP*, xxxi (1932), 315–31.

——, *The Triumph of the English Language* (London, 1953).

KERMODE, FRANK, 'The Defence of Poetry', in the *Observer*, March 12th, 1961, p. 31.

KRAPP, R. M., 'Class Analysis of a Literary Controversy: Wit and Sense in Seventeenth-Century English Literature', *Science and Society*, x (1946), 80–92.

LEWIS, C. S., *The Allegory of Love* (Oxford, 1936).

——, *English Literature in the Sixteenth Century, excluding Drama* (Oxford, 1954).

——, *Studies in Words* (Cambridge, 1960).

LLOYD, C., 'John Dryden and the Royal Society', *PMLA*, xlv (1930), 967–76.

McCLENNEN, J., 'On the Meaning and Function of Allegory in the English Renaissance', *Univ. of Mich. contrib. in Mod. Phil.*, vi (1947).

McKENZIE, G., *Critical Responsiveness: A Study of the Psychological Current in Later Eighteenth Century Criticism* (Berkeley, 1949).

McKEON, RICHARD, 'Literary Criticism and the Concept of Imitation in Antiquity', *MP*, xxxiv (1936), 1–35.

——, 'Poetry and Philosophy in the Twelfth Century: The Renaissance of Rhetoric', *MP*, xliii (1946), 217–34.

——, 'Rhetoric in the Middle Ages', *Speculum*, xvii (1942), 1–32.

MACLEAN, NORMAN, 'From Action to Image: Theories of the Lyric in the Eighteenth Century', in R. S. Crane (ed.), *Critics and Criticism* (Chicago, 1952), pp. 408–60.

MAHOOD, M. M., *Poetry and Humanism* (London, 1950).

MANLY, J. M., 'Chaucer and the Rhetoricians', *Proc. of the Brit. Acad.* (1926), pp. 95–113.

MARTZ, L. L., *The Poetry of Mediation* (New Haven, 1954).

MASON, H. A., *Humanism and Poetry in the Early Tudor Period* (London, 1959).

MILLER, PERRY, *The New England Mind: The Seventeenth Century* (New York, 1939).

MITCHELL, W. FRASER, *English Pulpit Oratory from Andrewes to Tillotson* (London, 1932).

MONK, S. H., *The Sublime: A Study of Critical Theories in XVIIIth-Century England* (New York, 1935).

NELSON, N. E., 'Peter Ramus and the Confusion of Logic, Rhetoric and Poetry', *Univ. of Mich. contrib. in Mod. Phil.* ii (1947), pp. 1–22.

NICHOLSON, MARJORIE, 'The Early Stage of Cartesianism in England', *SP*, xxvi (1929), 356–74.

OLSON, ELDER, 'The Argument of Longinus "On the Sublime" ', *MP*, xxxix (1942), 225–58.

ONG, WALTER J., S.J., 'The Province of Rhetoric and Poetic', *Mod. Sch.*, xix (1942), 24–27.

——, 'Hobbes and Talon's Ramist Rhetoric in English', *Trans. of Camb., Biblio. Soc.*, I, pt. iii (1951), pp. 260–9.

——, 'Psyche and the Geometers; Aspects of Associationist Critical Theory', *MP*, xlix (1951), 16–27.

——, *Ramus and Talon Inventory* (Camb., Mass., 1958).

——, 'Ramus and the Transit to the Modern Mind', *Mod. Sch.*, xxxii (1955), 301–11.

——, *Ramus, Method and the Decay of Dialogue* (Camb., Mass., 1958).

——, 'Ramus; Rhetoric and the Pre-Newtonian Mind', *Eng. Inst. Essays*, ed. A. S. Downer (New York, 1952), pp. 310–41.

——, 'Wit and Mystery: A Revolution of Medieval Latin Hymnody', *Speculum*, xxii (1947), 310–41.

PAETOW, L. J., *The Arts of Discourse at Medieval Universities, with special reference to Grammar and Rhetoric, Univ. of Ill. St.*, iii (1910).

RASHDALL, H., *The Universities of Europe in the Middle Ages*, new edition by F. N. Powicke and A. B. Emden (3 vols., Oxford, 1936).

RISKE, E. T., BREDVOLD, L. I., STROUP, T. B., and LLOYD, C., 'Dryden and Waller as Members of the Royal Society', *PMLA*, xlviii (1931), 951–61.

ROSENBERG, A., 'Bishop Sprat on Science and Imagery', *Isis*, xliii (1952), 220–2.

SAINTSBURY, GEORGE, *A History of Criticism and Literary Taste in Europe* (3 vols., London, 1900).

SHARP, R. L., *From Donne to Dryden* (Chapel Hill, 1940).

SINGLETON, C. S., 'Dante's Allegory', *Speculum*, xxv (1950), 78–86.

SMITH, A. J., 'The Metaphysic of Love', *RES*, ix (1958), 362–75.

——, 'An Examination of some claims for Ramism', *RES*, vii (1956), 349–59.

——, 'On Metaphysical Poetry'; in *Determinations*, ed. F. R. Leavis (London, 1934).

SPINGARN, J. E., *A History of Literary Criticism in the Renaissance* (New York, 1899).

SWEETING, J., *Early Tudor Criticism* (Oxford, 1940).

THORNE, J. P., 'A Ramistical Commentary on Sidney's "An Apologie for Poetrie" ', *MP*, liv (1957), 158–64.

THORPE, C. DeW., *The Aesthetic Theory of Thomas Hobbes* (Ann Arbor, 1940).

TUVE, ROSAMUND, *Elizabethan and Metaphysical Imagery* (Chicago, 1947).

——, 'Imagery and Logic: Ramus and Metaphysical Poetics', *JHI*, iii (1942), 365–400.

——, *A Reading of George Herbert* (London, 1952).

USTICK, W. L., and HUDSON, H., 'Wit, "Mixt Wit" and the Bee in Amber', *HLB*, viii (1935), 103–30.

VAN DOREN, MARK, *John Dryden: A Study of his Poetry* (New York, 1946); orig. pub. as *The Poetry of John Dryden* (New York, 1920).

VAN HOOK, LA RUE, 'Greek Rhetorical Terminology in Puttenham's "The Arte of English Poesie" ', *Trans. of Amer. Phil. Ass.* xlv (1914), 111–28.

WALLACE, K. R., *Francis Bacon on Communication and Rhetoric* (Chapel Hill, 1943).

WALLERSTEIN, RUTH, 'The Development of the Rhetoric and Metre of the Heroic Couplet, especially 1625–1645', *PMLA*, l (1935), 166–210.

——, *Studies in Seventeenth Century Poetic* (Wisconsin, 1950).

WEINBERG, BERNARD, *A History of Literary Criticism in the Italian Renaissance* (2 vols., Chicago, 1961).

——, 'Robortello on the Poetics', in *Critics and Criticism*, ed. R. S. Crane (Chicago, 1952) pp. 319–48.

——, 'Castelvetro's Theory of Poetics', in *Critics and Criticism*, ed. R. S. Crane (Chicago, 1952), pp. 349–71.

——, 'The Poetic Theories of Minturno', in *Studies in Honor of Frederick W. Shipley* (St. Louis, 1942), pp. 101–29.

——, 'Scaliger vs Aristotle on Poetics', *MP*, xxxix (1942), 337–60.

——, 'Translations and Commentaries of Longinus 'On the Sublime' to 1600: A Bibliography', *MP*, xlvii (1950), 145–51.

WILLEY, BASIL, *The Eighteenth Century Background* (London, 1940).

——, *The Seventeenth Century Background* (London, 1934).

WILLIAMSON, G. E., 'The Restoration Revolt against Enthusiasm', *SP*, xxx (1933), 571–603.

——, 'The Rhetorical Pattern of Neo-Classical Wit', *MP*, xxxiii (1935), 55–81.

——, *The Senecan Amble: A Study in Prose Form from Bacon to Collier* (London, 1951).

——, 'Senecan Style in the Seventeenth Century', *PQ*, xv (1936), 321–51.

——, 'Strong Lines', *English Studies*, xviii (1936), 152–9.

Index of Names

The more important references are indicated by italic type